OXFORD REVISION GUIDES

AS & A Level

RELIGIOUS STUDIES: PHILOSOPHY & ETHICS

through diagrams

Greg Dewar

OXFORD
UNIVERSITY PRESS

OXFORD
UNIVERSITY PRESS

Great Clarendon Street, Oxford OX2 6DP

Oxford University Press is a department of the
University of Oxford. It furthers the University's objective
of excellence in research, scholarship, and education by
publishing worldwide in

Oxford New York

Auckland Cape Town Dar es Salaam Hong Kong Karachi
Kuala Lumpur Madrid Melbourne Mexico City Nairobi
New Delhi Shanghai Taipei Toronto

With offices in

Argentina Austria Brazil Chile Czech Republic France Greece
Guatemala Hungary Italy Japan Poland Portugal Singapore
South Korea Switzerland Thailand Turkey Ukraine Vietnam

Oxford is a registered trade mark of Oxford University Press
in the UK and in certain other countries

First published 2002

British Library Cataloguing in Publication Data

Data available

ISBN-13: 978-0-19-915079-3
ISBN-10: 0-19-915079-6

10 9 8 7 6 5 4 3 2

Typeset and DEsigned by Fakenham Photosetting Ltd

Printed in Great Britain by Bell & Bain Ltd, Glasgow

Contents

3

Contents (cont.)

A number of pages also contain advice relating to revision and to the exam itself:

Match to the specifications

	WJEC	OCR	AQA	Edexcel
Philosophy of religion				
Plato's Forms		AS		
Aristotle's cause and purpose		AS		
Judaeo-Christian origins – the Bible		AS		
Arguments for the existence of God	AS/A2	AS	AS/A2	AS/A2
Science and religion	A2 (incl. Miracles)		AS	AS
Problem of evil	AS	AS	A2	AS
Challenges from psychology and sociology		AS		
Body and soul – life after death	Synoptic	A2	A2	A2
Religious experience	A2 (incl. revelation)	A2	AS/A2	AS (incl. miracles) A2
Religious language	A2	A2		A2

	WJEC	OCR	AQA	Edexcel
Ethics				
Ethical theory	A2 (incl. emotivism and egoism)	AS		A2
Virtue ethics	A2	AS	A2	
Situation ethics	AS	AS		AS
Natural Law	AS	AS		
Medical ethics – including abortion and euthanasia	A2	AS		
Right to life		AS		
Utilitarianism	AS	AS	AS	AS
Absolute and relative morality		AS		A2
Categorical imperativism	A2	AS	AS	
Free will and determinism		A2	A2	
Conscience		A2		
Religious ethics		A2	AS/A2	AS
Practical ethics: environment, sex and war	AS/A2	A2		AS

Specifications are liable to change. For up-to-date information on examinations, please visit the appropriate website:

WJEC: www.wjec.co.uk

OCR: www.ocr.org.uk

AQA: www.aqa.org.uk

Edexcel: www.edexcel.org.uk

Plato and the Forms

Plato (428–347BCE)

Plato was a pupil of **Socrates**, who was executed by the Athenian authorities for 'corrupting the youth of the city': he had been encouraging people to challenge the views and opinions of the city elders. After Socrates was executed, Plato travelled around the eastern Mediterranean, before setting up his university in Athens.

The allegory of the cave

Imagine some prisoners in a cave. They are chained to the floor so that they can only see the back wall of the cave, and the shadows of things passing the mouth of the cave. One man escapes, and is dazzled by the 'real' objects that were casting the shadows. He sees colours and shapes – he returns to tell his fellows, but they reject his news.

The allegory of the cave suggests that people are 'philosophically ignorant', and are like the prisoners chained to the floor of the cave. They can only see the shadows playing on the back of the cave. They assume that these shadows are in fact the whole of reality.

The world outside represents the world of the **Forms**. The prisoner who escapes is like the person who achieves 'philosophical enlightenment'.

This entire allegory, I said, you may now append, dear Glaucon, to the previous argument; the cave is the world of sight, the light of the fire is the sun, and you will not misapprehend me if you interpret the journey upward to be the ascent of the soul into the intellectual world according to my poor belief, which, at your desire, I have expressed – whether rightly or wrongly, God knows. But, whether true or false, my opinion is that in the world of knowledge the idea of good appears last of all, and is seen only with an effort; and, when seen, is also inferred to be the universal author of all things beautiful and right, parent of light and of the lord of light in this visible world, and the immediate source of reason and truth in the intellectual; and that this is the power upon which he who would act rationally either in public or private life must have his eye fixed.

http://www.utm.edu/research/iep/text/plato/rep/rep-7.htm

Plato's 'Forms' are sorts, kinds or types of things. They were not created, and they do not do anything. They are simply 'there'. The forms are timeless, unchanging and beyond space.

The created world, by contrast, is made of **contingent**, imperfect 'stuff', subject to change and decay.

This idea of **Form** and **matter** is central to Plato's view of the world. There are basically two worlds:

The finite world

Here the material objects exist, subject to change and decay. They take their identity from the way that they conform to their corresponding idea in the world of the Form.

The finite world is a shadow of The 'real' world of the Form.

The world of the Form

Here the patterns for the objects and concepts for the material world exist in a state of unchanging perfection.

It is the job of the philosopher to break free from the shackles of the finite world and find the world of reality in the world of the Form.

Plato and the Forms (continued)

Many Greek philosophers believed that the soul was trapped in the material world – they thought of the body as a prison. Plato believed that the soul broke free from the body on death and returned to the world of the Form, which is where it came from in the first place. The **Demiurge** created the universe using changeable 'chaotic' material, and using the Forms as a model. The material that the universe is made from is constantly changing and being redistributed. Plato believed that we categorise the objects that we experience using our knowledge of those eternal Forms. A thing has its identity according to the way that it conforms to its corresponding Form. Plato believed that the Forms exist independently of anything in the finite world.

Demiurge (Greek: craftsman)	Plato believed that the Demiurge was the maker of the universe. However, the Demiurge was not the same as the Christian God – the Demiurge was not omnipotent.

For example:
A person sees a horse. He recognises it as a horse because of its characteristic 'horseness'. This is how he knows it is not a dog, or a lion, or an elephant.

The Form of the Good

Plato thought that the highest Form was the Form of the Good. Through an understanding of the Form of the Good, we can understand the value of all things. Any good act that we carry out in this world is a pale imitation of the perfect Good that exists in the world of ideas.

This idea of the Form of the Good was understood by later (Christian) thinkers as a way of explaining God. The idea of the Good is also important for an understanding of Plato's (and Augustine's) view of the nature of evil.

Plato believed that ordinary things gain their nature by either:

Imitating		Participating
This would mean that the Forms are independent of the physical world – they **transcend** or go beyond the material. The ordinary object simply imitates the eternal Form.	or	This would mean that the Forms are present in the objects of the physical world, and are much less mysterious. The ordinary object has something of the eternal Form in it.

Plato believed that we understand something to be 'good' – we are born with a dim recollection of the 'Form' of justice, or goodness, or whatever. Plato talks of the **a priori** knowledge of mathematics. For example, '2 + 2 = 4' is something that we know before we find four things to add together. Plato thought that this knowledge was a recollection of things known in an earlier existence.

a priori	Knowledge that is held *before* sense experience is gathered

a posteriori	Knowledge that comes *after* sense experience

Plato on mind and body

Plato argued that the soul is immortal – a part of the world of the ideas. The body is a part of the material world. The soul is immortal and imperishable. The body, of course, is not!

Plato could argue this by basing his thinking on the idea of the Form. The soul is the essential, immaterial part of a human, temporarily united with the body, before returning to the world of the Form.

The body is a physical thing, existing in time and space. As such, it has **extension**. The mind has no such extension – it does not exist in time and space. Because it exists in the realm of the Forms, the mind can access universal truths from the world of ideas. This distinction between the mind and the body is called **dualism** – the distinction between thinking soul and doing body.

Dualism
The mind dwells in the body rather like the driver of a car.

Materialism
The mind is an extension of the body, a form of its activity. The phenomenon that we identify as 'the mind' is actually nothing but a collection of chemical responses.

The Greeks distinguished between different aspects of human existence as follows:

soma
The body as a whole, its activities, personality and so on

nous
The thinking mind

sarx
Flesh and blood – the physical body

pneuma
The spirit, thought, spirituality, reason

psyche
Emotions and sensations

The aim of the soul is to return to the world of ideas – the soul survives the body, and with it survives the identity of the individual.

Aristotle

Cause and purpose

Aristotle (384–322BCE) disagreed with his teacher, Plato. He argued that knowledge of the Form was **a posteriori** – we only develop knowledge of the Form of a horse after contact with lots of horses. The Form exists within the object itself. Where Plato thought that the natural world was a reflection of the world of ideas, Aristotle thought that what was in the human soul was simply a reflection of the real world. Reality is made up of several things, comprising Form and matter. The matter of a thing can exist after the thing itself has ceased to exist.

Form	A thing's specific characteristics

Matter	The 'stuff' that a thing is made of

The Form is the range of characteristics that combine to define the object for what it is. The matter can come together to make a range of different objects without changing – it is the Form that changes. Matter contains the **potential** to become a specific Form.

> For example:
> A chicken is made of a variety of materials – cells of different sorts. Its characteristics – clucking, laying eggs and so on – make it a chicken. When it dies, it becomes a dead chicken – the matter is maintained, but the Form has changed.
> From this idea of Form and matter, Aristotle went on to define his idea of **causality.** He believed that there are four *aitiai* (causes)
>
> **Material Cause**
> The matter from which the thing is made. ⇨ *For example:*
> *The bronze that the statue is made of*
>
> **Efficient Cause**
> The agent that brings something about. ⇨ *The sculptor and his chisel*
>
> **Formal Cause**
> The kind of thing that something is (i.e. its Form). ⇨ *The shape or design that the bronze is being sculpted into*
>
> **Final Cause**
> The goal or purpose that a thing moves towards. ⇨ *The purpose of the sculpture*

This idea is important for two significant philosophical theories:

The cosmological argument for the existence of God	The Natural Law theory of ethics
This theory argues that God is the 'First Cause' of the universe.	This theory tries to define good in terms of the Final Cause, or purpose, of a thing.

Aristotle argued for a **teleological** explanation of natural things – he defined objects in terms of what they are for. Some goals are **extrinsic** – they are achieved by an action external to the object. A knife's goal is to cut, and its success is determined by the way it cuts. Other goals are **intrinsic**. A person's goal is to live a rational life – the whole make-up of a person is to achieve this. The essence of each biological kind is determined by its goal or purpose.

τελος (**telos**)
Goal, the final purpose, or aim, of a thing

> **So** each object or being has two aspects to its existence:
> 1. There is one fundamental feature of a thing that causes its other features to be organised in the way that they are. *For example, its horseness.*
> 2. This feature is based on the purpose of that thing.
>   *Horseness is defined by the purpose of a horse – its final goal.*

Mind and body

> πσυχη (**psyche**)
> This is the word the Greeks gave to the **animator**, the living force in a living being. Aristotle counted nutrition, reproduction, movement and perception as powers of the psyche.

> νους (**nous**)
> This is how Aristotle referred to **reason**. This is the highest form of rationality. Aristotle believed that the 'unmoved mover' of the universe was a cosmic **nous**.

Aristotle believed that the soul is the **Form** of the body. The soul is simply the sum total of the operations of a human being.	As such, the soul is not immortal – it is simply the Form of the body, and not capable of existing without the body.

The concept of God as Creator

There are two basic accounts of the Creation of the world. The first is the well-known 'six days' version. The second gives the story of Adam and Eve.

Genesis 1

This is the account of the Creation of the world in six days. It speaks of the earth being 'without form and void', and of the 'Spirit of God' moving over the face of the earth. God creates different parts of the earth on each day. In each case the creating action is 'God said':

- Light and dark
- Waters above and below sky
- Heaven separated from earth
- Land and sea, vegetation
- The sun and moon, and the stars
- Living creatures – man (and woman)

This story appears to have a Greek influence:

The **Spirit of God** came to be identified with the 'logos', the Wisdom or Word of God, the intelligible part of God's mysterious being. This is reflected in the way that God creates simply by command. The logos is sometimes compared with Plato's Forms.

The account clearly shows that God pre-exists the creation of the world, and shows God's complete sovereignty over the created order.

Isaiah 40:22–23

It is he who sits above the circle of the earth, and its inhabitants are like grasshoppers; who stretches out the heavens like a curtain, and spreads them like a tent to live in; who brings princes to naught, and makes the rulers of the earth as nothing.

There are other texts that support this idea that God is 'in control'. In a mysterious world, with life fragile and at the mercy of bewildering powers, belief in God as being in charge brought meaning to chaos.

An important part of the Jewish and Christian beliefs about God and Creation is that God created the universe **ex nihilo** – out of nothing.

Genesis 2–3

The second part of the Genesis Creation story (Chapters 2–3) involves the creation of Adam and Eve, and the 'Fall' and eviction from the Garden of Eden.

The account is different to the first Creation story:

- God is pictured in a more super-human way.
- He walks and talks, and gets angry.
- The creating activity is much more 'hands on'.
- Adam is created 'of dust from the ground, and breathed into his nostrils the breath of life'.
- God provides for His Creation, and becomes angry when He is disobeyed.
- God is more involved in Creation – He 'gets His hands dirty'.

Adam and Eve are put in the Garden of Eden as keepers.

Genesis 2:15

The Lord God took the man and put him in the garden of Eden to till it and keep it.

However, there is a command – that the couple do not eat from the **tree of the knowledge of good and evil**, on threat of death.

Eve is created as a helper for Adam. The couple exist in a state of innocence until the **serpent** tempts Eve to pick a fruit from the tree. They then realise they are naked, and are ashamed. God evicts them from the Garden.

The goodness of God

Exodus 20: the Ten Commandments

Moses receives the Decalogue while on Mount Sinai. The Commandments break into two parts:

Positive
- Keep the Sabbath day holy.
- Honour your parents.

Negative
- Do not worship other gods.
- Do not make graven images (statues) and worship them.
- Do not take the Lord's name in vain.
- Do not murder, commit adultery, steal, lie about someone in court or be jealous.

God is terrifying – the people ask to be represented by Moses. God's message is that loyalty will be repaid: 'In every place where I cause my name to be remembered I will come to you and bless you.'

In Exodus 20, God is shown to be setting up a system that will provide for his people.

- People must remain faithful to God, and not worship other gods.
- The Ten Commandments explain exactly what a person's duties, both religious, and social, will be.
- This provides for everyone in society. The Commandment about the Sabbath says that the day of rest applies to everyone, even the non-Jew (and animals!).
- The rest of the Torah extends the Ten Commandments and provides a complete social security system for God's people.
- God is a benevolent dictator, fond of his children when they are good, but swift to anger when they are bad. God is 'a jealous' God.

God's activity in the world

Joshua 10:1–15

During a battle with various enemies, the Jewish armies are helped through the direct intervention of God.

> *And the Lord threw [the enemies] into a panic*
> *... The Lord threw down great stones from heaven on them*
> *... And the sun stood still, and the moon stayed*

God is credited with the victory against the enemies of the Jews.

Unlike the Greek idea of God being associated with the world of the Form, the Biblical God is closely involved in the world of humans:

- He intervenes directly in events.
- He is prepared to intervene in the 'laws of nature' in order to help his people.
- The Jewish army's victory is attributed to God, not to any military skill.

Miracle	Usually defined as an event that goes against the laws of nature. Often associated with incurable illnesses, or events that are 'out of the ordinary'. The word can be used trivially – 'It's a miracle that Norwich City won again'. The classic definition (from David Hume) is that a miracle is a 'Violation of the Law of Nature by a Divine Agent (God)'.

Conclusion
- The Bible shows God's involvement in the world to be **dynamic**.
- The world was created through God's intelligent decision.
- The world was created with a purpose in mind, and God is closely involved in this purpose.

Anselm's ontological argument

Anselm's argument was based on the premise that God does exist – he set out to show that not believing in God is an absurd position to hold. This was a **reductio ad absurdum** argument – it tried to show that the existence of God could not be denied because to do so would involve adopting a nonsensical argument.

Anselm (1033–1109) was a Benedictine monk and Archbishop of Canterbury. He therefore started from a theistic ('believing') stance.

Anselm's starting point was to propose a definition of the word 'God'. From this point, he tried to show that it is absurd to suggest that God does not exist. His argument was in two parts, formed around an objection raised by another monk.

'God is the thought than which nothing greater can be thought.'

Even the suggestion that there is no God requires the **concept** of God. Since the greatest thought *must* have an equivalent reality to be greater than even the least significant thing in reality, for God to be the greatest thought, God must exist.

But
Would this argument not also prove the existence of anything 'perfect'? Anselm quoted one of his own critics – a monk named **Gaunilo**:

• Suppose someone proposes 'the most perfect island'.
• Since it is perfect, Gaunilo argued that Anselm was saying that it must exist. Since part of the perfection Anselm was arguing about included existence, the island *must* exist – otherwise even the grottiest island was better than the imaginary one.

For when a painter thinks ahead to what he will paint, he has that picture in his thought, but he does not yet think it exists, because he has not done it yet. Once he has painted it he has it in his thought and thinks it exists because he has done it. Thus even the fool is compelled to grant that something greater than which cannot be thought exists in thought, because he understands what he hears, and whatever is understood exists in thought.

'The Fool has said in his heart, there is no God'

Anselm's reply **was** that he was not arguing about temporal, **contingent** things (such as islands, which are rooted in time and space), but of '**the greatest thing that can be thought**'. Islands have no 'intrinsic maximum' – a notional island can always be bettered (see the section on **Plantinga**). God is not in the same category. God is not contingent or temporal. As such, God's existence is **necessary**.

Descartes's ontological argument

René Descartes (1596–1650) set out his argument in his *Meditations*. He began by defining God as:

a supremely perfect being

From this definition, Descartes tried to prove God's existence.

Descartes is famous for his approach to establishing the extent of his knowledge. He began by doubting that he knew anything, and then concluded that the only thing that he could know was that he was thinking. '**Cogito, ergo sum**' – I think, therefore I am.

Because God is a supremely perfect being, He possesses all perfections.

This perfect state includes existence, which is a perfection in itself. Existence is a predicate of a perfect being.

Therefore God exists.

There are some things that an object has to have for it to be that object.
- The two wheels are essential to a bicycle
- A bachelor has to be unmarried.

Descartes argued that God must exist in the same way that a triangle must have three sides and three angles that add up to 180°.

Predicate
To predicate something is to ascribe to something a quality or property.

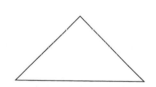

But, nevertheless, when I think of it more attentively, it appears that the existence can no more be separated from the essence of God, than the idea of a mountain from that of a valley, or the equality of its three angles to two right angles, from the essence of a [rectilinear] triangle; so that it is not less impossible to conceive a God, that is, a being supremely perfect, to whom existence is awanting, or who is devoid of a certain perfection, than to conceive a mountain without a valley.
http://www.cola.wright.edu/DesCartes/Meditation5.html

- This argument cannot apply to objects affected by space and time (such as Gaunilo's island).
- It can only apply to something that is perfect.

- Only God can have absolute perfection – there cannot be two absolutes.

- Descartes argued that to deny the existence of God is as absurd as saying 'the existing such and such does not exist'.
(Mackie, p.42)

- All arguments that try to establish the necessary existence of other things, including Martians (Mackie) or unicorns (Russell), are trying to establish the necessary existence of *contingent* objects. But only an absolutely perfect being can have *necessary* existence.

The responses of Kant, Russell, and Hume

Descartes had said that God had existence in the same way as a triangle has three sides.

Immanuel Kant (1724–1804)
- *If* you have a triangle
- then it *must* have three angles.
- *But* if you do *not* have the triangle, you have neither its three angles nor its three sides.

- **If** you accept that there is a God, it is logical to accept also that His existence is *necessary* (as opposed to *contingent*, something that happens by chance).
But you do not have to accept that there is a God.

Analytic statements	**Synthetic statements**
are true or false in terms of the words used: *A vixen is a female fox.*	look to empirical evidence for their verification: *All foxes are carnivorous.*

Kant was distinguishing between **analytic** and **synthetic** statements. Necessity is about logic, whereas existence is about experience.

Predicate	**Necessity**	**Existence**
To predicate something is to ascribe to something a quality or property.	$2 + 2 = 4$ This *has* to be so!	I saw four. But there might have been five.

- Existence is not a predicate – you can describe something perfectly, and then add that it exists. It is not a quality in a list of qualities.
- Kant argued that adding reality to a concept does not make it any better. He put it like this: 'a hundred real thalers (*German silver coin*) does not contain the least coin more than a hundred possible thalers.'

  Describing someone as 'tall' adds to our understanding of that person – it ascribes a quality to them.

  Describing someone as 'existing' does not.

- Stephen Davis pointed out that something imaginary does lack 'practical value' when compared with its real counterpart.

Bertrand Russell (1872–1970)
- Russell argued that Anselm's use of the notion of necessary existence represented a **syllogism**.
- Existence cannot be a predicate – if it was, Russell argued that the following could be constructed: Men exist – Santa Claus is a man – therefore Santa Claus exists.
Therefore
- Existence is not a property of things.
It is, rather, a numerical concept: comparing cows and unicorns brings you to the point where you conclude that there are many cows, but no unicorns.
Existence is not a quality or attribute that unicorns lack.

Syllogism
is the inference of one proposition from two premises.
- All Greeks are men
- All men are mortal
- Therefore all Greeks are mortal.

David Hume (1711–1776)
- Hume argued that the description of a thing can contain every detail possible, but we must go beyond the description itself to determine whether or not that thing exists.
- A thing cannot be 'defined into existence'; no matter how perfect we imagine that being to be, we cannot simply derive existence from its assumed perfection.
- All the ontological argument does is place God's existence in philosophically rational terms *if* He did exist.

Other responses to the ontological argument

Plato (c.428–347BCE)

The allegory of the cave

Imagine some people living in a cave. They are tied up so that they can only see the back wall of the cave. The only things that the people can see are the shadows of things passing the mouth of the cave.

One man escapes, and is dazzled by the 'real' objects that were casting the shadows. He sees colours and shapes – he returns to tell his fellows, but they reject his news.

This famous passage from *Republic* explains Plato's **idea of the Form**. Objects in our world are imperfect copies of the 'Form' of that thing. The most important 'Form' is the 'Form of the Good'.

All things in the material world are derivatives from the universals that they represent. Anselm regarded the 'greatest thought' as an Idea.

Iris Murdoch (1919–1999)

Murdoch argued that Anselm's idea of necessary existence was a part of the Platonic view of degrees of reality (see the allegory of the cave, left).

Anselm was pointing towards a spiritual reality beyond human reasoning. From this failure of reason, we are able to catch a glimpse of the nature of God as a transcendent being.

René Descartes (1596–1650)

- God is the absolute of all possible perfections.
- This perfect state includes existence, which is a perfection in itself.

Predicate

To predicate something is to ascribe to something a quality or property.

There are some qualities that are essential to a thing – a triangle must have three sides, and God must have existence.

Norman Malcolm (1911–1990)

Malcolm argued that necessary existence cannot be affected by anything external to itself. It cannot be brought about, nor can it be terminated, by anything.
- Therefore, God's existence is either **impossible**, or **necessary.**
Because
- Since necessary existence cannot be affected by anything beyond itself, God cannot be 'made' to come into existence.
- For God not to exist becomes logically absurd.

If God does **not** exist, He cannot be brought into existence, therefore His existence is impossible.

If God **does** exist, He cannot have been brought into existence, nor can He cease to exist.

Platinga (1932–present)

- For **Alvin Plantinga** a possible world is a complete way that things can be, not merely a different world elsewhere in the galaxy.
- There are an infinite number of possible worlds. In this one you chose A-Level Religious Studies – in another you could have chosen something else.
- There is one of these possible worlds in which there exists a being with **maximal greatness**. A being can only have maximal greatness if it exists in every possible world.

Therefore this maximally great being *must* exist in every possible world. Since our world is a possible world, God must exist here.

Possible worlds

A possible world differs in some possible way from our 'actual' world. Philosophers use the concept to decide on the **'modality'** of a statement. Modality refers to the statement's necessity, possibility or impossibility.

A non-realist view of the existence of God

Vardy points out that the various arguments argue for God's existence as though he was an **object** (see Gaunilo's objection).

Garth Moore

compares the existence of God with the existence of the equator – no-one claims that the equator does not exist, but there isn't a line drawn around the planet! In The same way, God's reality is as real for believers as is the equator for geographers. God is therefore a reality in the believer's life.

Aquinas's cosmological argument

Plato (428–347BCE)
- Motion and change are brought about by something external to the things that they happen to.
- There is a **self-moving principle** from which all change and motion originate.

This principle is the soul. It is the soul that is responsible for the world as it is.

Cosmology
κοσμος (*cosmos*) *the Greek word for the world*
The cosmological argument argues from the existence of the world, and its perceived state of order, to the existence of a Creator, or God.

Thomas Aquinas (1225–1274)
The classic version of the cosmological argument is found in Thomas Aquinas's ***Summa Theologica***, where he proposed **five ways** to argue for the existence of God.

1 The unmoved mover
- Everything that is moving or changing (i.e. more or less everything!) is moved or changed by something outside itself.
- The instigator of the motion or change in a thing is also changing or in motion.
- And so on . . .
- And so on . . .
- This process cannot go back infinitely, since then there would be no 'First Mover'.

Therefore there must be a First Mover, independent of anything else. This is what everyone understands to be God.

2 The uncaused causer
- Every effect has a cause.
- Nothing that we experience is caused by itself.
- As with (1), there cannot be an infinite regression of causes.

Therefore there must be a First Cause. This is what everyone understands to be God.

Aquinas based his argument on Aristotle's views on **causation** (see p.9):
1. Material Cause
2. Efficient Cause
3. Formal Cause
4. Final Cause

3 Contingency and necessity
- All things in nature are subject to change.
- It is possible for a thing not to be, then to come into existence, and then to cease to exist.
- If this is so, then at some time there was nothing at all.
- If *this* is so, then there must be something that brings contingent things into existence, since nothing can come from nothing.

Therefore there must be a being that necessarily exists to bring the contingent world into being. This is what everyone understands to be God.

4 Excellence
- Everything in the world that exists is more or less good. There are varying degrees of excellence.
- There cannot be an infinite scale of good.

Therefore there must be something that is perfection. This is what everyone understands to be God.

5 Purpose (strictly speaking, a **teleological** argument)
- Everything works to some purpose or other.
- This cannot just be luck, since things that have no rational powers still have purpose. They must be directed by some external power.

Therefore there is an intelligent being which directs everything towards a purpose. This is what everyone understands to be God.

Responses to Aquinas

Vardy sees Aquinas's **third way** (from contingency and necessity) as the most important:

The third way is taken from possibility and necessity, and runs thus. We find in nature things that are possible to be and not to be, since they are found to be generated, and to corrupt, and consequently, they are possible to be and not to be. But it is impossible for these always to exist, for that which is possible not to be at some time is not. Therefore, if everything is possible not to be, then at one time there could have been nothing in existence. Now if this were true, even now there would be nothing in existence, because that which does not exist only begins to exist by something already existing. Therefore, if at one time nothing was in existence, it would have been impossible for anything to have begun to exist; and thus even now nothing would be in existence – which is absurd. Therefore, not all beings are merely possible, but there must exist something the existence of which is necessary. But every necessary thing either has its necessity caused by another, or not. Now it is impossible to go on to infinity in necessary things which have their necessity caused by another, as has been already proved in regard to efficient causes. Therefore we cannot but postulate the existence of some being having of itself its own necessity, and not receiving it from another, but rather causing in others their necessity. This all men speak of as God.

http://www.newadvent.org/summa/100203.htm

- The world is made up of **contingent** things (things subject to change and decay).
- Contingent things need not exist. They depend on something other than themselves for their existence.
- If all things were contingent, then there would be a time when nothing contingent existed.
- If there were a time when nothing existed, then without there being some (non-contingent) agency to bring contingent things into being, there would still be nothing.
- Everything that is contingent is dependent on something else for its existence.
- Each contingent thing must be preceded by something else to bring it into existence. Yet this sequence cannot stretch back infinitely.

There must therefore be a non-contingent agent which is responsible for bringing the contingent universe into being. Aquinas refers to this 'being' as God.

Criticisms of Aquinas

N.B. Vardy claims that Aquinas tries to establish **dependence**, rather than a stretch back in time.

N.B. Developments in modern physics have begun to consider the idea that matter may not be eternal.

- Why not an endless series of causes?
- Can there not be something that has always existed, but may cease to exist at some time in the future?
- Why should the chain of causes lead back to a single origin – might there not be a whole collection of separate origins?
- Aquinas based his argument on a contingent universe – but in some ways the universe is not contingent. The matter and energy in the universe are eternal, though they are distributed through the universe in different ways at different times.

Revision Advice 1: Basic organisation

Make sure you have a list of all the topics that you need to revise. Get a copy of the specifications for your course – either ask one of your tutors or visit the appropriate exam board's website.

Read through the specification content. Look at the topics that are included in your course, and list them.

Use this topic list as an index to organise the notes and essays you have written throughout your course.

Highlight the sections of the specification that you are confident with. Using a different colour, highlight the sections that you think you will need to work on.

The Kalam argument

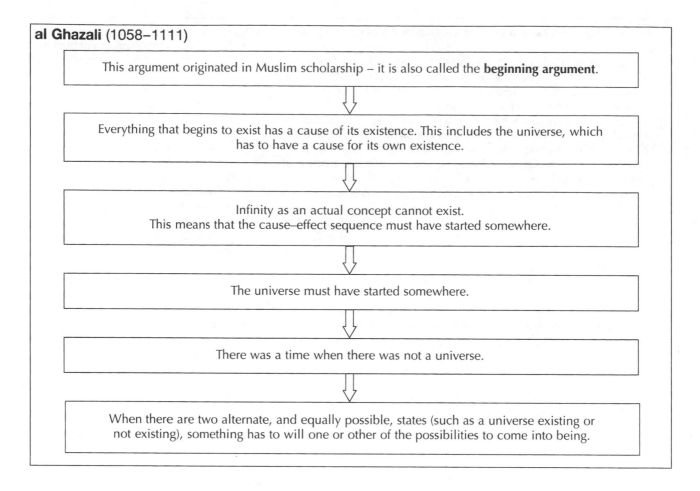

al Ghazali (1058–1111)

This argument originated in Muslim scholarship – it is also called the **beginning argument**.

Everything that begins to exist has a cause of its existence. This includes the universe, which has to have a cause for its own existence.

Infinity as an actual concept cannot exist.
This means that the cause–effect sequence must have started somewhere.

The universe must have started somewhere.

There was a time when there was not a universe.

When there are two alternate, and equally possible, states (such as a universe existing or not existing), something has to will one or other of the possibilities to come into being.

William Lane Craig (1949–present)

Craig argued that the universe cannot be infinite, because you cannot add to an actual infinite amount. The past can be regarded as a succession of events added one on another.

Potential infinity
Like the future – events are constantly being added to the sum total.

Actual infinity
A mathematical concept from **set theory**, referring to the idea of infinite numbers of parts within a set.

- Since the universe *is* finite, it must have had a beginning.
- Whatever exists must have a cause.
- Therefore the universe had a cause to its existence.
- If the world had a beginning, this beginning was either caused or uncaused.
- **It either came about naturally, or through a 'personal choice'.**
- The laws of nature did not exist before the world came into being – there were no natural causes to bring the world about.
- **Therefore it cannot be that the world came about due to random forces of nature. There must have been some personal agency involved.**
- This personal agent must have existed outside space and time, since these came into being at the point of creation. Therefore the 'personal agent' is a transcendent being.
- The cause of the universe must be a 'personal being' who freely chooses to create the world.

Ed Miller
(1937–present)
This adaptation of the Kalam argument centres on time:

- An infinite universe would have an infinite number of days.
- The end of an infinite series of days would never be reached.
- This means that we would never reach today.

- Time began when the universe began.
- Events are caused.
- The beginning of the universe was an event.
- Therefore there must have been a cause.
- This First Cause was God.

The responses of Copleston, Russell, and Hume

Frederick Copleston (1907–1994) and Bertrand Russell (1872–1970)
Copleston argued that there are some things that do not have to have come into existence. They would not be, had the things that caused them not come together in the way that they did.

> Copleston's argument was proposed during a famous radio debate with Bertrand Russell on the BBC in 1947.

> The universe is basically the sum total of all things that exist, and these objects rely on things beyond themselves for their existence.

> Since the universe consists of everything that there is, and none of its contents can be the cause of its existence, the cause for the existence of the universe must be external to it.

> The cause for the universe must be self-causing. Copleston calls this a 'necessary being'. It must exist independently of anything else, and as such is outside the universe.

Russell replied:

> *The whole concept of cause is one we derive from our observation of particular things; I see no reason whatsoever to suppose that the total has any cause whatsoever. ...what I'm saying is that the concept of cause is not applicable to the total.*
>
> http://www.utas.edu.au/docs/humsoc/philosophy/ccc/slides/3g.html

Russell was denying that the universe needed any explanation at all for its existence. Russell's universe would appear to be entirely without reason. The religious person would reply that the universe is intelligible, and the cause of an intelligent creative power. Russell has attracted criticism for his apparent lack of curiosity about the cause and origin of the universe: his statement:

> *I should say that the universe is just there, and that's all.*

makes the existence of the universe a mere **brute fact**. Claiming that the universe has a cause because everything in it has a cause is like claiming that because every human being has a mother, the entire human race has a mother.

- Copleston criticised Russell, pointing out that the First Cause may not be in a linear time sequence, but a more **ontological** sequence.

Russell's lack of curiosity about the origins of the universe is odd, given his generally inquisitive and scientific approach!

David Hume (1711–1776)
Hume also argued against a First Cause for the universe. He maintained that the fact that everything *within* the universe has a cause does not necessarily mean that the universe itself must have a cause.
- He argued that we have no experience of universes being made, and so we cannot speak meaningfully about the creation of the universe. To move from 'everything that we observe has a cause' to 'the universe has a cause' is too big a leap in logic.

Other modern responses to the cosmological argument

John L. Mackie (1917–1981)

Mackie responded to the criticisms of Aquinas. Modern science and mathematics had moved on from the medieval world-view, which was very hierarchical.

- Mackie defended the idea that there cannot be an infinite regression of causes.
- It is not logical to think of a railway train consisting simply of an infinite number of carriages: the train must ultimately have an engine to drive it. Nor can you have a watch which has a movement determined by an infinite sequence of cogs and springs: the movement must begin with the mainspring and end with the hands on the face of the watch.

Anthony Kenny (1931–present)

Kenny bases his observations on Newton's Laws of Motion, and noted his **First Law of Motion**:

> *A body's velocity would remain unchanged unless some other force – such as friction – acted upon it.*

Kenny thinks that Newton's Law proves Aquinas wrong. It is possible that an object can be in one of two states – stationary or moving at a constant rate – without any external force acting on it.

This would appear to mean that Aquinas's statement that nothing moves itself is incorrect.

Gottfried Leibniz (1646–1716)

'Why is there something rather than nothing?'

Leibniz's argument is sometimes called the 'argument from sufficient reason'.

There must be an ultimate reason to account for the existence of the world itself. This cannot be from within the world. It must be external. For a sufficient reason for the world's existence, there must be a being that can create existence.

This being must **necessarily** exist.
This is what we call God.

Modern science

- Further challenges to Aquinas's ideas regarding the uncaused cause come from subatomic physics.
- Particles have been observed to disappear and reappear without any apparent cause.
- The Big Bang theory appears to support the idea of a time when the universe did not exist.
- Since it is not possible to add to an actual number of days (see the section on Ed Miller), the universe appears to be finite.

However, some say that the Big Bang did not mark the beginning of the universe, but simply the beginning of this particular phase of the universe. Some scientists argue for an **oscillating universe**, where this is only one of a series of expanding and contracting universes.

The teleological argument of Aquinas

The teleological argument, suggesting that there is evidence for design in the universe, argues **a posteriori**.

τελος (*telos*)
Goal, aim, purpose
The teleological argument looks at the idea of purpose and order in the universe.

a priori
The proof of the statement does not rely on external evidence.
For example:
All bachelors are unmarried.
Malcolm is a bachelor.
Malcolm is unmarried.

a posteriori
The proof of the statement relies on external evidence.
For example:
The girls in Year 11 achieved higher grades than the boys.

The teleological argument is based on the idea that the world was **designed.** Its main principle is that there is evidence for design in the world.

Aquinas (1225–1274)
See the fifth way (in the section on **The cosmological argument**). Aquinas argued that for non-intelligent matter to behave in a way that is beneficial, there needs to be an intelligent power to bring this state of affairs about. This is God.

Revision Advice 2: The examiner

Know your enemy! Well, not your enemy – the examiner is not there to catch you out but to see what you can do in response to the questions set in the exam. So it would be a good idea to find out what you need to do!

Take a look at the assessment objectives for your course (you'll find them towards the front of the specifications). These are what you will be tested on, so it's a good idea to understand what they want.

Look at the guidance notes that are published to support teachers – these are written by the examiners to help teachers to plan their courses, and might help you to understand how to approach the topics on your course!

The exam boards also publish 'specimen questions' and 'mark schemes' for their courses (more on these later). You might like to look at the mark schemes to see how your exam paper will be marked. *Don't be tempted to treat the mark schemes as 'correct answers' – the examiners are looking for any reasonable answer to a question, not just a 'right answer'.*

Once you understand what the examiners are going to be looking for, you can start planning your revision. More advice later.

Paley's argument

William Paley (1743–1805)

In **Natural Theology**, Paley used the famous analogy of the watch (an 'old-fashioned' mechanical watch, with a tremendously complex movement of cogs, wheels and springs, rather than the modern quartz watch):

- It is not reasonable to assume that a watch found on a heath came about without the agency of a watchmaker.
- It is equally unreasonable to suggest that the universe, with all its intricacies, came about without the agency of a God.

You could equally well apply the argument to other comparisons between nature and manufactured items. Consider:

- the eye, when compared to a sophisticated auto-focus camera
- the heart, and doctors' attempts to make an artificial heart to treat patients with heart disease
- engineers' efforts to make robots
- artificial intelligence and neurological research.

Design *qua* Purpose
The argument that the Universe appears to have been designed to fulfil some purpose.

The basis of the argument is that there is evidence of **design** in the universe around us. Everything appears to have been designed to fulfil some function. This argument is **Design *qua* Purpose**.

- The way that each aspect of the Natural World appears to fulfil its purpose well is further evidence of design.

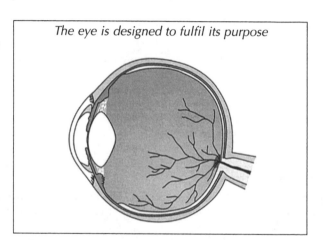

The eye is designed to fulfil its purpose

Paley therefore argues for a **Designing Creator** – God.

- Paley goes on to argue that there is further evidence for a Creator God in the **regularity** of the Universe.
- Astronomical discoveries, and Isaac Newton's Laws of Motion, demonstrated a controlled, rather than random, principle at work in the Universe.

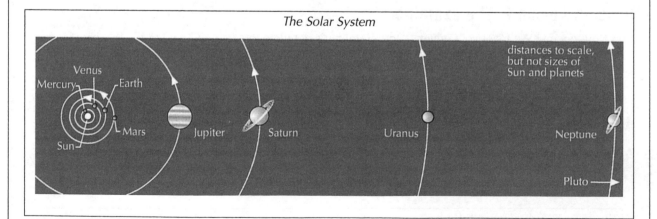

The Solar System

distances to scale, but not sizes of Sun and planets

Venus
Mercury — Earth
Mars
Sun
Jupiter
Saturn
Uranus
Neptune
Pluto

Design *qua* Regularity
The argument that the Universe appears to behave according to some order or rule.

In particular, Paley considered the motion of the planets in the solar system.

- The relationships between the planets, and the effect of gravity between them, could not have come about without a designing principle at work. This principle is God.

Modern versions from Tennant and Swinburne

F. R. Tennant (1866–1957)
Philosophical Theology (1930)
- It is possible to imagine a chaotic universe, where there are no rules.
- The universe is evidently *not* chaotic. In fact, it appears to be designed to support life. Further, it appears to be beautiful at all levels.
- Evolution itself, proposed by biologists as an unregulated principle, in fact works to the advancement of species, supported by a world that provides all that is necessary to promote life.

- There is more to life than mere existence. Humans appreciate aesthetic activity, such as art, music, and literature. This is not necessary for mere survival, so cannot have come about through natural selection. Therefore, life as we know it is the product of a designing creator.
- This last part of Tennant's argument is sometimes called the **aesthetic argument**.
- Tennant also formulated the **anthropic principle** (see below).

Richard Swinburne (1934–present)

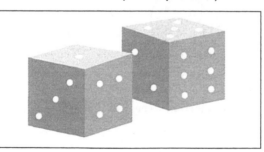

- The universe could easily be either ordered or chaotic.
- The fact that it appears ordered cannot be mere *chance*.
- It must therefore be a matter of **probabilities**.
- The sheer size of the universe makes it unlikely that it should just 'happen'.
- Further, the universe appears to operate by a series of laws.
- These laws do not account for the apparently ordered way in which the universe operates:

In scientific explanations we explain particular phenomena as brought about by prior phenomena in accord with scientific laws... from the very nature of science it cannot explain the highest level laws of all; for they are that by which it explains all other phenomena.

Swinburne, R. *The Existence of God*, 1979, p.138

Swinburne argued that the high degree of order that the universe demonstrates is evidence of a personal, conscious choice of God. From this order we can discern beauty (he claimed that we cannot have beauty without order) and the order is a 'good' thing.

Hume's and Mill's criticisms

David Hume (1711–1776)

Hume set out two versions of the design argument:

Hume's first argument	1. To speak of 'design' is to imply a designer. 2. Great design implies a great designer. 3. There is great design in the world, so ... 4. There must be a great designer.

This version relies on analogy. Hume argued that it in fact implies a superhuman, anthropomorphic concept of God, which is very limited and inconsistent. The world is imperfect and flawed, and as such it could suggest an imperfect and flawed creator:

The design of the 'wobbly' Millennium Bridge across the Thames is argued to suggest an incompetent design team.	The design of the world, with all its arbitrary suffering, is argued to suggest an incompetent creator.

Hume's second argument	1. The world is ordered. 2. This is either because of chance or because of design. 3. It is entirely possible that the world did come about through chance.

Further, there is nothing in the argument to suppose that there is only one creator – if many builders collaborate to build a house, why not many Gods?

Hume went on to support the idea of natural selection – he claimed that it is entirely plausible that adaptations made by animals to survive may be the result of random adaptations, rather than the agency of an intelligent designer.

Hume was arguing that *if* a person can discern order and purpose in the universe, all that this can legitimately lead to is the conclusion that there is order and purpose in the universe. To conclude that there is a God behind this presumed order would be, in **Mackie's** word, 'gratuitous'. Hume argued that there is no *need* to make that step from ordered universe to God.	Paley's analogy was to compare the world with a watch. Hume argued that a more accurate analogy would be to compare the world with a carrot – the 'mark' of design discerned in the world could be due to 'generation', 'self-regulation' and 'growth' rather than to design.
	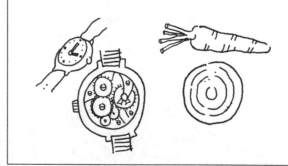

Darwin (1809–1882) supported this criticism with his work on natural selection – see also biologists such as Richard Dawkins.

J. S. Mill (1806–1873)

In *Nature and the Utility Religion* (1874) Mill argues that nature is 'guilty' of serious crimes for which she goes unpunished. The various 'atrocities' through which both humans and animals suffer would not go unpunished if they were the result of Human agency. *'Nearly all the things which men are hanged or imprisoned for doing to one another are nature's everyday performances'.*

Mill therefore concludes that the world cannot be ordered, and he rejects the idea that it is the result of intelligent design.

Darwin's criticisms

Darwin, evolution and the teleological argument
Origin of Species by Means of Natural Selection (1859)

Charles Darwin

- Random variations in a species become a feature of that species where they promote the survival of that species.

Darwin proposed a theory of the survival of the fittest (this theory was also proposed by Spencer in *Principles of Biology*, 1865).

Darwin called the principle by which species develop **natural selection**. The fittest, healthiest members of the species survive, and their characteristics become a part of the character of the species.

Darwin drew on the work of **Thomas Malthus**, who had argued that the world has a built-in regulator which controls the population levels of living creatures.

The Malthusian principle of population control		
Malthus's ideas apply to both humans and the animal kingdom.	Low population •	The species thrives with ideal conditions for survival.
	Population growth •	The population begins to grow – favourable conditions mean that infant mortality is relatively low, and there is relatively little disease.
	Overpopulation •	The environment begins to struggle to support the population. Disease and pestilence spread. Infant mortality and other factors increase.
	Fall in population •	The population level begins to suffer as famines and epidemics begin to reduce numbers.
	Low population •	See above

Natural selection

Organisms produce more offspring than can survive.

- There are variations between these individual offspring – they are not all alike.
- Some of these variations turn out to be favourable as the organism struggles to survive in its particular environment.
- These offspring therefore survive better than their siblings who do not have the variation. These successful variants are more attractive to potential mates, and the variation becomes an established characteristic of the species.
- The offspring with the variation therefore are more successful, and produce more offspring themselves. Meanwhile the less successful offspring (those without the variation) dwindle in number.

The variation becomes a part of the make-up of the organism.

Darwin saw this process as gradual and ongoing. It explains the variations within a species, and also the apparently close relationship between different species.

So what?

> Paley and Aquinas argued for intelligent design in the world.

> Darwin argued that the apparent design is in fact the result of a natural and random process. It is, in the words of the geneticist Steve Jones, **a series of successful mistakes** (*Almost Like A Whale*, 1999).

Dawkins's criticisms

Richard Dawkins (1941–present)
The Selfish Gene and other books

Dawkins proposes a purely mechanistic universe, in which biological impulses drive life forwards.

Altruism
Regard for others as
a principle of action People do not behave altruistically. They behave in order to enable human genes to survive.

'We are survival machines – robot vehicles blindly programmed to preserve the selfish molecules known as genes.'

The Blind Watchmaker (1986) (The title is taken from the introduction to Paley's *Natural Theology*.)
Climbing Mount Improbable (1996)
Dawkins sees the development of life on earth as inevitable because of the genetic foundations for that life.
- Each living thing carries a certain uniqueness that is defined by its genes.
- The evolutionary process is carried through by random and spontaneous mutations in the genetic make-up of living creatures. This genetic make-up causes each living thing to develop in the way that it does.

The process is not entirely random. While the initial mutation may be random, the process that follows is not. The evolutionary self-selection process affects the success of any particular genetic mutation.
The mapping of the human genome pushes back the boundaries of human knowledge about the nature of life. We know that a fertilised egg contains all the genetic information required for that egg to develop into a unique, sentient human being. DNA contains every instruction necessary for the egg to split and develop into an individual person.

The Selfish Gene (1989)

Dawkins does not mean selfish in a moral sense, but that genes are engaged in a struggle for survival.

Dawkins claims that our genes are 'selfish'.
- These selfish genes survive using the human body, which is, so to speak, a 'survival suit'.
At a fundamental level, genes are simply bytes of information, programs that are engaged in a struggle for survival. Evolution is this genetic struggle in practice.

Some responses to Dawkins and to materialist biology and neo-Darwinism:

- **Arthur Peacocke** (*physical biologist and theologian*) – Dawkins still does not address the need for an explanation of *how* our universe came into being, or why things are.

- **John Polkinghorne** (*physicist and priest*) – God *chose* to create a universe that is governed by chance and law.

- **Paul Davies** (*physicist*) – There is a reason for the organisation of the universe, and someone designed it. However, it is a matter of interpretation. 'Science deals with the facts of the world, religion deals with the interpretation of those facts.'

Davies, P. in Stannard, R. *Science and Wonders,* 1996

Is the universe really ordered?

Immanuel Kant (1724–1804)

- The design argument is based on the premise that there is design in the universe.
- The universe may be in a state of chaos and confusion.
- Our minds assimilate and organise sense experiences into a perceived order.

Kant's synthesis of empiricism and rationalism
All our knowledge of the world comes from sensation, but our reason determines how we perceive the world around us. We all wear the spectacles of reason, affecting the way that we perceive the world.

Sigmund Freud (1856–1939)

- In *The Future of an Illusion* (1927) Freud argued that religion arises from a fear of a chaotic and un-ordered world. A person's resolution of this traumatic perception of the world is to project onto it their memory of their father, who provided a world of order and regularity while they were a child.

Religious faith is therefore an illusion based on 'wishful thinking' rather than reality.

- We therefore impose a perceived order on a chaotic universe.
- Our minds are pre-disposed to see order, so we **project** order on to the universe.

Post-modernist philosophy has argued that we impose order on the universe by talking it all into place. Our words create an order out of chaos. However, modern science has also argued for an order of sorts:

The anthropic principle
The anthropic principle was first suggested by F. R. Tennant, who argued that life on earth exists because the laws that govern the universe have particular features that contribute to make life possible. For example:

Gravitational force is constant
- *if larger:* stars would be too hot; they would burn up quickly and unevenly
- *if smaller:* stars would be too cool; nuclear fusion would not ignite; no heavy element production

Expansion rate of the universe is stable
- *if larger:* no galaxy formation
- *if smaller:* universe would collapse prior to star formation

The anthropic principle has developed into a **strong** and a **weak** form.

Strong anthropic principle:
The conditions required for life are intrinsic to the nature of the universe. Life was *inevitable*.

Weak anthropic principle:
The conditions required for life in the universe *happen* to have occurred.

Some theists have argued that this apparent order is evidence for an intelligent creating power behind the universe.
Others argue that the weak form is merely an observation, and the strong form is based on flawed logic.

Various scientists have tried to estimate the odds against the existence of life on earth. Consider:

The physicist Lawrence Krauss compares the odds against gravity having precisely the value necessary for the cosmos to exist to the odds against someone guessing precisely how many atoms are in the sun.
http://www.unesco.org/courier/2001_05/uk/doss21.htm

According to Yale University's Harold Morowitz, a probability expert, this would be the equivalent of throwing 4 billion penny pieces into the air, and every one landing 'heads up'.

What is religious experience?

The various classic arguments about the existence of God would appear to be unconvincing, but they lend weight to the claim that God *might* exist.

However, most people do not defend their religious belief using philosophical argument. Rather, they refer to their experience of God.

What is a religious experience?

1. An experience in a religious context. For example, an experience of an act of worship, or of a religious building, would count as a religious experience in this sense.

2. A person's experience of something (a presence or power) beyond themselves.

- Religious experiences tend to be of something 'out of the ordinary'.
- There is often a problem in trying to explain the experience. Everyday language would appear inadequate.
- There are some experiences that are universal (such as the experience of hunger, or of seeing something objective). Religious experiences tend to be unique to the experiencer – not everyone has religious experiences.
- It is difficult to verify (check) a religious experience.
- Religious experiences provide insight into something other than the everyday, material world.
- Religious experiences are often said to be 'by permission' of God – an ordinary experience is available to anyone with the required equipment.

Richard Swinburne (*The Existence of God,* 1979)

identified **five** types of religious experience in which people seem to perceive God.

In having a private experience that can be described using everyday language *(e.g. a dream).*	In having a private experience that cannot be described using everyday language *(e.g. a mystical experience).*	The conviction that they were experiencing God, even though there are no public or private phenomena to be experienced.
In perceiving a perfectly normal phenomenon *(e.g. a night sky).*	In perceiving a very unusual public object *(e.g. a miracle such as the resurrection).*	

Mysticism

The name given to experiences that apprehend an ultimate reality, but that cannot be described using normal language. Well known mystics include:

Walter Hilton (d. 1396)

Hilton was a monk near Southwell. He is well known for his practical guidance for meditation – his own contemplative writing concentrates on the bitterness of Christ's suffering, and on his compassion for the human condition.

Margery Kempe (c. 1373–1439)

Kempe became well known for her writings on the nature of God using domestic imagery. She based her writings on a series of visions (described in vivid language).

See also notes of Julian of Norwich, Teresa of Avila and John of the Cross in the Religious Experience notes.

James's varieties of religious experience

William James (1842–1910) wrote a book called *The Varieties of Religious Experience* (1902).

Ineffability
The experience is so unlike anything else that the person cannot describe it to anyone else. The expressions *'the dissolution of the personal ego'* and *'a sense of peace and sacredness'* are meaningless to anyone who has not had such an experience.

Noetic quality
Despite their apparently inexpressible nature, such experiences produce a sense of insight into truths that are not attainable by the intellect alone. Rather than being understood through reason and intellectual discussion, these truths are attained through instinct and perception. They are eternal and universal, rather than trivial.

Transiency
The experience lasts only a short time (studies have suggested an average duration of around an hour). It may be that the memory of the experience dulls with time, though the experience is instantly recalled should it happen again. Where the experience is a part of a series, there is a progression towards increased understanding of the truths being revealed. The experience leaves the person with a sense of the importance of the experience.

Passivity
This is a sense of powerlessness in the face of the experience. People have spoken of a sense of having being taken over by some ultimate power. Often, the person can appear completely out of control – in particular, *speaking in tongues* or prophetic speech are associated with religious experience.

The experience need not be particularly spectacular – simply a sense that the 'penny has dropped', a growing sense of awareness of a truth that has been known for some time. It could also be a completely life-changing experience that causes the person to lose consciousness.

James noted that most religious experiences occur when the person is conscious – the person is able to tell that they are not simply experiencing a dream. He also noted that it is possible that the experiences that he recorded could have been induced through the influence of alcohol or drugs.

Revision Advice 3: Planning your time

You ought to be revisiting topics throughout your course. However, towards the end of the course you will need to plan carefully to make sure that you have a good understanding of the course as a whole, and to prepare for the exams themselves.

A write-on wall planner or a calendar will give you an 'at-a-glance' guide to your revision campaign.

Allow equal coverage for all your subjects – don't neglect your 'best' subject to concentrate on one that you feel less confident on.

Build important dates into your plan. If you know that you will not be able to revise, allow for this as you allocate days to subjects.

Once you have an overview, begin to build your plan for each subject, based on your findings from the first stage (page 17).

Break a revision session into 45-minute blocks, with 15-minute breaks. If you can't live without *EastEnders*, build your revision around it (you'll only end up resenting having to work during it! However, be realistic about how much TV to include!). Then allocate topics to revision sessions.

You won't be able to learn for much longer than 45 minutes, and the 15-minute breaks will prevent both information overload and back strain!

Conversion experiences

A conversion experience usually leads to some sort of change of life. The religious context for the term refers to the way that the experience brings about some sort of change from one set of beliefs to another (for example, the change from being an atheist to being a believer).

C. S. Lewis (1898–1963) was a Professor of Medieval English at Oxford and Cambridge. He wrote a series of books explaining Christianity, including the *Narnia Chronicles*.

You must picture me alone in that room in Magdalen College, night after night, feeling, whenever my mind lifted even for a second from my work, the steady, unrelenting approach of him whom I most earnestly desired not to meet. That which I so greatly feared had at last come upon me. In the Trinity Term of 1929 I gave in, and admitted that God was God, knelt, and prayed; perhaps that night, the most dejected and reluctant convert in all England.
Surprised by Joy, 1955, pp.228–229

One of the more remarkable features of conversion experiences is the unlikeliness of the conversion. The subject is often implacably opposed to the concept that s/he becomes associated with. The best-known example of this is **St Paul**, who persecuted the early Christian Church until a conversion experience on the Damascus Road caused him to become the greatest Christian missionary (**Acts 9:1–18**). Paul himself described the experience as being as though he were re-born, a new creation.

There have also been cases of gradual conversions, in which a person's life is gradually changed. Piece by piece, a new system of beliefs is constructed. The process may not be smooth – but it is hallmarked by a personal decision by the person to accept the belief system.

A. J. Ayer (1910–1989) was the 'arch atheist' of the twentieth-century philosophical world. He wrote a book called *Language, Truth and Logic*, in which he argued that any language that could not be verified either by logic or by direct sense experience was essentially meaningless. This would discount any metaphysical language; and in particular, religious language.

In 1988, the year before his actual death, Ayer choked on a bit of smoked salmon, passed out, and his heart stopped for fully four minutes. When, with the help of medical assistance, he regained consciousness, he reported having a so-called near-death experience—a red light supposedly responsible for the governing of the universe shone, something resembling the River Styx appeared, and other trimmings were included—that found its way into the National Enquirer. *He told an interviewer for the* Tatler *that the experience made him a bit more 'wobbly' on the question of the existence of an afterlife. Although this did not in any way qualify his lifelong atheism, it apparently made him, for the first time in his life, responsive to nature. 'Freddie has got so much nicer,' his wife said, 'since he died.'*
http://www.weeklystandard.com/magazine/mag_5_19_00/epstein_bkar_5_18_00.html
Ayer is quoted as having told his doctor that he would have to revise his opinions on life after death and God, since the experience was of his 'Creator'.

Revision Advice 4: Your tutor

Don't forget the people who have been teaching you the course! They may have planned a series of revision lessons, or they may offer some sort of revision clinic.

- If they tell you what they will be covering in such a session, read through your notes before you go.
- If you find a topic hard to follow, ask your tutor for advice. You could also share the burden with your fellow students – they may have a 'take' on the topic that 'clicks' with you. Check back through your notes and text books to make sure they got it right!
- Look for student websites that will support A Level revision.

Criticisms from Freud and Marx

Freud

Freud believed that religion is simply **wishful thinking**. The mind creates the illusion as part of its attempts to deal with the 'outside' world. Freud thought that religion is a **'universal obsessional neurosis'** which addresses fears about the world and about society.

Religion is a form of **neurotic illness** arising out of the unconscious mind. Neuroses arouse repressed memories that re-emerge into the conscious mind. Freud believed that these neuroses are sexual – he therefore concluded that religion is an illusion associated with repressed sexual memories. Freud believed that religion was an attempt to deal with a chaotic and frightening world.

In **The Future of an Illusion** Freud argued that religion provides a consolation (a sort of security blanket) for people. He also suggested that religion has been used to suppress people. **Karl Marx** made the same criticisms of religion. He called religion the **opium of the people** – a sedative that kept the people under control.

Marx

Marx argued that people have their self-determination removed through a process of de-humanising activities that only serve to line the pockets of the rich capitalist minority. Any work that the people undertake is to the benefit of the idle rich – they do not enjoy the fruits of their labours.
Therefore:
- All religious, moral and political life is rooted in economics.
- People have needs, and society is organised to meet those needs.
- However, some people have been able to establish a society that benefits the few.
- **Religion simply serves to maintain this system at the expense of the people.**

Revision Advice 5: Revision strategy

You need to know how best to approach your revision. Are you a visual learner, or do you work best with text? Do you prefer to make notes, or simply to read? Here are some suggestions for approaching your revision.

Take a plain A4 sheet of paper, and produce spidergrams for each topic. File each one carefully.

Break key theories down into stages, and write them onto paper or card. Cut each stage out, and then file. Later you can try to re-arrange the cards in the right order!

Make full use of past papers, or Specimen Questions (see the exam boards' websites). Use the questions as stimuli for notes, or try timed essays.

Read your notes on a particular topic. Then put your notes to one side, and write fresh notes. Check them for errors, then file carefully.

Read through your textbook (let's hope this isn't the first time you've done this!).

Buy a set of index cards and a box. Make brief notes on key theories, and file.

Use a highlighter or a coloured crayon to mark out Key Words. You will find the key words much more quickly later. (N.B. Only do this to your own books – your tutors will get a little grumpy if your returned textbooks look like a technicolour accident!).

More on page 32

The moral argument of Aquinas

Thomas Aquinas's **fourth way** can be taken as an argument for the existence of God that takes experience of morality as its starting point.

Summa Theologica
Part One, Question 2, Article 3
The fourth way is taken from the gradation to be found in things. Among beings there are some more and some less good, true, noble and the like. But 'more' and 'less' are predicated of different things, according as they resemble in their different ways something which is the maximum, as a thing is said to be hotter according as it more nearly resembles that which is hottest; so that there is something which is truest, something best, something noblest and, consequently, something which is uttermost being; for those things that are greatest in truth are greatest in being, as it is written in Metaph. ii. Now the maximum in any genus is the cause of all in that genus; as fire, which is the maximum heat, is the cause of all hot things. Therefore there must also be something which is to all beings the cause of their being, goodness, and every other perfection; and this we call God.
   http://www.newadvent.org/summa/100203.htm

This means
• Everything in the world that exists is more or less good. There are varying degrees of excellence.
• There cannot be an infinite scale of good.
Therefore there must be something that is perfection. This is what everyone understands to be God.

• Aquinas was not arguing for the existence of God from experience of morality.
• He was arguing that we experience things that are good, true and noble. These things must take their goodness, truth and nobility from something that is more good, true and noble.
• There cannot be an infinite regression of goodness, etc.
• There must be something that is ultimate good. This is what we know as God.
• This idea derives from ideas about **causation** – something must be the cause of the noble things that we experience.
• The goal towards which all humanity strives is this ultimate good.

The idea that everything strives towards the ultimate good is based on
Aristotle's Four Causes.

This striving towards ultimate reality is also the basis of **Augustine's theodicy** (see section on **The problem of evil**).

Ultimate reality

The Created Order striving towards ultimate reality

....

Revision Advice 5 (continued)

Try using sticky notes to display important ideas and quotes.

Keep a book of quotations – while you won't need to quote word-for-word, it helps to know what certain philosophers actually said!

More on page 44

Kant's moral argument

Immanuel Kant (1724–1804)

Kant did not regard the moral argument as an argument for the existence of God. He believed that God's existence could only be established through faith.

- Happiness is the natural reward for virtuous behaviour.
- Therefore, behaving morally should lead to happiness.
- However, this appears never actually to happen.

There must therefore be something else that leads people to behave morally.

The achievement of the Highest Good in the world is the necessary object of a will determined by the moral law ... [which] ... commands us to make the highest possible good in a world the final object of all our conduct.
Kant, I. ***Critique of Practical Reason***

There must therefore be a reward for moral behaviour in the next world.

BUT

Since this promise of reward for moral behaviour is too far away to motivate moral behaviour, there must be something else that causes a person to behave morally. Kant argued that there must be some sort of sense of obligation that causes moral behaviour. This obligation is the source of moral behaviour, regardless of any reward or consequence. He argued that there were certain rationally discernible, objective laws that we are bound to follow. He called these laws **categorical imperatives**.

The categorical imperative
- People must be subject to something other than the prospect of future reward to encourage them.
- People must be subject to some sort of **obligation**.

These obligations could be understood through rationally discoverable laws. Kant called these **categorical imperatives**.

Categorical imperative	**Hypothetical imperative**
Do not tell lies.	To get to London, go this way.

- Being moral is a case of following this categorical imperative.

The basic principle that informs this is:

Act according to a maxim which can be adopted at the same time as a universal law.
Kant, I. *Fundamental Principles of the Metaphysics of Ethics*, 1785
http://www.knuten.liu.se/~bjoch509/works/kant/intr_morals.txt

This means I am never to act otherwise than so that I could also will that my maxim should become a universal law. I should do nothing that I would not want to have turned into a law that applies to everyone.

33

The categorical imperative as an argument for God's existence?

Our moral experience tells us that we are under an obligation to strive for the Highest Good.

> 1. Morality demands that we strive for this Higher Good.
>   - If it is our **obligation** to follow the law, it is our **obligation** to aim for the highest goal of this law.

> 2. It is not possible for a human being to achieve this Higher Good without assistance.
>   - Since we are not the 'cause of the world', we cannot bring about the Highest Good. Even if we could achieve perfect morality, we could not ensure the 'necessary connection' for the perfect happiness that would follow. Humans therefore lack the necessary power to bring about the Highest Good.

> 3. God must exist to assist us in achieving this Higher Good.

It is illogical to have a Highest Good that is impossible to achieve. Kant therefore argued that it was logically necessary to accept both the existence of God, and of eternal life. God is the being that brings about happiness as a reward for virtue. Since happiness clearly does not come about in this life for the majority, there must be a life beyond death in which the reward comes.

H. P. Owen (1926–1996)

Either morality is a product of impersonal – or chance – existence, or it comes from a personal source, such as God.

'It is impossible to think of a command without ... a commander'

(Owen, H.P. ***The Moral Argument for Christian Theism,*** p.49).

J. L. Mackie (1917–1981)

Mackie argued that there are no objective moral values.
- Somehow, moral judgements have come to include the claim that there are objective moral standards.
This became known as the 'Error Theory'.
- Without any objective moral standard, many people believe that there is no place for God in moral discourse.

While this does not prove there is no God, it does make the moral argument more difficult to maintain.

Dom Illtyd Trethowan (1929–present)
- Morality is a form of **religious experience**.
- Every time we make a moral choice, we choose between different actions.
- We are guided in making these choices through a sense of obligation.
- This obligation can be traced back to the fact that each person has value.

This value must come from somewhere:

> *We have value because we receive it from a source of value. This is what I mean by God. That is why the demand upon us to develop ourselves is an absolute, unconditional demand.*
>
> Trethowan, I. *Absolute Value,* 1970

We have a sense of moral obligation because we have value.

Freud's criticisms

Sigmund Freud (1856–1939)
The conscience is in fact a product of the unconscious mind.
- The super-ego also plays a part.
- These two aspects of psychological activity represent the moral decision-making mechanisms. They are 'pre-rational', in that they are independent of rational reflection.

The super-ego
The conscience
– creates feelings of guilt

The ego-ideal
Creates feelings of pride and satisfaction

Freud divided the mind into three parts:

The pre-conscious
Those things that we cannot necessarily remember now, but which we can normally recollect

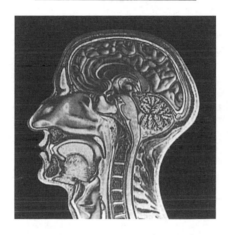

The conscious
The part of which we are aware

The unconscious
This includes memories that are too traumatic to remember, or which are too embarrassing, or which we were too young to remember

A person's moral sense comes from their super-ego. This is a psychological development that results from the Oedipus complex. The super-ego is an 'inner parent' which rewards good behaviour and punishes bad. The 'conscience' is, in fact, the action of the super-ego. Actions normally thought to be a matter of conscience are therefore determined by unconscious influences.
- Life is a series of challenges producing tension. If these tensions are not resolved, they become repressed. They reappear in later life in the form of neuroses. Behaviour that is repetitive and compulsive is called an **obsessional neurosis**.

Religion is an obsessional neurosis. Often so-called religious influences can be ascribed to such obsessive neurotic behaviour.

Criticism
Freud's ideas of the development of the conscience owe much to his idea of the **Oedipus complex**. Freud believed that a child will develop a sexual attraction to their opposite-sex parent. This then develops into an attraction for the same-sex parent after fears arise over the jealousy of the other parent.

Since Freud introduced the idea of conscience as guilt, psychologists have developed a theory that distinguishes between the mature and immature conscience.

Mature conscience
The mature conscience rationalises its decisions. It works out what is right and wrong through an evaluation of values.

Immature conscience
The immature conscience is more concerned with 'fitting in' and approval. It bases its decisions on emotion, rather than reason.

J. L. Mackie argued that evidence of biological, sociological and psychological explanations for conscience means that the moral argument no longer has a valid defence.

Newman's argument and modern criticisms

J. H. Newman (1801–1890)

Newman was a Roman Catholic theologian writing during the late nineteenth century. In **An Essay in Aid of a Grammar of Assent** (1870), he argued that we have an **illative** sense of moral judgement, which is where we get feelings of guilt and responsibility.

- Our conscience is evidence of 'One Supreme Master'. Newman **inferred** the existence of God from his experience of **conscience**.

Conscience is the 'Voice of the Lawgiver'. The existence of this voice, and its 'commission' of right and wrong, is sufficient evidence for the existence of God.

Newman was not proposing an argument for the existence of God from the existence of morality. Rather, his argument was based on the actual **experience of conscience**.

I assume, then, that Conscience has a legitimate place among our mental acts; as really so, as the action of memory, of reasoning, of imagination, or as the sense of the beautiful; that, as there are objects which, when presented to the mind, cause it to feel grief, regret, joy, or desire, so there are things which excite in us approbation or blame, and which we in consequence call right or wrong; and which, experienced in ourselves, kindle in us that specific sense of pleasure or pain, which goes by the name of a good or bad conscience. This being taken for granted, I shall attempt to show that in this special feeling, which follows on the commission of what we call right or wrong, lie the materials for the real apprehension of a Divine Sovereign and Judge.

http://www.newmanreader.org/works/grammar/chapter5-1.html

His argument relied on three points:

Conscience is authoritative.	There is a higher power behind conscience.	The person experiencing conscience is intelligent or rational.

Since sociology and psychology have claimed to provide apparent scientific explanations for the existence of the conscience and our experience of it, Newman's argument appears to have been proved wrong.

But supporters of Newman's idea argue that psychological theories for the existence and experience of conscience have provided an apparently scientific explanation only for its existence – not for its origins or purpose.

Brian Davies
- Why should it be God alone that can only bring about the Highest Good?
- Why not a **pantheon of angels**?
- Also, Kant argued that 'ought' implies 'can'. But does it? We ought to aim for the Highest Good, but we may not be able to attain that Good. John *ought* to learn French, but it does not necessarily follow that he *can*. However, it is desirable for John to try. (Davies, B. *An Introduction to the Philosophy of Religion,* p.176).

Bertrand Russell (1872–1970) in *Why I am not a Christian* (1957)
- Russell argued that human maturity required that we get rid of religion.
- A truly free rational choice is incompatible with religious concepts such as sin and reward for virtuous behaviour.
- To obey out of fear or from a desire to secure a reward (such as eternal life) is hardly the same as making a free moral choice.

Joseph Fletcher (1905–1991) *Situation Ethics* (1966)
- Morality is far more complicated than simply obeying an objective duty.
- A person responds to a moral situation in the most loving way.
- There are no absolute rules – how you act depends upon the situation.

Knowledge a priori and a posteriori

These two terms are used to refer to two types of knowledge, and also to two types of propositions, or statements, made about knowledge.

---

a priori
'prior to experience'
- Statements made a priori do not look to external sense experience for authority.
- A priori knowledge is defined without reference to anything other than itself.

An experienceable event
i.e. something that can be experienced

---

a posteriori
'subsequent to experience'
- Statements made a posteriori look to external sense experience for authority.
- A posteriori knowledge is defined with reference to something other than itself.

Many people claim that knowledge that is **a priori** is 'innate'. This would mean that it is 'built in' to human existence – we are born with it.

The field of mathematics is often held to be a priori – there is a sense that '2 + 2 = 4' without having to find four oranges to sort into various groups to see whether the sum is correct.

In fact, our knowledge of mathematics would appear to be acquired through experience. We experience groups of things, and we develop a knowledge of the relationships between groups of different sizes.

However, the mathematical knowledge that may be acquired can be verified without recourse to sense experience. Mathematical knowledge can be verified through reason and logic.

> *Kant used an a priori argument in his moral argument. He believed that a priori knowledge concerns only necessary truths, whereas a posteriori knowledge concerns contingent truths.*

A priori knowledge and religion
Several philosophers claim that knowledge of God is derived from a special form of awareness that stands alongside cognitive, moral and aesthetic forms of knowledge. Religious expression may be subject to cultural conditioning, but there is a core of knowledge that is irreducible.

Friedrich Schleiermacher (1768–1834)
Religion is not a matter of knowing or doing, but is a 'feeling of absolute dependence'.

Ernst Troeltsch (1865–1923)
Religion is a 'science' that must be analysed in its own terms as a completely independent phenomenon, and a 'qualitatively distinct aspect of human consciousness'.

Deductive and inductive reasoning

Constructing an argument

An argument comprises a series of **premises** leading to a **conclusion**. For the argument to be **valid**, it needs to obey the rules of logical argument.

Premise:	Premise:	Conclusion:
Water is wet.	*My foot is in water.*	*My foot is wet.*

This argument obeys the laws of logic – the two premises state what is the case, and the conclusion is drawn based on these premises. This is a **sound** argument.

However, not all arguments are as cut-and-dried as this!

Premise:	Premise:	Conclusion:
This water is frozen.	*It froze at 0°C.*	*Water freezes at 0°C.*

The water need not freeze at 0°C on every occasion. Scientists are prepared to accept a conclusion based on observation only when it becomes intellectually dishonest to deny the conclusion any further.

- The first approach is **deductive** – it is a sound piece of argument.
- The second approach is **inductive** – it is based on observation.

The two approaches are different.

Deductive	**Inductive**
An argument that draws its conclusion from a set of premises. No claims of truth are made, simply of logic.	A method of arguing that starts with observation and makes its conclusion 'on the balance of probability'.

> *Note that Sherlock Holmes does not deduce his legendary conclusions – his approach is more **abductive** (the process of using evidence to reach a wider conclusion).*

David Hume (in his ***Enquiry Concerning Human Understanding***, 1748, 1758) argued that the inductive approach depended upon a uniform and predictable world. There is no basis for this other than 'habit or custom of mind'. The sun rises every morning, and we have no reason to believe that it will not continue to do so. However, there is nothing to say that the sun won't stand still tomorrow.

The **problem of induction** is the problem of finding something 'rationally compelling' about the conclusion being inferred.

Deductive argument also has its critics:
- It is difficult to establish the premises.
- Arguing the conclusion from the premises is often merely stating the obvious.

Some scientists have argued that inductive argument will not lead to the truth, but it provides the best way to arrive at the truth.

Faith

Faith	1 Confidence, reliance, belief esp. without evidence or proof. Belief based on testimony or authority. 2 What is or should be believed; a system of firmly-held beliefs or principles; a religion. ME. 3 *Theol.* Belief in the doctrines of a religion, esp. such as affects character and conduct. LME. The spiritual apprehension of divine truth or intangible realities. LME. 4 The power to convince; authority, credibility. Attestation, confirmation, assurance.[1]

Fides quae
Faith as object of belief
• *'The Faith'* – the content of what is to be believed.
For example:

> Do you believe and trust in God the Father, source of all being and life, the one for whom we exist?
> All   *I believe and trust in him.*
> Do you believe and trust in God the Son, who took our human nature, died for us and rose again?
> All   *I believe and trust in him.*
> Do you believe and trust in God the Holy Spirit, who gives life to the people of God and makes Christ known in the world?
> All   *I believe and trust in him.*
> This is the faith of the Church.
> All   *This is our faith. We believe and trust in one God, Father, Son and Holy Spirit.*
> *Common Worship – Church of England Service Book, 2000*

Faith becomes dogma (doctrine, teaching or opinion) – a person 'opts in' to a 'faith community' by accepting the teachings of that community.

> This is known as *fides quae* (i.e. faith in terms of its content).

Fides qua
Faith as trust
• In response to the Roman Catholic emphasis on the body of teaching that had to be accepted, the **Reformation** came to emphasise the element of **trust**.
This view led to a more 'subjective' view of faith:

Faith as subjective	**Faith as objective**
The faith by which we believe.	The faith that we believe.

Faith healing
Some Christians believe that a strong faith can be rewarded with 'signs'. Consider the '**Toronto Blessing**', where worshippers at a charismatic church near Toronto Airport experienced 'manifestations of the spirit' – dramatic outbursts of uncontrollable laughter and physical movement. They believed these outbursts to be a sign of their faith in God.

[1]Excerpted from *The Oxford Interactive Encyclopedia*. Developed by The Learning Company, Inc. Copyright © 1997 TLC Properties Inc. All rights reserved.

'Belief in' and 'belief that'

- The debate between subjective and objective faith can be summed up as a debate between **'belief in'** and **'belief that'**.

Recent Protestantism has made the following distinctions:

Notitia	**Assensus**	**Fiducia**
Knowledge of what is to be believed	Intellectual acceptance of its truth	Personal commitment to that truth

- 'Belief that' implies no commitment to the statement, simply an assertion that it is a true statement.
- 'Belief in' implies both an acceptance of the truth of the statement, and a personal commitment to the truth contained in the statement.

> 'I believe in God, the Father Almighty' – the first statement in the Nicene Creed – implies trust in God, rather than simply an acceptance that there is a God.

Karl Rahner
(1904–1984)
Faith is the answer to man's search for meaning – the Catholic Church acts as guarantor to individuals' faith commitments.

Wolfhart Pannenberg
(1928–present)
Faith is grounded in history – there is a verifiable historical event behind Christian faith, based on the Resurrection. Faith (**fiducia**) is the trust that God will honour His eschatological promises – the promise of life eternal is grounded in the Resurrection of Christ.

Søren Kierkegaard (1813–1855)
Philosophical Fragments (1844)
Existentialism starts with the self, but sees it as 'engaged' with the world. This engagement gives each individual a unique point of view. Kierkegaard was critical of the society of his day: he saw individuals flocking together to form 'the public', and the characteristic of this group was its non-committal 'talk'. Kierkegaard saw people as being little better than sheep, being herded along without any real thought about, or engagement in, the world around them. This non-commitment was particularly evident in the Danish Lutheran Church, where Kierkegaard saw a kind of 'Sunday Christianity'. Kierkegaard believed that Christianity was so important that a person could not be non-committal about it. It was 'either/or'.

Three stages:

1. The **aesthetic stage**, where people live for the moment, with enjoyment the guiding principle. Everything that is boring is bad. At this stage, a person can experience **angst**, or a sense of dread and emptiness. This angst can be the springboard to a higher level, or it can lead to a decline deeper into the aesthetic stage. The leap to another stage requires commitment – it is a personal choice.

2. The next stage is the **ethical stage**. Life at this stage is serious and responsible. The person chooses to have an opinion on what is right and wrong.

3. Sometimes a person can become tired of the life of duty and responsibility – they may relapse into the aesthetic stage, or they may leap to the **religious stage**, the life of faith.

Are faith and reason connected?

Faith and reason

There is something inherently 'unreasonable' in the main tenets of Christianity.

• The concept of 'truly God and truly man' is paradoxical.

> We believe in one Lord, Jesus Christ, the only Son of God, eternally begotten of the Father, God from God, Light from Light, true God from true God, begotten, not made, of one Being with the Father; through him all things were made. For us and for our salvation he came down from heaven, was incarnate from the Holy Spirit and the Virgin Mary and was made man.
>
> Nicene Creed – Common Worship – *Church of England Service Book*, 2000

Theologians and philosophers attempted to use Classical Greek philosophy to reconcile the paradox – they used the Greek term *'homo-ousios'* (of one substance), borrowed from Platonism. It came to denote the sharing of a single form of being.

> Some philosophers point out that faith is the acceptance of what is precisely 'unreasonable'. For instance, Kierkegaard saw faith as authentic when it grasped what is most absurd to reason, the Incarnation. To Kierkegaard, reason was, in fact, an obstacle to faith. He was suspicious of the 'cold logic' of Athens, and argued that a passionate commitment was required.
>
> Faith is the opposite of reason, rather than a search for understanding.

Anselm (1033–1109)

Anselm believed that reason could be used to try to understand the nature of the existence of God. His **ontological argument** (see *Proslogion 2*) relied on reason to demonstrate the reasonableness of the existence of God, though he began with revealed truths. His starting point is the revelation contained in the Bible that there is a God, before moving on to use reason to explain how it could be so.

> His 'catchphrase' in trying to apply reason to his Christian belief was **fides quarens intellectum** (faith seeking understanding – the original title for his work **Proslogion**).

> 'I long to understand in some degree thy truth, which my heart believes and loves. For I do not seek to understand that I may believe, but I believe in order to understand.'
> 'I do not seek to understand that I may believe, but I believe that I may understand. For this too I believe, that unless I first believe, I shall not understand.'
>
> Anselm, quoted in the *Lion Handbook of Christian Belief*

Augustine of Hippo (365–430)

• Faith comes before reason.
• It must be a freely-taken option.

> 'I believe in order to understand'

> Augustine believed that Faith was paramount, but that it was incomplete without Reason. Augustine believed that all knowledge begins with faith, and that God-given reason should then be employed to emulate God and seek understanding. Augustine's motto is often said to be 'Fides Quarens Intellectuum' – Faith seeking Understanding – a quotation from Anselm.

Are faith and reason connected? (continued)

Thomas Aquinas (1225–1274)

Aquinas believed that reason could demonstrate the existence, and to some extent the nature, of God.

> Reason is the God-given tool for discerning what is good. Ethical decisions require reason to understand what is a thing's **Final Cause** (see the section on **Natural Law ethics**).

> However, a full understanding of the nature of God relies on the use of revelation.
> • Reason can only take man so far – revelation is required to acquire a fuller understanding of the nature of God.

Aquinas' famous **five ways** were formulated to show that faith and reason were consistent with each other.

Martin Luther (1483–1546)

> The **Reformers** were concerned that reason was beginning to replace revelation as the basis for Christian faith – the **Scholastics** (such as Aquinas) appeared to be rejecting the Bible in favour of pure reason.

> Luther argued that the Scholastics were making reason the foundation on which faith is built – this made it a human action, and therefore a 'work'.

• For faith to be effective in the Christian scheme of the Redemption of man, it needs to be a free act. It cannot be guaranteed by human reason.

Luther followed Augustine's belief in the **Fall** (the Fall from Grace as represented by the story of Adam and Eve in the Garden of Eden). The Fall corrupted human reason – it therefore could not provide true knowledge of God.

Blaise Pascal (1623–1662)

Pascal took a rather cynical view of human nature – people were more concerned with everyday life than with impenetrable philosophical truths. He proposed a more practical approach, **Pascal's wager**.

There is no way to guarantee the truths claimed by Christianity. The claims are that there is a God, but it is impossible to guarantee this. Therefore, life would appear to be a gamble.
• If you live your life as though there is *no* God, but in the end it turns out that you were wrong, then eternal punishment in hell awaits!
• If you live your life as though there *is* a God, but in the end it turns out that you were wrong, then you have lost nothing!

But
• If you live your life as though there is a God, and in the end it turns out that you were right, you will be rewarded with eternal life.

The gamble is therefore how you live your life in anticipation for the possible rewards promised by Christianity.

• Pascal was not being as callous as it appears – he was himself deeply religious in his way.

The only choice available is to make a sensible risk – the way taught by Christ.

The scientific revolution

According to Genesis:
> In the beginning when God created the heavens and the earth, the earth was a formless void and darkness covered the face of the deep, while a wind from God swept over the face of the waters. Then God said, 'Let there be light' and there was light.
>
> Genesis 1:1–3 *(New Revised Standard Version)*

God is pictured as a 'hands-on' creative power, responsible for the construction of the planet (see section on **Judaeo-Christian influences**). God is directly involved in Creation.
The Christian view of the planet was also influenced by **Ptolemy** (c.90–168).

Ptolemy was an astronomer based in Alexandria. He modified Aristotle's classical **terrocentric** view of the universe by introducing epicycles to explain why planets move backwards in the sky.

His writings provided Christianity (and Judaism) with a scientific basis for the Biblical claims for a universe with the earth at its centre.

This view held sway in the scientific community for over a millennium.

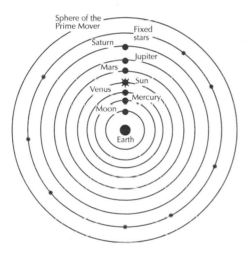

Aristotle's universe with the Earth at the centre

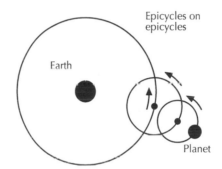

Aristotle's universe could not explain why planets moved backwards in the sky. It was suggested that planets moved around points which moved in circles around the Earth. These circles were called epicycles. Ptolemy later proposed epicycles on epicycles!

Nicolas Copernicus (1473–1543)

In 1543 Copernicus published his book *De Revolutionibus Orbium Coelestium* (The Revolution of the Heavenly Orbs). He proposed a **heliocentric** universe – the sun stands at the centre of the universe.

His arguments were based on mathematical calculations.

Galileo Galilei (1564–1642)

Galileo pioneered the scientific method: observation, hypothesis, experiment and conclusion.

He showed that motion was not uniform, but subject to change. Having been introduced to the telescope, he improved it, and observed craters on the moon, phases in Venus and satellites around Jupiter. Further astronomical work led Galileo to propose that the sun was the fixed body at the centre of motion, and that the earth orbited the sun along with all the other planets.

The Church of Rome considered Galileo's work heretical; he was tried by the Inquisition in 1633 and forced to spend the last years of his life under house arrest. His response to the Church's position is reputed to have been: *It is the Church's job to tell people how to get to heaven, not how the heavens go.*

The scientific revolution (continued)

Johannes Kepler (1571–1630)

- Kepler cast further doubt on medieval cosmology, developing three laws of planetary motion (these laws were subsequently explained by Newton). His laws described the geometrical behaviour of planets around a central star.

René Descartes (1596–1650)

- Descartes argued for the use of reason, rather than appeals to authority.
He separated mind and matter, which led to **deism:** God is entirely separate and remote from the created order. God created the universe, and then left it – a self-regulating mechanism – to run itself.

Isaac Newton (1642–1727)

Philosophiae Naturalis Principia Mathematica (1687)

- Newton's work influenced science for the next three centuries. He devised a system of physical laws based on mass, force, velocity and acceleration.
- The universe was like a long-case clock, with cogs, springs and levers all working together. To explain any aspect of the universe required only observation – no longer was it necessary to rely on an external authority. Newton proposed that God's role was simply to make minor adjustments – rather like the clockmaker returning to regulate the movement of his clock. God's role was reduced to explaining only those things which science could not explain – hence the '**God of the gaps**'.

> **Newton felt that this system fitted his Christian world-view. The mechanical order of the universe reflected the perfections of its maker.**

Pierre Simon, Marquis de Laplace (1749–1827)

- Laplace argued that the world could be explained in terms of chance and mechanism. God was not needed to explain the motion of the planets. When asked about this he replied:

> *God? I have no need of that hypothesis.*

He proposed '**scientific determinism**' – a set of laws that would govern the development of the universe given a certain configuration at a certain time.

Revision Advice 5 (continued)

One of the best ways to learn is to teach it to others – try explaining a theory to a friend!

Important – Keep to the 15-minute break system – don't overload your brain!

Organise your notes into a new set of binders – use a set of index pages to help. Write a contents list, and highlight areas where your notes are not so good.

Set targets – 'by 9 o'clock I will have revised the Ontological argument' – and set rewards to encourage yourself. Not too much liquid, though, and avoid alcohol.

Convert an essay into a set of bullet points, or a spidergram.

Read a section from a textbook, then write a short essay. Check it against the book for accuracy.

More on page 47

Modern science

In 1900 **Max Planck** introduced his 'quantum mechanics', the physics of very small particles.

Five years later, **Albert Einstein** defined relativity, the physics of the very large. Newton's mechanics were replaced by Einstein's view of the universe.

With the formulation of the **Big Bang theory** and the discovery of the radiation 'echo' that the theory predicts, it appears that the traditional religious world-view is discredited. **Georges Lemaître** first proposed the theory in 1927, and **Edwin Hubble** offered certain refinements.

Fred Hoyle proposed an alternative to the Big Bang, the Steady State theory, in 1948. He argued that there is a continuous destruction and renewal of matter within a fixed and constant universe.

It is now generally accepted by scientists that the universe began with a Big Bang around 20 billion years ago. The point at which this bang took place is the point *from which* space and time originate. It is as though the universe is contained within an expanding bubble.

Further evidence for this has been found by a microwave telescope on Antarctica. It has detected 'ripples' in the microwave background radiation often referred to as the echo from the Big Bang. The Cosmic Microwave Background Radiation is believed to have formed when the Universe was only 300 000 years old, and is the effect of radiation and matter separating out as part of the birth of the universe.

Scientists such as **Richard Dawkins** (see section on evolution in **The teleological argument** and **Science and religion**) adopt an implacably atheistic stance. They claim that there is no evidence that can support belief in God.

Dawkins appears to suggest that religion and science are rivals in providing explanations for the existence of the universe.

The religious response to science

Negative responses

Henry Morris

> Morris was the spokesman of a group of ultra-conservative Christians who proposed that the creation of the world was exactly as written in Genesis.

He tried to formulate **scientific creationism**. This maintained the six-day Creation, the Fall and consequent decay of the created order, the Flood, and the Tower of Babel (accounting for the multiplicity of languages).

Thomas Chalmers

Chalmers proposed the **gap theory**. He noted an apparent gap between the first verse of Genesis (Genesis 1:1) and the rest of the account.
He argued that between the first verse and the rest of the account there was an extended period of time that included the fall of Satan. Only after that did the six-day creation of the earth take place.

A. J. Monty White

In *How Old is the Earth?* (1985), White argued that any evidence that shows that the earth is older than the Bible suggests is superficial and misleading.

Positive responses

Hans Kung

Kung argued that the challenge from new scientific theories was *existential*. The debate was not one of *how* the cosmos came into being, but whether there is *meaning* to the universe.
The debate can be reduced to this:
Is the universe planned, or unplanned?
If the universe came about by accident, there can be no meaning to life, whereas if there is an overall plan, meaning can be discerned.

C. Stephen Evans

Philosophy of Religion (1982)
- There is no conflict between religion and science – rather than replacing religion, science has replaced *myth and magic* (see sections dealing with Richard Dawkins).

This idea maintains religious belief without the closed-minded approach of the fundamentalists. It is also more in line with the nature of the development of Christian thought, which has been anything but dogmatic and closed-minded.

Keith Ward

Holding Fast to God (1982)
- Religion (and theology in particular) aims to provide a theological explanation for the universe, rather than a causal explanation.

The final explanation of why the universe should have come into being is beyond the scope of science. Scientific discoveries have added to the claims of theology by opening up an ever more complex explanation of the universe.

Adam Ford *Universe: God, Man and Science* (1986)

- Science and religion can co-exist.
- Many scientific theories were being discussed in religion long before the birth of modern science (for instance, Augustine of Hippo appeared to suggest the possibility of evolution).
- While the universe appears to be subject to random chance, it is still a part of a game whose rules were formulated by God (see Einstein's statement, in his letter to Max Born, that God does not play dice).
- Everything in the universe is subject to God's will – not just at the point of Creation, but throughout history.

The more science discovers about the world, the more we discover about God.

Russell Stannard *Grounds for Reasonable Belief* (1989)

- Science can only deal with physical explanations.
- Science (especially evolutionary theory) appears to have discounted the designer God (spoken of in the teleological argument for the existence of God). However, while the evolution of life might be random, the conditions required to provide for this evolution are not. This is an echo of the **anthropic principle** (see **Is the universe really ordered?**).

Science engages the intellect; religion addresses the whole person in a personal quest for meaning in the universe.

The religious response to science (continued)

John Polkinghorne
Science and Creation (1988)
Reason and Reality (1991)
- Religion seeks to provide a 'total' view of the world. It takes into account all forms of knowledge, including the scientific.
- There is a convergence in method between theology and science – the old scientific method is being abandoned as the universe turns out to be more complex.
- God is a 'subject' (a **thou**); the world is an 'object' (an **it**).

Truth can be seen as 'correspondence' and 'coherence'. Science deals with correspondence, where hypotheses are shown to be accurate. Religion deals with what 'makes sense' – what provides coherence for the individual.

The challenge of physics
The new cosmology has caused religion to re-examine its claims for a Creator God. In an increasingly materialist **WYSIWYG** world, the role of religion, which addresses the metaphysical, has been challenged both by science and by issues relation to religious language (see the section on **Religious Language**).

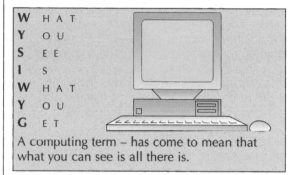

W	H A T
Y	O U
S	E E
I	S
W	H A T
Y	O U
G	E T

A computing term – has come to mean that what you can see is all there is.

In the face of these challenges, theology has had to reformulate the traditional claims of religion– and language about God has had to become more aware of the physical world.

Revision Advice 5 (continued)

Try more active approaches to your revision. If there are a number of philosophers who have contributed to the theory that you are revising, try making a matching exercise to help you to remember who said what:

Anselm	*'God is the thought than which nothing greater can be thought'.*
Descartes	*'God is a Supremely Perfect Being'*
	and so on......

Cut the boxes out and jumble them up. Then try to match up the different boxes to get the theory straight. You can try this technique to revise the various contributions to a particular theory, or a single philosopher's contributions to a range of theories (this would be particularly useful for David Hume, who seems to have something to say on lots of things!).

Throughout your revision and exam programmes, make sure that you eat properly. Include plenty of fruit and fresh veg!	Don't forget the experts – your tutors are an excellent source of advice and support. Make full use of them!

The origins of life on earth

Sir Charles Lyell (1797–1875)
Principles of Geology (1830)

- Lyell established the principles of the formation of the earth.
- He noted that rock formations were much older than had previously been thought. He showed that the formations were formed out of a slow process taking millions of years.
- Geographical features such as valleys and mountains were the result of natural processes such as sedimentary deposition and orogeny
- This was in direct contradiction to the claims of the Bible – there it is claimed that the world as we have it is the direct result of God's creative activity.
- **Bishop Ussher** (Bishop of Armagh) had calculated that (based on the genealogical details and the ages of the Biblical prophets) the planet came into being in 4004BCE.

Robert Chambers (1802–1871)
Vestiges of the Natural History of Creation (1843)
- Chambers studied fossil records, and recognised that time and nature had played a part in the formation of life.

However, he wanted to preserve the role of God in the creative process.

Thomas Malthus (1766–1834)
Essay on the Principle of Population (1798)
- Malthus was an economist.
- He argued that population, whether of human beings or of animals, was subject to variations.
- These variations were caused by natural processes.
In effect, population is controlled by famine, pestilence and death.

The Malthusian principle of population control

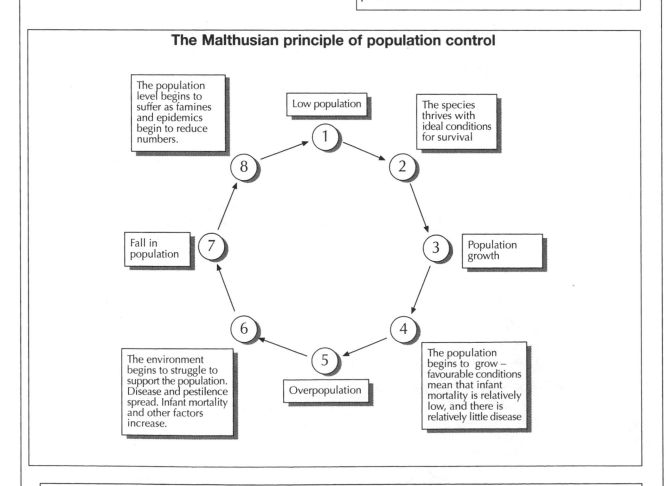

The population level begins to suffer as famines and epidemics begin to reduce numbers. — 8

Low population — 1

The species thrives with ideal conditions for survival — 2

Fall in population — 7

Population growth — 3

The environment begins to struggle to support the population. Disease and pestilence spread. Infant mortality and other factors increase. — 6

5

Overpopulation

The population begins to grow – favourable conditions mean that infant mortality is relatively low, and there is relatively little disease — 4

Malthus's principle gave Darwin the foundation for the idea of natural selection – the environment is not always conducive to the survival of a species, and survival can become a struggle.

Darwinism and neo-Darwinism

Charles Darwin *The Origin of Species* (1859)

During his famous expedition to the Galapagos Islands in 1839, Darwin noted that there were variations between animals on each of the islands.

He attributed these differences to the variations in conditions between the islands themselves. Each group of animals appeared to have adapted to the conditions on their island.

Darwin devised his theory of evolution to explain how these variations could have come about.

Natural selection
⇨ Organisms produce more offspring than can survive.
⇨ There are variations between these individual offspring – they are not all alike.
⇨ Some of these variations turn out to be favourable as the organism struggles to survive in its particular environment.
⇨ These offspring therefore survive better than their siblings who do not have the variation.
⇨ The offspring with the variation therefore are more successful, and produce more offspring themselves. Meanwhile, the less successful offspring (those without the variation) dwindle in number.
The variation becomes a part of the make-up of the organism.

Richard Dawkins

Neo-Darwinism
Genetic research, which has demonstrated the impact of random mutations being adopted as characteristics within the evolutionary process, has modified Darwin's initial proposition.

Richard Dawkins is the Charles Symonyi Professor of the Public Understanding of Science at Oxford University. His books about evolution and science include *The Selfish Gene, The Extended Phenotype, The Blind Watchmaker, River Out of Eden, Climbing Mount Improbable*, and most recently *Unweaving the Rainbow*.

Dawkins has redefined the principles of evolution – he introduced the concept of **random genetic mutation**.

Living organisms have extremely complex genetic codes. When a new organism is formed (by whatever means the species has at its disposal), sometimes random genetic mutations creep in.

The more advantageous genetic mutations give some an advantage.

The less advantageous genetic mutations make no difference to an individual's chances.

The Selfish Gene (1989)
• Dawkins argues that the human gene is essentially **selfish** – it is engaged in a struggle for survival.
• He calls the human body a **survival suit** for its genes.
As the genetic code for human beings is decoded, Dawkins' argument becomes more powerful – see information on the mapping of the human genome.

You may have seen Richard Dawkins on discussion programmes, speaking in favour of a neo-Darwinian view of the origins of life on earth. His views on '*The Selfish Gene*' have clear implications for free will, determinism, and human responsibility.

Creationism as a response to Darwin

The theory of evolution appears to remove the need for a God in the process of the creation of life. Some scientists have tried to reconcile the scientific theory with the Genesis account.

These scientists have taken a **literal** interpretation of the Genesis account. At the same time, religious fundamentalists have campaigned to preserve the Genesis story as the 'official' account.

In some states in the USA, Christian fundamentalists have succeeded in having the theory of evolution banned from schools and colleges. Some commentators have estimated that *100 million* Americans believe that the world was created in six days, and is around 10 000 years old.

Scopes Trial 1925

A high school biology teacher who taught the theory of evolution was prosecuted in Dayton, Tennessee. The teacher, John Scopes (1900-70), was accused of having broken a law in the state of Tennessee, which forbade the teaching of the theory of evolution in public schools because it contradicted the account of creation in the Bible. The trial attracted attention from around the world – the press called it the **Monkey Trial** and parodied the theory of evolution as meaning that humans were descended from monkeys. Clarence Darrow appeared for the defence, and former US Secretary of State William Jennings Bryan for the prosecution. Scopes was convicted and fined $100, but the verdict was later reversed on technical grounds by the state supreme court. The Act that Scopes was tried under remained on the books until 1967.

The **Conservative Creationists** believe that the Genesis story is to be interpreted in a strictly literal way. The world was created exactly as the Bible says. Fossil and geological evidence is dismissed as irrelevant since God may have 'planted' the rocks as a test of faith.

In the nineteenth century this debate was taken to apparent extremes. One lively topic of discussion was whether Adam had a navel, and if so, why.

The **Progressive Creationists** take a more liberal interpretation of the Genesis account. They feel that they can accommodate the fossil record and geological evidence through this interpretation.

For example, the word 'day' in Genesis 1 is taken to refer to a more general period of time rather than 24 hours. Thus the scientific data that suggests a world that is considerably older than Archbishop Ussher's estimate can be accommodated.

These approaches seemed to many at best to be hopelessly optimistic, and at worst naïve, if the scientific evidence is as compelling as is suggested.

Many people felt that, for intelligent educated people, science had replaced the superstitions of religion. At the same time, philosophers were embracing movements such as logical positivism, which were arguing that religious language was meaningless, and Marxism, which argued that religion had been no better than a sedative blinding the masses to their own exploitation.

The apparent clash between scientific and biblical views of the origins of life on earth can be seen best in the world of education. The State of Kansas has recently been involved in a controversial move to exclude the teaching of Darwinian Evolution from state schools. Some schools have placed warning stickers on science textbooks warning that evolution is 'only a theory, standing alongside that of the Bible'. Other schools have glued offending pages together.

A school in Gateshead has also been the subject of scrutiny after it was reported that science lessons were preceded with a warning that the scientific theories were inferior to the biblical accounts of creation.

Other religious responses to Darwin

Darwin had appeared to refute the old dualistic view of the universe. In its place there was a more materialist view. Religion has had to face this challenge and adjust the way that it talks about the origins of life.

Many critics have focussed on the lack of fossil evidence – the body of evidence is limited, and there is no continuous fossil link from prehistory.

In reply, some have suggested that the fossil evidence is sparse because of gaps caused when circumstances were not favourable for the formation of fossils.

Others have argued that evolution is not a continuous process, but one that progresses in fits and starts.

For some, this has meant the traditional views of God and Creation have been lost forever. A more naturalistic view has been adopted – the **Sea of Faith** movement in England has argued for a non-dualist universe.

Some have found ways of accommodating both the religious and scientific views in a world-view that uses **evidence** to answer the 'how' questions, and **myth** to answer the 'why' questions.

Others have found the scientific claims unconvincing, and retain their traditional Bible-based view of the universe.

Charles Kingsley (1819–1875)
- Kingsley supported Darwin's conclusions.
- He thought that evolution was a 'noble conception' of God, in that human beings were capable of self-development. He compared this to the God that was credited with having intervened in Creation to produce new species.

Darwin quoted Kingsley in the preface to the second edition of *The Origin of Species*.

Bishop Wilberforce (1805–1873)
Quarterly Review (1860)
- Wilberforce questioned the evidence for evolution.
- 'Is it credible that all favourable varieties of Turnips are intending to become men?'

Wilberforce met with T.H. Huxley, a humanist and one of Darwin's supporters, to debate the issue. Wilberforce's line was to ridicule the idea that human beings were descended from apes.

Bishop Wilberforce

T.H. Huxley

Types of evil

evil | iv()l, -vl | *n.* OE. [f. the adj.] **1** Wickedness, moral depravity, sin; whatever is censurable, painful, malicious, or disastrous; the evil part or element of anything. OE. **2** A wrongdoing, a crime, a sin. OE–E17. **3** *the evil,* (collect. pl.) people. ME. **4** A disaster, a misfortune. ME–L18. **5** A disease, a sickness. *obs.* exc. *dial.* in *gen.* sense. ME. **b** Hist. *the evil, the king's evil,* scrofula. LME. **6** Any particular thing that is physically or morally harmful. ME.*

Evil = whatever is painful, malicious or disastrous

Natural evil Suffering caused by natural disasters	**Moral Evil** Suffering caused by human selfishness
e.g. a volcano erupts in the Congo, destroying a city and making thousands homeless	e.g. Hitler's Germany engineers the killing of millions of people, including Jews, homosexuals and Gypsies.

Thomas Hobbes (1588–1679)
'The Life of Man, solitary, poor, nasty, brutish and short.'

Leviathan, 1651, pt 1 ch.13

> *Man . . .*
> *Who trusted God was love indeed*
> *And love Creation's final law – Though Nature, red in tooth and claw*
> *With ravine, shrieked against his creed.*
> Tennyson, *In Memoriam*

Life is fragile – every living thing is engaged in a constant struggle to survive. Creatures survive at the expense of other creatures, and nature involves a great deal of suffering. There is disease, famine, accident and death.

Humans also play a role in this scenario. They cause each other pain and suffering through their selfishness and violence. Despite all this, religion claims that the world was created by an omnipotent God. Either God is incapable of preventing evil (and therefore not omnipotent) or unwilling to prevent evil (and therefore unworthy of worship).

For many people, the existence of evil is persuasive evidence for the non-existence of God.

It may be worth remembering that Thomas Hobbes was writing during the English Civil War. This was a time of great upheaval, and life was indeed 'nasty, brutish and short'!

Epicurus and Hume on evil

Epicurus (342–270BCE)
This is the classic formulation of the 'problem of evil': it is often referred to as **the inconsistent triad**.

- Is God willing, but not able, to prevent evil? Then he is not omnipotent.
- Is God able to prevent evil, but not willing? Then he is nasty.
- Is he both able and willing? Then why do we suffer?

An all-loving God?
If God is all-loving, he would not tolerate the suffering of even a single one of the creatures he created. He would either not have created a world in which such a creature would suffer, or would step in to prevent it.

e.g. where was God in Auschwitz?

An omnipotent God?
If God is omnipotent, he would have been able to create a universe without suffering, or would be able to step in to prevent it.

e.g. there is a God, but is He worthy of worship?

It would appear reasonable to conclude that God is all-loving, but impotent – he can do nothing in the face of evil.

The problem of evil suggests that either God is not omnipotent and all-loving, or he does not exist.

David Hume
In his *Dialogues Concerning Natural Religion*, Hume looked at the qualities of omnipotence, omnibenevolence (all-lovingness) and evil.

1. God is not omnipotent,
or
2. God is not all-loving,
or
3. Evil does not exist.

He concluded that
- there was too much direct evidence for the existence of evil for the third option;
- God must therefore be either impotent or malicious.

In either case, the classical definition of God as omnipotent, etc. appears redundant.

He therefore concluded that God does not exist.

Revision Advice 6: D-Day minus five

Many examiners believe that exams are passed and failed in the twelve hours up to the exam, rather than in the exam itself. Remember why you've been working so hard for so long, and keep a sense of perspective!

Don't plan any heavy revision sessions during the exams. Aim for a summary of revision notes.

Check the details for your exams – which one is first, where is it being held, what time and so on!

Make sure your pens are in full working order – there's nothing worse than running out of ink!

Set a good night's sleep, followed by a healthy breakfast.

Aquinas on evil

Thomas Aquinas (1225–1274) presented an argument that stated that the existence of God is logically impossible in the face of the existence of evil. He then set out to prove this position to be false.

> It seems that God does not exist: because if one of two contraries be infinite, the other would be altogether destroyed. But the name of God means that He is infinite goodness. If, therefore, God existed, there would be no evil discoverable; but there is evil in the world. Therefore God does not exist.
>
> *Summa Theologica*

Aquinas defined God as infinitely good: the existence of evil constitutes a challenge to the existence of such a God. Even the smallest amount of evil removes the possibility of infinite goodness.

His argument stands if we accept that God is infinitely good, and if we use the word 'good' in the same way for God as for humanity.

Aquinas was an **Aristotelian** – he believed that goodness is wrapped up in cause and purpose. An act is good in so far as it achieves its potential.

Aquinas's application of Aristotelian causation is the foundation of Roman Catholic morality. Every action has a purpose given it by God. (See the section on **The teleological argument for the existence of God.**)
For example:

- The purpose of sexual intercourse is to have children.
- Any sexual activity that denies the possibility of conception is therefore 'wrong', because it falls short of the potential for life.

In keeping with the Augustinian theodicy (see **The classic theodicies** below), evil is seen not as an objective ontology, but as a *privation*, or an absence of Good.

Sin and repentance
Two Greek (koine) words used in the New Testament may be relevant to the debate

ʿαμαρτια *(hamartia)*	μετανοια *(metanoia)*
This is the word used for **sin** – it means (roughly!) to 'fall short of the mark', or to 'fail to achieve the potential'.	This is the word used for **repentance** – it means to 'turn around', or to 'turn the back on'.

Thus moral evil could be seen as a failure to achieve potential – this could be in the Aristotelian sense, or it could refer to the potential for humanity to behave in a compassionate way.

The theodicy of Augustine

Augustine of Hippo (354-430)
Augustine based his theory on his reading of key Biblical passages: Genesis 3 and Romans 5:12-20.
He also based it on two assumptions:

1. Evil is not from God – God's creation was faultless and perfect.

2. Evil came from within the world.

Genesis 3 is the story of Adam and Eve and their 'Fall' in the Garden of Eden. In it the 'Serpent' convinces Eve to pick a fruit from the tree of the knowledge of good and evil (a tree that she was forbidden by God to pick from). She picks the fruit, and passes some to Adam. In punishment, God has them evicted from the garden.

In ***Romans 5:12–20*** St Paul describes the Christian belief that Jesus's sacrifice on the Cross wipes out the sin committed by Adam and Eve. Jesus's self-sacrifice has made available a boundless gift, the gift of righteousness.

Augustine's theodicy in summary

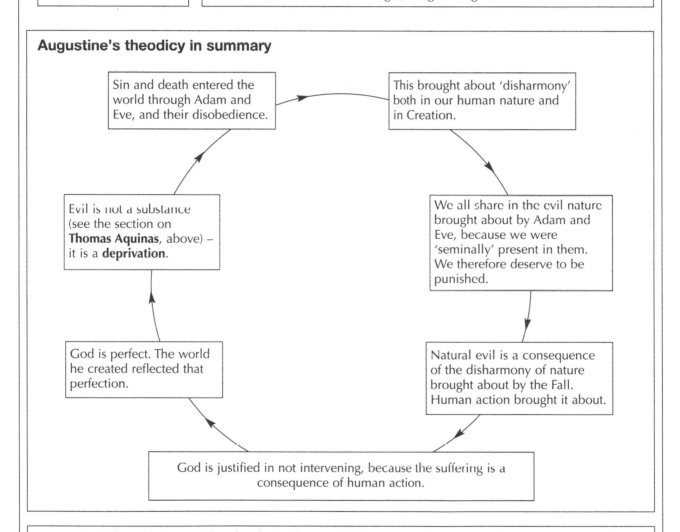

Sin and death entered the world through Adam and Eve, and their disobedience.

This brought about 'disharmony' both in our human nature and in Creation.

We all share in the evil nature brought about by Adam and Eve, because we were 'seminally' present in them. We therefore deserve to be punished.

Natural evil is a consequence of the disharmony of nature brought about by the Fall. Human action brought it about.

God is justified in not intervening, because the suffering is a consequence of human action.

God is perfect. The world he created reflected that perfection.

Evil is not a substance (see the section on **Thomas Aquinas**, above) – it is a **deprivation**.

- Augustine's theory hinges on the idea that evil is a **privation**.
He uses the analogy of blindness – blindness is not an 'entity', but an absence of sight.
Augustine accounts for evil by ascribing it to human agency. Evil came about as a result of the misuse of **free will**.

All suffering is therefore a consequence of this abuse of free will.

Natural evil is caused by the imbalance in nature brought about by the Fall.

Moral evil is caused because the world has become estranged from God, and immorality has been able to thrive.

- However, God has not relinquished any responsibility for the world. If God were simply just, everyone would be suitably punished. Instead, God's grace brought about the possibility of reconciliation through Jesus Christ, whose crucifixion saved a certain number from eternal punishment.

The theodicy of Irenaeus

Irenaeus (130–202)
Peter Cole summarises the two classic theodicies as follows:

The Augustinian theodicy is a **soul-deciding** theodicy.	The Irenaean theodicy is **soul-making**.

Cole, P. *Philosophy of Religion*, 1999, p.70

This means that the Augustinian theodicy is concerned with judgement. Irenaeus is more concerned with the development of humanity.

Suffering is a necessary part of God's created universe – it is through suffering that human souls are made noble – the world is a **'vale of soul-making'** (John Hick, from a letter from John Keats to George and Georgiana Keats in 1819: 'Call the World if you please a Vale of Soul-Making').

One of the ways in which this 'test' is carried out is through faith – God's purpose cannot easily be discerned, but believers continue to believe despite the evidence. This faith becomes a virtue. John Hick calls this lack of understanding an **'epistemic distance'**.

Humans were created in the image and likeness of God.

We are in an immature moral state, though we have the potential for moral perfection.

Throughout our lives we change from being human animals to 'children of God'. This is a choice made after struggle and experience, as we choose God rather than our baser instincts. There are no angels or external forces at work here.

God brings in suffering for the benefit of humanity. From it we learn positive values, and about the world around us.

Suffering and evil are:
1. **Useful as a means of knowledge**. Hunger leads to pain, and causes a desire to feed. Knowledge of pain prompts humans to seek to help others in pain.
2. **Character-building** (see Keats). Evil offers the opportunity to grow morally. If we were programmed to 'do the right thing' there would be no moral value to our actions. 'We would never learn the art of goodness in a world designed as a complete paradise' (Swinburne). Hick agrees.
3. **A predictable environment**. The world runs to a series of natural laws. These laws are independent of our needs, and operate regardless of anything. Natural evil is when these laws come into conflict with our own perceived needs. There is no moral dimension to this. However, we can be sure of things in a predictable world!

Heaven and hell are important within Irenaeus's Theodocy as a part of the process of **deification**, the lifting up of humanity to the divine. This process enables humans to achieve perfection.

Criticisms of the classic theodicies

Problems with Augustine's theodicy

Augustine suggested that there was a state of blissful ignorance in the Garden of Eden, which was then knocked off balance by the Fall. Biologists have formulated the theory of **natural selection**, in which the innate selfishness of creatures becomes a virtue in the battle for survival.

However, if God can be held responsible for the system by which the natural world works, he should be held responsible for the suffering that his system causes.

A more complicated problem is associated with the idea of collective responsibility. Why should people suffer for the misdemeanours of past generations? Even the Bible argues this: see Jeremiah 31: 27–34 (should the children's teeth be set on edge because the Fathers have eaten sour grapes?).

Augustine makes much of the idea of hell – as a part of Creation, God must be responsible for its creation, so he must have foreseen the need for punishment.

Problems with Irenaeus's theodicy

Irenaeus argued that everyone goes to heaven. This would appear **unjust**, in that evil goes unpunished. Morality becomes pointless. ⟹ It is not orthodox Christianity. It denies the Fall, and Jesus's role is reduced to that of a moral example.

Why should 'soul-making' involve suffering? The 'suffering is good for you' argument seems unjust, especially in the suffering of innocents.
- Hume was critical: 'Could not our world be a little more hospitable and still teach us what we need to know? Could we not learn through pleasure as well as pain?'
- Swinburne argues that our suffering *is* limited, by our own capacity to feel pain, and by our lifespan.

Can suffering ever be justified on the grounds of motive? Suffering does not sit easily with the concept of a loving God.

Some philosophers offer the **free will defence (FWD)** as an answer to the problems posed by the theodicies.

The FWD argues that God has made human beings **free agents**, free to love God, but also free to choose evil.

Others propose a **process theodicy.**

Process theologians have adopted a **panentheist** view of God. They believe that God and the world are inextricably linked. God suffers alongside His Creation.

John Hick's reformulation of the Irenaean theodicy

Hick's theodicy is a modern reformulation of the Irenaean theodicy. It is based on the idea that free choice is better than compulsion.
- For human beings to love God, they have to be free to choose to do so.
- Love cannot be forced.
- The capacity to love God is a quality that has to be developed.

Peter Vardy's story of the king in love with the peasant illustrates this idea well! (See section on **The free will defence**, below.)

In order to allow for this development, humans have been created imperfect.

There has to be room for improvement in order for development to be possible.

*Hick called this distance between God and man an **epistemic distance**. It is a distance in knowledge and understanding.*

This distance allows humans the room to develop – if God were too close, humans would find it impossible not to be influenced.
- They would be unable to make a free choice, and would not benefit from the developmental experience of being morally free.

For humans to be free to make moral choices, there must be a full range of alternatives to choose from. The world must include the possibility for suffering, or moral choices would be meaningless.

Hick therefore proposed that suffering is a necessary condition in this process of free choice. The world is a forge in which humans are changed – it is a world in which the soul is refined. Hick illustrates this with a phrase from a letter by John Keats:
'Call the world if you please a Vale of Soul-Making'

A world without problems, difficulties, perils and hardships would be morally static, for moral and spiritual growth comes through responses to challenges; and in a paradise there would be no challenges.

Hick, J. *Evil and the God of Love*, 1968, p.372

One way in which humans can develop is through their response to suffering.
- One of the ways in which this 'test' is carried out is through faith – God's purpose cannot easily be discerned (the **epistemic distance**), but believers continue to believe despite the evidence. This faith becomes a virtue.

The free will defence

Peter Vardy (*The Puzzle of Evil*) suggests a parable.

- **Richard Swinburne** also lends support – he argues that mass-suffering (such as the Holocaust) cannot be prevented by God without compromising the freedom of humanity.
- Swinburne also argues that death, the cause of a great deal of suffering, is necessary because without mortality it would not be possible to take genuine responsibility for our actions. If we were immortal, there would be no consequence to our actions.

> *Imagine a King falls in love with a peasant girl. He could simply demand her love. However, love cannot be compelled – it must be earned. Love for God cannot be compelled – it must come about freely.*
>
> Vardy, P. *The Puzzle of Evil*

For human beings to have free will, we have to have a totally free choice.

- In a free world, a person should be free to act wrongly as well as to act in accordance with a moral code.
- It is illogical to propose that a person can be 'infallibly guaranteed always to act rightly' (Hick, J. *Philosophy of Religion*, p.38).
- To suggest that God should not have created beings with the capacity to sin is to suggest that God should not have created people.

J. L. Mackie suggested that it is possible that a person should choose to do good on every occasion.

The choice that faced God was not only between obedient robots and willfully disobedient free agents.

Rather, there was also the opportunity to create beings that would act freely but always do right. Mackie held that God's failure to do this is inconsistent with His being an omnipotent and wholly good God.

John Hick argues that if human beings appear to be able to make a completely free choice while only choosing good, then they do not really have completely free choice.

Humans who have their choice limited in this way are no better than robots.

This has implications for our ideas about free will and determinism – if God knows what choice we will make, He is guilty of tolerating evil. If God does not know, it limits His omniscience.

The most powerful objection to the free will defence comes from the Russian author **Fyodor Dostoyevsky** (in his book *The Brothers Karamazov*).

Dostoyevsky catalogued a series of atrocities visited on innocent children. He asked whether human free will is worth the price of the suffering of innocent children, and he suggested that God is responsible for evil. He therefore concluded that if God has created a world in which free will leads to such suffering, then God is not worthy of worship:

'It's not worth the tears of that one tortured child who beat itself on the breast with its little fist and prayed in its stinking outhouse, with its unexpiated tears to 'dear, kind God'! It's not worth it, because those tears are unatoned for. They must be atoned for, or there can be no harmony....Too high a price is asked for harmony; it's beyond our means to pay so much to enter on it. And so I hasten to give back my entrance ticket, and if I am an honest man I am bound to give it back as soon as possible. And that I am doing. It's not God that I don't accept, Alyosha, only I most respectfully return him the ticket.'

www.kosiek.com/dostoevsky/library/karamazov.txt

Process theodicy

Jurgen Moltmann justifies the suffering of humanity with the Christian belief that God suffered on the Cross. Evil is something to be fought constantly, with the knowledge that God has suffered alongside his creation.

David Griffin (after A. N. Whitehead) argues that God is *not* omnipotent. The universe is an uncreated process which 'includes' the deity. God is therefore a part of the world, and confined by it. His involvement in creation was as initiator alone.

Panentheism
'All is in God'
God is held to be 'true perfection'.

'True perfection' – absoluteness, immutability, eternity and independence, but also perfect relationality, mutability, etc.

God includes the world, so God's experience is related to the world, altered by changes in the world and involved in the process of the world. The best analogy is that of the mind and the body.

- God, as part of the world, is affected by it, but unable to control it. God is therefore the 'fellow sufferer who understands' (Whitehead).

God's creative choice was either to create a universe with suffering in it, or for there to be no universe at all.

> **Note that** the God in process theodicy is *not* omnipotent. God's role in creation is limited – He is bound by the laws of nature. However, God is still held responsible for evil, since He began the process knowing that He would not be able to control it.

> **Problems with process theodicy**
> It simply replaces an omnipotent God with an impotent (if sympathetic) God: rather than trying to reconcile the classic concept of God with the existence of evil, it simply 'sacks' him.

Revision Advice 7: D-Day

On the day of your first exam, you will naturally be nervous. Just remember all the careful preparation, and try to keep a cool head.

> Arrive in good time for the exam, but not too early. You will find that time hangs heavily on your hands!

> In the same way, don't arrive so late that you are in a rush. Try to be 'cool, calm and collected!'

> Try not to talk about the exam with your colleagues. They are just as nervous as you (though they may be better at hiding it). Pre-exam discussions almost always convince you that you haven't revised properly, so take no notice of them. You know how well you have revised, so be confident!

Freud's challenge

Freud is well known as the pioneer of research into the unconscious mind. He based much of his research on his treatment of a number of middle class, middle aged Viennese women, where he believed that their unhappiness was based on the repression of infantile sexuality.

According to Sigmund Freud (1856-1939)
- Religion is **wishful thinking** – human minds create the illusion to combat psychological turmoil.
- This turmoil stems either from stress which originates from the way that society functions, or from fear of the natural world.
- The human mind creates images and beliefs to fulfil basic needs and desires.
- Freud described religion as an **illusion** – not necessarily false, but something that answers inner needs.

Religion is a form of **neurotic illness** arising out of the unconscious mind. Neuroses arouse repressed memories that re-emerge into the conscious mind.
Freud believed that these neuroses are sexual – he therefore concluded that religion is an illusion associated with repressed sexual memories.

- Freud's work on religion centres on its function as a means of overcoming inner fears and turmoils.
- This process was closely associated with the way that the human mind develops into adulthood. Throughout childhood there are different experiences, some of which are traumatic. If the traumatic experiences are not resolved, they are 'locked away' in the subconscious mind.
- Where the locking away is unsuccessful, the memory can re-emerge, and lead to trauma.

Freud arrived at this conclusion from his work with his patients as he practised as a doctor in Vienna.

For example:
Freud noted in particular the neurotic attitudes some of his patients had towards hygiene. As children are being brought up, their parents take great pains to instil in them the importance of cleanliness. As an adult, the individual still feels 'unclean' and washes, even though they are clean. Alternatively, a person could be brought up in an untidy and chaotic household – the unresolved difficulties that this provides manifest as an obsessive tidiness in their adult home.

- Freud's treatment for these neuroses was to allow the patient to investigate their repressed memories, and to see their obsessions for what they truly were.
- Religion operates on a similar level – the ritualistic nature of religious activity is a compulsive obsessive neurosis – he called it the **universal obsessional neurosis**.
- In *The Future of an Illusion* (1927) Freud argued that religion arises from a fear of a chaotic and un-ordered world. A person's resolution of this traumatic perception of the world is to project on to it their memory of their father, who provided a world of order and regularity while they were a child.

Religious faith is therefore an illusion based on wishful thinking rather than reality.

The best-known aspect of Freud's explanation of religion is the involvement of sexual trauma. In *The Aetiology of Hysteria* (1896) he argued that premature sexual experience, often in infancy, is the source of 'every case of hysteria'. This arises out of the body's most basic urges.

As the child develops, the parent becomes increasingly concerned about manifestations of their child's sexual nature. As the child begins to explore their own sexuality, the parent tries to prevent them; in particular, by instilling feelings of guilt in their child.

There are also more complicated emotions at work. Freud traced these conflicts back to when the child is being breast-fed. Once it is weaned, the child becomes more aware of a world beyond its mother. It sees its father apparently replacing it in its mother's affections, and it experiences feelings of jealousy towards him. Freud calls this the **Oedipus complex**.

- The child represses the conflict into its subconscious mind.
- Throughout its adult life, this repressed memory then takes the form of a neurotic obsession. In particular, the jealousy felt towards the father manifests itself in the apparent religious obsession with God as a father figure.

Freud's challenge (continued)

Religion and the primal horde

The work of various naturalists and anthropologists gave Freud the idea that in primitive human society there were **hordes**. Dominant males, who have 'first pick' of the breeding females, head these groups. Younger male members of the horde become resentful – this comes from their jealousy coupled with their respect for the dominant male as head of the horde. Freud called their attitude to the father **ambivalent**. Eventually, they plot to kill him.

After his death, they begin to idolise the father figure, setting him up as a **totem**. The horde experiences a traumatic collective guilt, which is transferred to some object or animal: the mind deflects the feelings of guilt onto the new totem.

The totem becomes a way of controlling guilt. This stage of the process is called **animism**. Freud then traced the process through to its second stage, which he called **religious**, in which the reputation of the slaughtered father grows to divine proportions, though the ambivalence and respect remain. To illustrate this, Freud referred to the **mass**.

In the mass, the slaughter of the God is recreated, and the representatives of the original horde eat the symbolic body. In this way, the guilt feelings are dealt with.

Freud was arguing that religion is a way of dealing with the inner guilt that is experienced as a result of the Oedipus complex (with its feelings of sexual repression), coupled with the natural fear of a disordered universe. Feelings of powerlessness are dealt with through the totemic projection of a father figure and the ritualistic practices of religion.

Criticisms of Freud's views of religion

Freud offered a critique of his own position in *The Future of Illusion*. A protagonist argues that religion has done much that is positive; for instance, religion has offered people real consolation in difficult times. Religion has provided certainty and order in an otherwise anarchic society.

- Freud's own response was to concede that religion has been of some use. However, religion is not simply a benign 'security blanket'. Rather, it has been the vehicle for social repression.
He argued that religion should be replaced by a more scientific view of the world.

Freud's mythological handling of the father guilt complex (through his idea of the horde) has been criticised in particular.

Freud's idea would only work if guilt could be passed down generationally. The ambivalence and guilt that lead to religious activity would need to be present in every generation. Even if the primal crime of patricide actually happened, guilt for the act cannot be passed on. While the Oedipus complex theory might account for some remarkable attitudes to sexuality and sexual activity in society, it creaks under the weight that Freud places on it.

> **Bronislaw Malinowski** (1884–1942) pointed to anthropological evidence counting against the Oedipus complex; for example, matriarchal tribes where the fathers played the role of nurse rather than patriarchal hunter-gatherer. He also noted that the animal kingdom lacks this Oedipus complex. Malinowski argued that the complex arises out of religion, rather than being the cause of it.

Therefore Freud's argument that religion arises out of repressed sexual guilt appears to be bogus.

- It was also pointed out that Freud's argument that religion arises out of the worship of a father figure neglects to consider the religions in which the point of worship is a woman, or the religious systems that have no deity at all.

Ana-Maria Rizzuto argues that religion is no more an illusion than science, since both involve the interpretation of data, and the subsequent imposition of an order onto the world.

Jung

Carl Gustav Jung (1875–1961) worked with Freud from 1907 until they disagreed over the idea of sexuality causing psychological problems. Jung's contribution to psychoanalysis is mainly based on his idea of **archetypes**.

Jung was more positive about the role of religion. He was also more positive about sexuality.

Jung noted similarities between the imagery used by various of his patients. He concluded that there was a division between parts of the unconscious mind: the **personal** and the **collective unconscious**.

The collective unconscious involves the sharing of a series of images, or **archetypes**. Religion provides many of these images: the individual shares in the cultural life of their group, and personal identity is wrapped up in this sharing.

Jung argued that God is an archetype. Each of us is born with the tendency to generate religious images. We share in these archetypes through the **collective unconscious**. Individuals participate in their cultural heritage through these archetypes.

An archetype is a set of images developed by a culture or society.

Jung argued that there is no way to prove the existence (or non-existence) of God – all that can be asserted is that God exists as a psychic reality.

Whereas Freud saw religion as the product of neurosis, Jung argued that religion is a necessary safety feature, acting as a balance, preventing disparity between different archetypes and thereby preventing neurosis. This process is called **individuation**.

However, Jung's claim that *all* archetypes are religious has been criticised by atheists. Jung countered by suggesting that atheism is a form of religion. This is not necessarily so!

Conclusion – the challenge to religious belief from psychology

John Hick argues that the verdict is 'not proven': while Freud and Jung offered valuable insights into the mechanisms that lead to religious belief, there is nothing compelling in either account to lead us to conclude that religion is a construct of mental activity.

Durkheim's sociological challenge

Sociology of religion

This is a relatively recent discipline – as an analysis of religion, sociology has only addressed the phenomenon of religion in the last 30 years. Sociology has focused attention away from a

For much of the twentieth century, sociology regarded religion as peripheral to the study of human society.

general critique of religion in terms of religious truth claims, towards addressing the question: Why are people religious?

Emile Durkheim (1858–1917) attempted a complete social explanation of religion as a social phenomenon. He looked at the following aspects of religion and society:

| origins | meaning | function |

He came to define religion in terms of its **function** within society as a **means of social cohesion**.

In ***The Elementary Forms of the Religious Life*** (1912), Durkheim noted that religion is an important part of the stability and integration in a society.

He defined religion as follows:

> Religion is a unified system of beliefs and practices relative to sacred things, that is to say, things set apart and forbidden – beliefs and practices which unite into a single moral community called a church all those who adhere to them.

> Religion gives a framework for the values and ideas held by society.

> Religion does not exist independently of the people who practise it. It is not a set of beliefs and practices, but a community activity.

> The group activities that religion involves act as a means whereby society is strengthened.

> Religion is therefore not so much about God, but more about the consolidation of society. Religion provides a particular society with its **sense of identity**.

Religion expresses something of the purpose of a society, and can often provide a society with a distinctive identity. It is very much a group activity.

Marx's challenge

Karl Marx (1818–1883) believed that:

All religious, moral and political life is rooted in **economics**.

People have needs and desires (material, social, and so on), and society structures itself to meet those needs and desires.
This has given rise to a **capitalist** society, where the workers produce goods and services, and rich industrialists and landowners profit from their labours.
This in turn forces the individual to view their labour, and therefore themselves, as an object, producing goods within the capitalist system, and results in their **alienation**. This alienation prevents the individual from being truly human, and creates a tension in society.

Marx was influenced by **Georg Wilhelm Friedrich Hegel** (1770–1831), who taught that history has been a long series of reflections. A thought is usually proposed as a development of previous thoughts. Others then reflect and respond to this thought, and a possibly contradictory thought is proposed, creating a tension between the new and the original thought. This tension is then resolved by a third proposal, which takes the best of the first two.

Thesis
The original thought

Antithesis
Its opposing thought

Synthesis
The resolving thought

Hegelian dialectic

Marx saw that this dialectic was leading to a state of revolution, where the tension of society itself would become resolved, before becoming a part of a further tension. The tension was caused by the alienation of the individual by the oppression of capitalism, which prevented the individual from being truly human.

Although Marx was himself religious, he came to see religion as a part of the oppressing structures that were alienating humanity.

He saw organised religion as
• dehumanising
• disempowering
• authoritarian
• stifling free social self-expression

Self-conscious self-determinism, the true character of humanity, was being frustrated by both capitalism and religion. Religion replaced this self-determinism with empty meaningless imagery, devoid of dignity.

Marx's writings

The chief themes in Marx's writings include the view that economic forces were increasingly oppressing human beings, and his belief that political action was a necessary part of philosophy. The essays also show the influence of the philosophy of history developed by Hegel.

The Communist Manifesto

This was a pamphlet written jointly with Engels on the eve of the German revolution of 1848: its full title is the ***Manifesto of the Communist Party***. It presents the authors' political and historical theories. The Communist Manifesto considers history to be a series of conflicts between classes. It predicts that the ruling middle class will be overthrown by the working class. The result of this revolution, according to Marx and Engels, will be a classless society in which the chief means of production are publicly owned.

Das Kapital was Marx's major work. In it, he described the free enterprise system as he saw it. He considered it the most efficient, dynamic economic system ever devised. But he also regarded it as afflicted with flaws that would destroy it through increasingly severe periods of inflation and depression.

The most serious flaw in the free enterprise system, according to Marx, is that it accumulates more and more wealth but becomes less and less capable of using this wealth wisely. As a result, Marx saw the accumulation of riches being accompanied by the rapid spread of human misery.

Marx's challenge (continued)

Marx's theories

Marx's doctrine is sometimes called **dialectical materialism**. This term was taken from Hegel's philosophy of history.

1. The basis of Marxism is the conviction that socialism is inevitable. Marx believed that the free enterprise system, or capitalism, was doomed and that socialism was the only alternative.

2. Marx believed that the individual, not God, is the highest being. People have made themselves what they are by their own labour. They use their intelligence and creative talent to dominate the world by a process called production. Through production, people make the goods they need to live. The means of production include natural resources, factories, machinery, and labour.

3. The process of production, according to Marx, is a collective effort, not an individual one. Organized societies are the principal creative agents in human history, and historical progress requires increasingly developed societies for production. Such developed societies are achieved by a continual refinement of production methods and of the division of labour. By the division of labour, Marx meant that each person specialises in one job, resulting in the development of two classes of people – the rulers and the workers. The ruling class owns the means of production. The working class consists of the non-owners, who are exploited (treated unfairly) by the owners.

The class struggle

Marx believed there was a strain in all societies because the social organisation never kept pace with the development of the means of production. An even greater strain developed from the division of people into two classes.

According to Marx, all history is a struggle between the ruling and working classes, and all societies have been torn by this conflict. Past societies tried to keep the exploited class under control by using elaborate political organisations, laws, customs, traditions, ideologies, religions, and rituals. Marx argued that personality, beliefs and activities are shaped by these institutions. By recognising these forces, he reasoned, people will be able to overcome them through revolutionary action.

Marx believed that private ownership of the chief means of production was the heart of the class system. For people to be truly free, he declared, the means of production must be publicly owned – by the community as a whole. With the resulting general economic and social equality, all people would have an opportunity to follow their own desires and to use their leisure time creatively. Unfair institutions and customs would disappear. All these events, said Marx, would take place when the proletariat (working class) revolted against the bourgeoisie (owners of the means of production).

Marx today

It appears that Marx has been discredited by events in the early 1990s, when the Communist countries of the Eastern Bloc crumbled and fell, and the new governments embraced free-market capitalism.

However, many religious people recognise that Marx was identifying an important social phenomenon, and Christianity and Marxism have a great deal in common. Christian Socialism is taught by many Church leaders, and Christian action to alleviate the hardships of the poor is based on Marx's socialist principles. However, the Christian ideal is one of voluntary participation in the socialist (with a small 's'!) activity, rather than one of compulsion.

Weber

Max Weber (1864–1920), a German sociologist, is thought by many to be the most influential sociologist to have examined the role of religion in society. He believed that the power of religion is wrapped up with the power of the charismatic leaders who begin religious movements, and with the people who continue their work. He made some distinctions between mainstream religion and the 'sect'. He tried to find a positive role for religion in the development of society.

Religion
- Mainstream religious institutions (such as the Church) are **inclusive** – they are accessible to all.
- The **priest**'s authority comes from the community, and is endorsed by appeals to historic orthodoxy.
- The Church is **universal** and its claims for salvation are available to anyone.

Sect
- Sects are **exclusive** and introverted. They often seek to isolate believers from other groups in society.
- The **prophet** is often charismatic – appeals to authority are made on this basis alone.
- The sect makes exclusive claims about salvation – there is often an **elect** few.

Durkheim argued that religion was a social glue that bound society together.
- Weber thought that religion had a more active role – religious movements could often be important agents of social change.

Weber also looked at the relationship between religion and economic activity. He looked at the way that Protestantism gave rise to the development of capitalism.

He noted that capitalism is not simply a money-making system.	Rather, capitalism is a 'way of life', with its own ideology and ethical system of duties and obligations.	He noted that Protestantism emphasised the individual, and the individual's need to work for God's glory.

For Religion must necessarily produce industry and frugality, and these cannot but produce riches. We must exhort all Christians to gain what they can and to save what they can; that is, in effect, to grow rich.
John Wesley, quoted by Weber in *The Protestant Ethic and the Spirit of Capitalism*

The Protestant work ethic
The Protestant ethic, also called the work ethic, is a code of morals based on the principles of thrift, discipline, hard work, and individualism. It came to be known as the 'Protestant' work ethic after its promotion by leading Protestant theologians such as Calvin. The work ethic provides a strict moral and spiritual framework in which a person can strive to live a 'good' life.

The Reformers were anxious not to give the impression that these 'good works' gave a person access to Everlasting Life. This could only come about through the Grace of God. However Luther believed that God calls individuals to work in some capacity or other, and we fulfill our vocation when we perform the tasks God gives us.

Plato on mind and body

Plato (428–347BCE)
Plato believed that the body is **physical**. It is rooted in the four dimensions of time and space. As such, the body is a part of the world of sensations. It is subject to change and decay.

The soul is different – it is a part of the realm of ideas.

For every physical thing there is a blueprint. It defines the thing as being what it is. A car is a collection of bits of metal and plastic. The components could equally well combine to make a domestic appliance. It is the object's conformity to the pattern (or **Form**) of a motor vehicle that defines it as a car, and not a washing machine. The Form of the car is changeless – the car isn't. It rusts, it wears and loses its value, whereas the Form remains unchanged.

As such, the soul is unchangeable. It is the Form of the human being – it is what defines the loose collection of chemicals as a human being, and not a loose collection of chemicals. An important part of the Form of a human being is our ability to reason, and to apprehend universals. Universals are the general, abstract qualities such as goodness that individual objects participate in.

Through the knowledge of universals, humans can come into contact with the eternal. In this way, we come to understand concepts such as justice and goodness through our experiences of things that are just and good.

The Greeks believed that the soul was in some way trapped and imprisoned in the body. Without the soul's ability to reflect on the universals, the person's experiences would be fleeting and meaningless. When the person dies, the various components that make up a human being are separated – this includes the separation of the soul.

Plato reasoned that the soul was pure (or 'simple'). The body was composite, and disintegrated on death. Since disintegration means (literally) to remove the integrity of a thing, Plato believed that only composite things could disintegrate. The soul, which was not composite, could not be reduced into constituent parts – it was simple, and so changeless.

σαρχ **sarx**	σωμα **soma**	ψυχη **psyche**
The physical part of the person – the flesh and blood. The components that are needed to make a person. You could almost say, the ingredients!	The sum total of the components of the body, including its activities and characteristics – in a sense, the collective. The ingredients mixed together!	The emotions and physical sensations and experiences. Animals also have a psyche. This is the animating element, the spark or energy that makes the body work.

πνευμα **pneuma**	νους **nous**
The spirit – the rational part of the human being. Also the activity of the mind.	The thinking mind

Plato did not believe that the mind contains a separate world made up of experiences of the real world. There is no separation between the object and the experience of that object. This is different to the more modern idea that we exist in a world contained in our minds, made up of internal impressions of external experiences.

The existence of the soul had an important implication for Plato's beliefs in the afterlife, and of the rewards for a virtuous life. Plato appears to have believed that the soul will be reborn in a new body (i.e. a belief in reincarnation), and that those who live virtuous lives will somehow be rewarded, but his opinions varied across his various works.

This view about the soul and the body became integrated into Christian orthodox theology. In particular, Aquinas wrote about an incorruptible soul which does not break down into smaller parts. The human soul is immortal.

Aquinas saw the soul as the animator of the body, and also the defining element of the body – that which makes it a human being and not a hamster or an aardvark.

Towards neo-Darwinism

Darwin and Wallace noticed that individuals within a species demonstrated variations in their characteristics. Since each set of parents produce more offspring than are needed, and since it would appear that circumstances work against their survival, these variations provide a means whereby the species can survive.

Some variations are helpful for the survival of the species, and become embedded in the characteristics of the species.

Survival is a matter for the strongest and best-adapted, while the less well-adapted die, taking their weak characteristics with them.

The stronger, fitter individuals mate and produce stronger, fitter offspring, while the weaker characteristics are simply bred out.

For example, consider the giraffe: as random genetic mutations caused longer-necked creatures, these creatures were able to exploit the higher food sources. As a result, longer-necked creatures mated with each other, and the mutation became part of the characteristic of the species. Meanwhile, the shorter-necked creatures either failed to thrive, or found some other specialism.

Evolution is the continuation of the characteristics that make a particular variation more viable.

The survivors from each generation pass on the characteristics that made them survive, and these become more and more refined.

Genetic studies have given rise to a 'new and improved' version of this theory, neo-Darwinism.

neo-Darwinism

Genetic research, which has demonstrated the impact of random mutations being adopted as characteristics within the evolutionary process, have modified Darwin's initial proposition. It has also been demonstrated that all life is built on DNA, and on the genes that DNA contains.

- 98.4% of human genes are the same as the genes of a chimpanzee.

- 75% of human genes are the same as the genes of a mouse.

- All humans are 99.9% genetically identical.

Source: www.knowledgegene.com

Dawkins's biological materialism

Richard Dawkins argues for a biologically materialist system for life – any evidence of 'divine activity' is an illusion.

The teleological argument for the existence of God
The argument is in two stages.

It tries to establish that there is order and purpose in the universe.	It then makes the step to the conclusion that there is something divine behind this order and purpose.

Darwin offers a mechanical explanation for the perceived design – previously this was thought of as the role of God.

- Recent developments in quantum mechanics, meanwhile, suggest that the design in the universe can be explained in terms of Einsteinian physics.

The role of God appears to have been explained away!

Dawkins's view

Dawkins's position is that of biological materialism. He holds the view that life amounts to bytes of digital information contained in DNA.

Dawkins holds that the 'soul' is nothing more than a mythological concept, invented by primitive people.

The genetic code is not a binary code as in computers, nor an eight-level code as in some telephone systems, but a quaternary code with four symbols. The machine code of the genes is uncannily computerlike.

Dawkins, R. *River out of Eden*, p.17

He has been quoted as saying that the concept of soul is nonsense for the weak-minded, and stifles creative endeavour. Rather than being enfleshed souls, Dawkins believes that there is simply no such thing as the soul.

There is no spirit-driven life force, no throbbing, heaving, pullulating, protoplasmic, mystic jelly. Life is just bytes and bytes and bytes of digital information.

Dawkins, R. *River out of Eden*, p.18

Dawkins's view is that living creatures are simply 'survival machines' with a program to replicate.

It could be argued that this replaces the spiritual concept of the soul with a more modern myth.
The evolutionary drive to 'propagate the digital database that did the programming' could be called the life-force that drives the universe –
Aquinas might simply add the phrase 'this is what everyone understands to be God'.

John Hick

In a letter written in 1819 the poet John Keats wrote: *Call the world If you please 'The vale of soul-making'.*

John Hick develops this theme in his treatment of the Irenean theodicy. His idea of eternal life, and of the soul continuing beyond death, can be called the **replica theory**.

Stage one
He asks us to imagine that 'John Smith', a resident of America, suddenly disappears, and an exact replica of John Smith appears in India. This replica is exact in every detail, even memory and emotion. The replica thinks of himself as being the John Smith who disappeared in the USA. His friends (who are naturally sceptical) carry out a series of tests, and are forced to conclude that this is indeed John Smith despite the problem of his mysterious disappearance.

Stage two
Hick then asks us to imagine that instead of disappearing, John Smith dies, and at that exact moment a replica appears in India. Even with Smith's cadaver on a slab, we would be forced to conclude that the replica is John Smith – we would have to admit that had been miraculously re-created in another place.

Stage three
Finally, Hick asks us to imagine that when John Smith dies, his replica is created on another world altogether. This world occupies its own separate space. It is a 'Resurrection World' populated by resurrected persons. It is:

> ... not situated at any distance or in any direction from the objects in our present world, although each object in either world is spatially related to every other object in the same world.
>
> Hick, J. *Philosophy of Religion* (1973), p.101

Hick claims the support of orthodox Christianity for his theory, citing St Paul (1 Corinthians 15) and Irenaeus in his argument. Hick argues that we do not need a direct link in space and time between earthly existence and the afterlife.

1 Corinthians 15:39–41
Not all flesh is alike, but there is one flesh for human beings, another for animals, another for birds, and another for fish. There are both heavenly bodies and earthly bodies, but the glory of the heavenly is one thing, and that of the earthly is another. There is one glory of the sun, and another glory of the moon, and another glory of the stars; indeed, star differs from star in glory. So it is with the resurrection of the dead. What is sown is perishable, what is raised is imperishable.

Unlike **Plato**, Hick believes that the body and the soul are one.
He also rejects the idea that the soul survives the body at the point of death.
He argues that what lives after death is a duplicate, a **replica**. The replica comes to life in heaven as an exact copy of the person who dies on earth. God creates this replica to live on after death.

BUT ...
- Even an exact replica is not the same as the original person.
- A replica would be, in effect, a completely new biological organism which is identical to the original, having had the original's experiences and psychological make-up superimposed upon it.

  > *Imagine my computer – it contains a great number of 'experiences' saved on its hard drive. If I were to buy an identical replacement, and then copy all the files across from the old computer, would the new one be a 'replica' of the old? Would I be able to think of it as the 'same computer'?*

- If it is possible to recreate a single replica, what is to prevent a whole army of replicas? If it were possible (even if it does not happen) it casts doubt on our being able to identify the replica as the afterlife existence of the original. If it were possible, how can identity be 'pinned' on any one replica?

  There has to be some sort of **continuity** between the original and the afterlife existences.

Hick's argument is supported to a certain extent by **Peter Vardy** in *The Puzzle of God*:

Vardy types some comments on a student's essay, saves the file on his computer, and prints a copy for the student. *He can print a second copy, in every way identical to the original, though printed on a different piece of paper.*

In the same way, God could produce an exact 'reprint' using every piece of information about us. This new 'us' would be an exact copy, using new materials. Only one copy is made in order to preserve the identity of the individual.

Vardy claims that this is in line with traditional Christian teaching, in which St Paul writes about a transformed body. Critics are concerned about the transfer of identity from the original body to the 'transformed' body.

Descartes and dualism

René Descartes identified the 'mind' as being the seat of all the feelings and sensations that he experienced and could not locate physically.

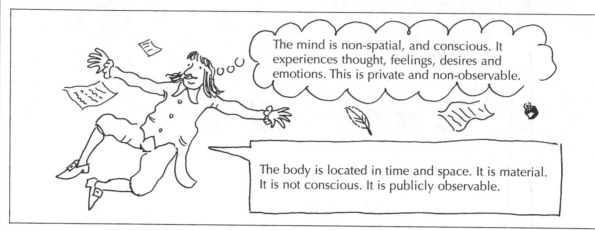

The mind is non-spatial, and conscious. It experiences thought, feelings, desires and emotions. This is private and non-observable.

The body is located in time and space. It is material. It is not conscious. It is publicly observable.

The mind is not the same as the brain. The mind is pure thought. Its essence is 'to think'. Ideas are purely mental phenomena – they do not exist in the empirical world. The point of interaction between mind and body is in the brain. (Descartes believed that the actual point of interaction was the **pineal gland**, though he did not go into details about the nature of this interaction.)

Plato believed that ideas existed 'out there' in the world, but could be understood by the mind.

Variations on the dualism theme

Interactionism
The body can affect the consciousness. Emotions can have physical effects.

Epiphenomenalism
Mental events cannot cause physical events – the mind cannot control the body. The electrical and chemical activity in the brain is experienced as mental activity.

if we liken the brain to a computer, man has a computer, not is a computer

Wilder Penfield, http://custance.org/Library/MIND/chapter5.html

This is a one-way process.

Gilbert Ryle and materialism
Materialism is a 'nothing but' approach – it takes a reductionist view of the mind–body approach.
- Gilbert Ryle described the dualist theory of the mind as a **category mistake**.
- This would be like visiting Chester-le-Street and asking where Durham County Cricket Club is – the club is not simply the ground, but the team, the members, the staff and so on. The 'club' is the sum total of all these things, and does not exist as a separate entity. Ryle uses the example of a collegiate university.

In the same way, there is no 'mind' that exists above and beyond the sum total of mental activities.

Beliefs in life after death

Jewish beliefs about life after death

The Old Testament does not have much to say about the afterlife. When *Apocalyptic Prophecy* became more mainstream, imagery about the afterlife was used to illustrate the prophet's point about the fate of the Hebrew people.

During the later periods of the history of Israel, many Jews believed that the souls of the dead went to live in *Sheol* – the place of shadows. This was a consequence of the 'Fall' when Adam and Eve were thrown out of Eden.

By Jesus's time, opinions were divided about the afterlife. The *Sadducees* appear not to believe that there is an afterlife, while their rivals the *Pharisees* argued for a bodily resurrection. Sheol became a place of waiting – the wicked suffered eternity in *Gehenna* while the righteous would enter Paradise. There are several passages in the Gospels where Jesus, who appears to have some Rabbinical training, refers to many of these beliefs.

Traditional Christian beliefs

The Apostles' Creed clearly states Christian belief in the resurrection of the body. The 1662 *Book of Common Prayer* (the defining book of the Church of England) states that Christians expect this bodily resurrection to occur followed by everlasting life.

There are also Biblical passages that support the idea:

> *I believe in the Holy Ghost;*
> *The Holy Catholic Church;*
> *The Communion of Saints;*
> *The Forgiveness of Sins;*
> *The Resurrection of the Body;*
> *And the Life everlasting.*

> *The tombs broke open and the bodies of many holy people who had died were raised to life. They came out of the tombs, and after Jesus's resurrection they went into the holy city and appeared to many people*
> Matthew 27:52–53

However, Christ often appears to talk of a more spiritual resurrection.
- There was a growing tradition in Jewish literature for an understanding of resurrection that did not involve reanimating dead bodies.
- **St Paul** wrote about the resurrection as involving the transformation of the person – he wrote about the differences between a 'natural body' and a 'spiritual body'. Resurrection will involve the 'glorifying' of the body.

The apparent disagreement between ideas of a bodily resurrection and a more spiritual resurrection may stem from the differences between Greek and Jewish traditions.

Current Christian views

Some thinkers reject the idea that there is any continuation of individual psychological or physical identity.	**D. Z. Phillips** *(Death and Immortality)* – The language of eternal life used by the Christian religion should be reinterpreted as a moral language – 'everlasting life' is a moral quality that is only attainable in this life.
Other theologians have argued that only God is eternal, and any concept of eternal life should be connected to that fact.	**Charles Hartshorne** *(The Logic of Perfection)* – What survives after death is simply the memory of the individual, preserved in the mind of God.
Fundamentalists maintain a belief in a bodily resurrection, based on Biblical authority.	Liberal Christians have placed greater emphasis on the Greek distinction between body and soul, arguing for a spiritual resurrection.

Some Christians have rejected the idea of life after death completely, seeing it as a mythological construction seeking validation of the virtuous life.

Beliefs in life after death (continued)

Resurrection	Reincarnation
The raising of the body after death	The rebirth of the soul in a new body after death

If it can be said that Henry VIII will (or even has been) resurrected, there needs to be something that shows clearly that the 'new' person is Henry VIII.

John Hick proposes his **replica** theory. He claims that when a person dies, a replica is created somewhere else:

John Smith disappears from a lecture in London, and reappears in New York. If he is identical in every respect, we'd be happy to confirm that it is John Smith.	John Smith *dies*, and is recreated in New York. If he is in every respect identical to the original, would we confirm that it is John Smith?

The problem is whether the resurrected body is **identifiable** as the person supposed to have been resurrected. Further, for that body to be truly identifiable, it would need to be situated in an environment that enables it to behave as though it is the person that it appears to be.

Another difficulty with the idea of resurrection is the fact that the body is in a state of constant change. If a person were to be resurrected, it is difficult to see how a body could exist in some realm of eternal life. Bodies are subject to change and decay – eternal life is supposed to be about freedom from this. It can be argued that part of being a person is this location.
This location could be as simple as a cultural background, or it could be that experience is essential to existence – without a body (with nerves and a brain) there can be no existence.

A body requires **location** – bodily existence is rooted in time and space. Contingent existence involves constant change, both through time and in space – the body is situated somewhere.

This is also a problem with the concept of heaven – for heaven to be the home of bodily-resurrected people, it needs to be located somewhere.
Some people try to explain this in terms of parallel dimensions, or alternative universes.

The Christian view is that the body will be resurrected after death – this is a reward for the righteous. St Paul speaks of a recreation – a resurrection with a glorified body.

So will it be with the resurrection of the dead. The body that is sown is perishable, it is raised imperishable; it is sown in dishonour, it is raised in glory; it is sown in weakness, it is raised in power; it is sown a natural body, it is raised a spiritual body. If there is a natural body, there is also a spiritual body.

1 Corinthans 15:42–44

Muslim beliefs about life after death

Islam teaches that the life on earth is a test – every believer in God will be judged when they die to see whether they are fit to be reborn in Paradise. The wicked will be punished in Hell.

Muslims believe that any believer in God (Muslim, Christian and Jew) will be judged. Those who follow the teachings of Allah and His Prophets will be welcomed into a wonderful garden, while those who ignored Allah's teaching will be punished in eternal fire. That said, many Muslim scholars acknowledge that it is impossible to describe heaven and hell, since they are 'not of this world'.

Reincarnation

Samsara – the Hindu belief in the cycle of rebirth

Hindus believe that the atman or soul is eternal. It can appear in many different bodies.

A more sophisticated view from Hindu philosophy is that the soul is at one with the whole of creation.

Many people see this idea as being like the replacement of a worn coat, or buying a new car. When the old body is worn out, or too damaged to go on, it is replaced with a nice new one.

It could be said that the soul is freed from the body to be at one with life itself.

Reunification with life itself (Brahman, the Godhead) is the aim of the rebirth cycle. This reunification is called **moksha**, and is wrapped up in a complex system based on ethical behaviour, and religious and community duties, all affecting the process of samsara.

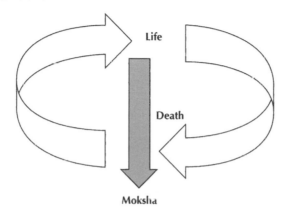

At birth, a Hindu is given a complex chart mapping out their duties – these are based on their caste (status), their birthdate and so on.

The individual must keep their **dharma** or duty – religious, ethical and family. Doing all this accumulates good **karma** (action).

A reborn soul carries no memory of its past life. However, its state, whether rich or poor, is based on the karma from its previous life.

Good karma builds up, and influences the quality of life enjoyed in the next life.

Disabilities and hardships are borne without complaint – they are due to bad karma in a previous life.

The Hindu belief considers that it is not the conscious self that is reincarnated. Rather, it is an eternal spiritual reality that underlies the whole process of lives. With each new life there comes a new empirical self, rooted in time and space. The **jiva** underlies this series of selves, and is encased in various bodies. There is also the 'subtle body' (*linga sharira*) which survives death and attaches itself to a new human being. The subtle body carries the karma.

The only link between the bodies is the jiva. This carries the memory of the entire series of lives. Normally there would be no consciousness of these memories, but sometimes there can be a 'leakage' and the individual can become aware of some past memories.

Once the process of **samsara** has been completed, the **jiva** attains to enlightenment (**moksha**).

Then the person becomes aware of the entire sequence of lives. This is short-lived, because the person transcends self-centredness and becomes one with the Universal **Atman**, the Eternal, Absolute Reality.

Re-becoming – Buddhist beliefs about reincarnation

Buddhism teaches that there is no single eternal Atman. There is therefore nothing that can be passed from life to life.

- Buddhism does not view individuals as having a fixed identity – they are constantly adjusting to the environment and conditions that they encounter. Buddhism also has a different understanding of the word **karma**. The term is interpreted as the process of working through the effects of ethically significant past actions. The actions are not 'carried forward' to the next life, but do affect or influence it.

Philosophical problems with an afterlife

Assuming that there is something that can be carried on beyond death, there are certain problems that present themselves:
- Is it meaningful to talk of life after death?
- If there is some sort of existence after death, how can there be a link from before death?

How do the philosophical objections affect traditional Christian belief in eternal life?

The meaningfulness of language about life after death

The **Vienna Group** and the **Logical Positivists** argued that language could only be meaningful if there was either:
- **Internal logic** to support a statement.

or

- **External, direct sense experience** to verify the statement.

Clearly, there is no internal logic in a statement about life after death, and direct sense experience is difficult to come by! Therefore the Logical Positivists argued that talk of life after death is meaningless.

> If we take in our hand any volume; of divinity or school metaphysics, for instance, let us ask, *Does it contain any abstract reasoning containing quantity or number?* No. *Does it contain any experimental reasoning, concerning matter of fact or existence?* No. Commit it to the flames: for it can contain nothing but sophistry and illusion.
>
> Hume, D. *An Enquiry Concerning Human Understanding*, 1748

Once the Logical Positivists had been forced to admit that the verification principle might pose problems for language, and had introduced the 'weak' verification principle, John Hick was able to suggest an **eschatological verification principle**.

- Language about life after death can be seen as meaningful because it will be possible to verify statements about the afterlife when we get there (or not, as the case may be!).

> The statement 'There is life after death' will be verifiable because we can verify it when we die.

> Remember that 'verifiable' simply means 'checkable' – it does not mean 'true' or 'false'.

However, Hick's concept will only work if there is some sort of cognitive presence to experience death.

Plato (Phaedo)
When a thing decays, it 'disintegrates' – its constituent parts lose their integrity and the thing ceases to be.
The soul is immaterial, and does not occupy space. It therefore does not disintegrate. It is **immortal**.

Immanuel Kant
Acting morally only makes sense if there is some goal that the moral agent is working towards. Eternal life is the reward for moral behaviour.

Continuity and identity
However, both arguments (and the others that are similar) presuppose that there is an immaterial element to human existence.

> Religious sources clearly speak of some kind of physical existence beyond death. The Koran speaks of a paradise full of physical pleasures, and the Bible contains numerous references to a physical life after death (see the parables of the rich man and Lazarus, and of the sheep and the goats).

> When considering the possibility of life after death, many philosophers have argued that the body must be the basis of any life after death because the memory is notoriously unreliable.

> There can be no continuity of identity between life and the afterlife if it is based on such faulty memory – some sort of bodily continuity is required.

Philosophical problems with an afterlife (continued)

Another argument to support a bodily presence in the afterlife is that of **individuation**. This is an important concept in determining what constitutes an individual – it provides the means for identifying a thing as belonging to a particular category of things. Clearly, a thing must retain its membership of a category if it is to retain its identity:

A thing is identified as a tree It has a single trunk, leaves, bark and so on.	It is cut down by a timber company and sawn into planks.	Although the molecules of the tree still exist, it has lost its cohesion – is it still a tree?

Therefore, how can a disembodied mind be 'individuated' – how can it be identified as a separate existence, or even as a particular identity?

It is argued that a personal identity is wrapped up in bodily existence and (if such a thing exists) a spiritual existence.

This is not a problem if the copy does not need to be exact.
For example:
It is possible for a disease such as cancer 'spontaneously' to stop its progress or reverse itself, thereby removing the threat of immediate death to a physical body. The person is 'cured'. The transformation means that they are no longer 'Joe with cancer'. In the same way, the copy could be a 'restored' version of the physical body: they can be 'Joe, who had cancer'. The person need not have cancer in the next life to be an exact copy of the person in this life.
All that would be needed to preserve the 'link' between the physical body and its replica would be the memory of the disease and cure.

However, since the characteristics that define the physical body and give it its unique identity are themselves physical, it seems reasonable to doubt the identity of a non-physical being.

Therefore, it would appear that there are difficulties in speaking of a non-corporeal life after death. For there to be any link between the identity of an individual before death and their afterlife, there would appear to need to be some sort of bodily life after death.

This begs several questions:

Where are all the bodies of the resurrected?	In what form are we resurrected?	Are we resurrected in the form we had when we died?

Some theologians argue for some sort of restoration in the body after death – while this may be a possible answer, it leaves us again with the problems of **connection** and **identity**.
- Peter Van Inwagen (quoted on 'Infidels.org') uses analogy to explain this. He imagines that Augustine wrote a manuscript that was destroyed, but then miraculously recreated.
- The manuscript is no more the same as the original as the house built by a child from building blocks which is knocked over by the mother. She rebuilds the house, but it is no longer the same. It was not built by the child.

The manuscript God creates... is not the manuscript that was destroyed, since the various atoms that compose the tracings of ink on its surface occupy their present positions not as a result of Augustine's activity but of God's.
http://www.infidels.org/library/modern/keith_augustine/immortality.html

However, it may not be necessary for there to be a direct material continuity between the two existences. We are in a constant state of cellular recreation.
My car has a 'corporate identity'. Over the years, many parts have worn out and been replaced. Does *my* car cease to be if all the parts are replaced? Or does it retain its 'corporate identity'?

Philosophical problems with an afterlife (continued)

It may be logically possible for a bodily resurrection in which there is a restoration of the body to some sort of physical perfection. Any dislocation in time or space would be no different from my moving to live in Ulan Bator. I would carry with me my experiences of living in Norwich (in a culture that I am familiar with), and my experiences would expand to take in the new cultures that I encountered.

While it may be logically possible that there is a bodily resurrection, it does not follow that there actually *is* a bodily resurrection.

There needs to be some sort of identification of the 'essence' of the individual which is then recreated as a restored physical body in the afterlife. It would need to take the elements that combine to form that person's individuality (elements both physical and spiritual). However, this may seem unfair – one of the 'elements' that has become the essence of Stephen Hawking is his suffering from Motor Neurone Disease.

Exam Advice 1: Reading the exam paper

The format of the paper shouldn't be a surprise (you've been using specimen questions and past exam papers as part of your revision). You need to make sure that you answer the right questions based on your revision.

1. Read through the whole paper first, before making any decisions about which questions to answer.
2. Don't jump to any conclusions about what the questions are about. Read each one through carefully, noting in your mind what each question is about.
3. Make some notes about the questions that you've chosen.

> Notes are a good way of making sure that you include all the points you want to make. However, you are working in a limited timeframe, and the plan won't earn you marks! Just write down the points you want to use, and number them to remind yourself of the way you mean to use them.

4. Try not to scrawl. The examiner will be reading 300+ essays, and there's no need to make their lives any more difficult!
5. Time your answers carefully, making full use of the time available.
6. Keep an analogue watch beside you on your desk. The exam hall will be equipped with a clock – frequent glances at it will be unavoidable as you try to manage your time. If you have a watch on your desk, it will save looking up at the front of the room. Also, an analogue watch (one with hands) gives you an at-a-glance idea of the time left to the end of the exam. A digital watch would need a mental calculation to arrive at the same piece of information!

Some modern ideas on religious experience

David Hay *Inner Space* (1987)
Following research by Alister Hardy and the **Religious Experience Research Unit** at Oxford, Hay claimed that 25–45% of people in Britain claim that they have been made aware of a presence or power beyond themselves. This suggests experiences of things beyond the ordinary.

- The experience is wholly beyond the experience of the ordinary.
- Often it is not possible to explain the experience.
- The experience is not common to everyone.
- There are cultural influences in describing the experiences.
- Religious experiences are **subjective**, whereas most experiences are **objective**.
- It is difficult to check a person's claims regarding a religious experience.
- Often the experience brings some insight into matters that have been mysterious before.

Some people believe that such an experience can only happen if God allows it – God appears to be selective.

Richard Swinburne *The Existence of God* (1979)
Swinburne identifies five types of religious experience. A person seems to perceive God:

1. Through a perfectly normal non-religious object (e.g. a natural scene)

2. Through an unusual public object (e.g. the Resurrection of Jesus)

These are both **public events**, observable by all.

3. Through private sensations describable using normal language (e.g. a dream)

4. Through private sensations not describable using normal language (e.g. a mystical experience)

These are **private events**, and not observable by anyone else.

5. Through experiencing no sensation at all. Nothing appears to make the person conclude that they were experiencing God – however, the person is left with a strong sense of an encounter with 'the Holy'.

Caroline Franks Davies *The Evidential Force of Religious Experience* (1989)

Religious experience is 'something akin to a sensory experience'. It is perceived through signs similar to those that we receive through encounters with other human beings. From the signs that we receive in a religious experience, we arrive at a sense of spiritual reality. The person can usually note that the experience happened at a particular time.

Exam Advice 2: Avoiding basic mistakes

Examiners are not out to trap candidates, but often candidates set traps for themselves. There are some important points to follow:

1. The exam will be testing your knowledge of the topics, but also your understanding and your evaluative skills. However, don't assume that you can just prepare the knowledge part, and the rest will follow. You need the subject knowledge to demonstrate your philosophical skills!
2. Beware of the 'write all you know about…' approach to A Level essay writing. It is unlikely that you will actually answer the question!
3. Answer the question set, rather than the question you wish the examiner had set.
4. Avoid un-necessary information – e.g. don't write lengthy biographies of people, since this will not gain you any marks! Don't indulge in technicolour descriptions of abortion processes – the specifications (and the exam questions) simply don't ask for it!

Otto and the numinous

In *The Idea of the Holy* (1936) Rudolph Otto (1869–1937) said that religion *must* derive from a being separate from this world.
This being is totally unknowable – it is **awesome** (!) and terrifying, yet also fascinating.

> The object of religious experience can be described as
> ***mysterium tremendum et fascinans***.

Religious experience is not historical or sociological – it is a personal experience of the **numinous**.
This does make experience of God impersonal – yet for
many, religious experience is intensely personal!

> Otto used the example of a storm which partially destroyed a bridge over a river. When people came out after the storm, there was an eerie silence, and a feeling of awe at the power of nature.

> **Kant** distinguished between the **phenomenon** (an experience of the empirical) and the **noumenon** (an experience of something beyond the empirical). Otto argued that religious experience is of the numenous. This experience evokes feelings of **awe** and **wonder**. This experience is **intuitive**, rather than the result of rational thought.

- Otto's use of the word **numinous** to refer to an experience of the wholly other needs closer definition – there appears to be little to distinguish between an experience of God, and the experience felt when watching the *Blair Witch Project*.

> Otto noted that the experiences of the numinous are described using everyday words.

> Words that are used tend to 'get close' to the experience, but cannot 'pin down' the actual experience.

> Otto called the words used to describe an experience its **schema**, and the process by which a schema is developed, schematisation. It is important to understand a particular schema when analysing a claimed religious experience.

Exam Advice 3: What the examiner is looking for

1. In the first place, they are expecting you to demonstrate your knowledge of the topics you have been studying. You will need to use the correct terms, and you know who said what about the issues. You won't need to learn quotations 'off-by-heart'.
2. You will be expected to be able to argue a particular point of view. You need to do this by referring to the various scholars and philosophers who have something to say on the issues, and by using their contributions to construct your argument with comments of your own where appropriate.
3. Your essay will need to follow the rules of argument, showing appropriate organisation and development.
4. Try to be specific. Avoid generalised statements because they tend to demonstrate a lack of knowledge on the subject.

Mysticism

John of the Cross (1542–1591)

John was a Carmelite monk, and a reformer of his order. He believed that the Carmelites' discipline had become increasingly relaxed, and his reforms (which were not popular – he was imprisoned for nine months) led to a split in the Carmelites.

- John wrote extensively about the Christian mystical experience. In particular, John is known for his writing about the progress of the soul through meditation.

> The soul is purified through the experience of the 'night of the senses', in which the soul maintains itself through pure faith having been detached from the senses. This is followed by 'the night of the spirit', where the soul is spiritualised by divine action. This experience is often accompanied by anguish and suffering.
> - The process of the purifying of the soul prepares it for union with God.

Teresa of Avila (1515–1582)

> Also known as **Teresa of Jesus,** Teresa was a Carmelite nun and one of Roman Catholicism's best-known **mystics**. She received a series of **visions**, which she claimed to provide insights into the nature of God.
>
> - She was helped in her work setting up a monastery at Avila by John of the Cross. During this time her own religious life deepened, and she claimed to reach a state of **spiritual marriage** in 1572.
>
> She occupies an important position in the history of Christian mysticism – she was the first to catalogue stages in mystic experience, and her accounts of her own experiences give a scientific description of the 'Life of Prayer' of a Christian contemplative.

Teresa provided a 'protocol' for identifying religious experience:

The experience should be within the traditions of the Church.	*This means that the experience should not reveal anything that is outside the teachings of orthodox Christianity.*

The experience should be discussed with a spiritual advisor.	*This means that before the experience can be treated 'seriously' it must be talked through with someone respected as a spiritual authority. Teresa herself referred her experiences to her Priest Confessor.*

There should be some sort of change in the life of the person.	*This means that the experience should make some difference to the person.*

Teresa's rules provide a way that a Christian can 'test' their religious experience, and thereby allow the experience to be taken seriously by fellow Christians.

Mysticism (continued)

Julian of Norwich (1342–1416)

Mother Julian was a recluse from Carrow Abbey in Norwich, attached to St Julian's Church in King Street.

At the beginning of May 1373, Mother Julian became gravely ill. After a week, a priest was called to administer the last rites. He set a crucifix in front of her bed, telling her to gaze on the figure and meditate upon it. As she looked at the crucifix, she received 16 'showings'; the first 15 in five hours, and the last on the following evening.

'**Showings**' was Mother Julian's term for the revelations that she received.

All the blessed teaching of our Lord God was showed by three parts. That is to say, (1) by bodily sight, and (2) by word formed in my understanding, and (3) by ghostly sight. For the 'bodily sight' I have said as I saw, as truly as I can. And for the 'words', I have said them right as Our Lord showed them to me. And for the 'ghostly sight', I have said some deal, but I may never fully tell it.

Revelations of Divine Love

What was the significance of the revelations?

Mother Julian was concerned to show something of the **relationship** between God and man. She wrote powerfully about the nature of the Trinity, the Christian teaching about 'Father, Son and Holy Spirit'. She saw God as Maker, Keeper and Lover, or Might, Wisdom and Goodness. She stated that God functions as 'the Father may, the Son can, and the Holy Ghost will do whatever he wills'.

The main theme of Mother Julian's revelations is that God is **love**.

What would we learn from this thing? Learn it well: love was his meaning.
Revelations of Divine Love, Ch 86

Mother Julian saw the whole of Creation **sustained** by God's love. He is intimately involved in the process of Creation, 'closer is he than breathing; nearer than hands and feet'. God was seen as the perfect master or Lord, with Creation as his servant. The relationship is often strained by the servant's waywardness, but God is eternally patient. The image is of a benevolent but powerful medieval landlord, kindly but still daunting.

Mother Julian also talked of God as **Mother** (see Chapters 58-63), talking of the motherliness of God. God is 'our Mother in nature and grace', and mankind is seen as the child which can run at the first sign of fear to 'the sweet gracious hand of our Mother'.

Mother Julian also offered insight into the fact of man's sin in the context of God's love.

*And God answered 'Sin is inevitable, but **all shall be well, and all shall be well, and all manner of thing shall be well**'*

Revelations of Divine Love, Ch 27

James's analysis of religious experience

William James (1842-1910)   *The Varieties of Religious Experience* (1902)

Rather than considering the truth claims of people claiming religious experiences, James looked at the effects of religion on people's lives.

James identified four characteristics of religious experience:

> ### Ineffability
> This refers to the unutterable quality of the experience. It is beyond words.

> ### Noetic quality
> The experience offers some insight into deep and meaningful truths. The knowledge is acquired through intuition rather than reason –often it is said to have been **revealed**.

> ### Transciency
> The experience itself can be fleeting: generally, religious experiences have been observed to have lasted less than two hours. However, their effects can last a lifetime.

> ### Passivity
> The experience is out of the control of the person. In extreme examples, the person can appear 'possessed' by the experience, and behaviour can appear bizarre.

James recognised that some religious experiences can be **induced**. Certainly, the effects of mystical experience can be similar to the effects of substance abuse. However, James saw behavioural effects as only a small part of the whole experience.

The hallmark of religious experience is a movement from 'tenseness, self-responsibility and worry' to 'equanimity, receptivity and peace'. Religious experience involves a sense of inner peace – a sense of a Higher Order, and a sense of a revealed truth.

James agreed with Teresa of Avila – the acid test of a religious experience is in the actions of the person following the experience. He believed that the person's experience should be marked by a saintliness and holiness which rises from the personal (or even interpersonal – James noted that there was a two-way traffic in the experience).

He described four 'fruits' of religious experience:

1. The experience leaves the person with an awareness of something beyond the trivial material world.	2. Elation – the person is left feeling 'high'.
3. The experience leaves the person with the feeling of having come into contact with a benevolent and 'friendly' power. Their response to this is one of self-surrender.	4. The person experiences a change in the emphasis in their life. They move towards a more spiritual, charitable and morally-aware state, characterised by a sense of awe and wonder at the universe.

Other modern ideas on religious experience

Martin Buber (1878–1965)

In *I and Thou* (1937) Martin Buber categorised two different types of relationships: **I-It** and **I-Thou**.

I-It	I-Thou
Encounters are impersonal. Encounters are seen in detached, objective and functional terms.	Encounters are personal. Relationships are taken further, and are deeper.

Søren Kierkegaard (1813–1855)

Kierkegaard was interested in the truths relevant to an individual's life – 'the truth for me'. Kierkegaard wanted to set up the individual against the 'system', emphasizing the humanity of the individual.
He believed that religious experience was a matter of personal commitment.

He saw the experience as depending on the 'leap of faith' – the person must make a decision, a risk.
There is little room for rationalising the experience. The leap of faith is basically irrational!

Knowledge of God would depend upon:

The level of personal faith – whether the faith is 'blind' or informed by theological understanding.	The nature of that faith – whether the believer is a Muslim, a Jew or whatever.	The commitment of the believer – whether the person is a devout believer or a 'Sunday Christian'.

Kierkegaard was particularly critical of the 'Sunday Christians', the Danish Lutherans who drifted to church every Sunday but had little faith commitment.

Paul Tillich (1886–1965)

Tillich argued for two components to a religious experience:

Being itself

There is no encounter with empirical elements. These elements would normally provide you with the information that you would need to explain what you are experiencing (taste, smell and so on).
Rather, the encounter is with *more than* the mere physical sensation. It is with reality itself.
Therefore, the encounter might involve everyday sensations, but the person derives a sense of the divine from the encounter.

Ultimate concern

Encounters cause us to 'take stock' to a greater or lesser extent. Fleeting contact with a stranger makes little impact, while an encounter with a close personal friend might inspire far more profound concern in us.

Tillich proposed a scale of concerns: **superficial**, **important** and **essential**. For an experience to be religious, it must inspire 'ultimate concern'.

Different ideas about miracles

David Hume (1711–1776)

Miracles are a 'violation of law by a supernatural being'

The Christian religion not only was at first attended with miracles, but even at this day cannot be believed by any reasonable person without one. Mere reason is insufficient to convince us of its veracity: and whosoever is moved by faith to assent to it, is conscious of a continued miracle in his own person, which subverts all the principles of his understanding, and gives him a determination to believe what is most contrary to custom and experience

Hume, D. *An Enquiry concerning Human Understanding Of Miracles*, Pt 2

That is, the Christian religion is based on miracles, both when it started and today. Christianity is not reasonable, and any Christian belief flies in the face of ('subverts') all understanding and experience.

Therefore, all religious belief is contrary to human experience and reason.

Mel Thompson (in *Teach Yourself Philosophy of Religion*) sees this as a simplistic view of miracles, based on an eighteenth-century view of the universe. He suggests two other definitions:
• A natural process, but speeded up.
• A natural event, happening at just the right moment.
He refers to Aquinas, who stated things can be miraculous because they are thought to be impossible *in nature*. These events are unlikely to have happened in a particular way and at a particular time.

Thompson concludes that miracles are a matter for interpretation.

Attitudes to religious claims about miracles

Bultmann (a Biblical scholar) – All miracles are **'mythological'**. Bultmann held that the Biblical miracles were part of a story wrapped up in the 'mythical trappings' of the first century: demons, voices from heaven and so on. He set out to remove these trappings and to expose the historical Christ. He believed that the miracle stories were expressions relevant to the question of existence confronting everyone.

I. T. Ramsey – Miracles are a **'disclosure situation'**, an unusual complex of incidents with which a new insight into truth is inextricably bound up. *But not all miracles are disclosure situations, and not all disclosure situations are miraculous!*

C. S. Lewis – The Incarnation is the central miracle for Christianity, and all other miracles are related to this one event. Miracles are a type of **revelation**.

A definition of 'miracle' depends upon constancy in nature, since the miraculous appears to 'go against' nature. The development of science, especially of theoretical physics, now goes beyond the simply mechanistic, Newtonian view. Therefore Hume's definition would appear simplistic or even redundant. This leads to a consideration of miracles in the context of causality – a miracle caused by events beyond our understanding (cf. Thompson, *Teach Yourself Philosophy of Religion*, p.164). Miracles appear in the eye of the beholder – they are a way of interpreting an event in a religious, rather than a scientific, way.

Aquinas on miracles

Things that are done occasionally by divine power outside of the usual established order of events are commonly called miracles (wonders). We wonder when we see an effect and do not know the cause. And because one and the same cause is sometimes known to some and unknown to others, it happens that of the witnesses of the effect some wonder and some do not wonder: thus an astronomer does not wonder at seeing an eclipse of the sun, at which a person that is ignorant of astronomy cannot help wondering.

Now the cause absolutely hidden to every man is God, inasmuch as no man in this life can mentally grasp the essence of God. Those events then are properly to be styled miracles, which happen by divine power beyond the order commonly observed in nature.

Summa Contra Gentiles

Aquinas defines 'ranks' of miracle

'Miracles of the **highest** rank are those in which something is done by God that nature can never do.' Aquinas cited the example of the sun going backwards in the sky (compare Joshua 10, and see section on **Judaeo-Christian influences on religious philosophy**).

'Miracles of the **second** rank are those in which God does something that nature can do, but not in that sequence and connection.' By this, Aquinas meant that walking is an act of nature, but it is an act of God if someone who uses a wheelchair should be able to walk again.

'A miracle of the **third** rank is something done by God, which is usually done by the operation of nature, but is done in this case without the working of natural principles, as when one is cured by divine power of a fever, in itself naturally curable, or when it rains without any working of the elements.' For example, Aquinas suggested that a cure that doctors had considered impossible without the benefit of time and care could be considered miraculous.

Comments on Aquinas's views

None of the definitions that Aquinas gave seem to consider God's purpose in carrying out the miracles – **Swinburne** considers these miracles to be entirely arbitrary. There appears to be little religious significance in them – nothing is revealed about God's nature.

Exam Advice 4: Planning an essay

1. Make a brief plan. Jot down what you want to say in the form of numbered bullet points – try to make the order logical.
2. Begin the essay with a sentence or two to 'define your terms'. This is not for the examiner's benefit – it is a useful way to steady yourself and focus on the needs of the essay.
3. Follow a logical order:

   - Begin with an introduction to the topic. Keep it relevant to the title of the essay.
   - Take each point in turn, and analyse it (again keep it relevant to the title). Track the development of the issue through the various philosophers' contributions, and include the various responses.
   - Finish by answering the question, referring back to your discussion.

Hume's arguments against miracles

David Hume (1711–1776), an empiricist, argued that any claim of a miraculous event should be measured against available evidence.

Miracles are a 'violation of law by a supernatural being'.

- These 'laws of nature' are based on past human experience.
- It would therefore be reasonable to reject the claim of a miracle because it would be contrary to human experience.
- However, people do claim experience of miraculous events.

These testimonies would have to be weighed against the reasonable doubt raised by the sum total of human (scientific) experience. If they were to be taken seriously, accounts of miracles would need to be of such a quality that they were difficult to dismiss.

Hume was therefore arguing that it is always more reasonable to reject extraordinary events as being contrary to the weight of human experience.
- There is no evidence to count against this weight of human experience, because the testimonies of people who claim experience of the miraculous are rarely of any quality.
The evidence cited to support miraculous events is often contradictory, and (in Hume's estimation) always tainted with primitive superstition.

Hume described the accounts as being sourced from **'ignorant and barbarous'** people.

Hume would only accept evidence from educated and intellectual sources – people who would have something to lose. So:

Violation of the laws of nature	+	Poor quality testimony	−	Grounds to reject the claim

Hume also stated that all religions claim that their founding figures performed miracles – the religions base their claims for authority on these miracles. Yet they cannot all be right. The stories cancel out the claims of the religions.

Hume provided **four** arguments against miracles:

i. There are insufficient witnesses of 'good-sense, education and learning'. Witnesses tend to be uneducated, ignorant peasantry.	ii. The witnesses tend to be sympathetic to the idea of miracles, and therefore more likely to describe an event as miraculous.	iii. Miracles tend to be observed by 'ignorant and barbarous nations'.	iv. Religions base their truth claims on the miraculous – they all experience miracles, but they can't all be right.

Does Hume have a point?

The laws of nature *are* based on human experience. However, these laws are based on experience *to date*. Scientific knowledge is based on observation, and many (so-called) facts have been overturned following further evidence. Hume assumes that the 'laws of nature' are constant, whereas science moves knowledge ever onward.

> *For example:*
> *Scientific fact up to the seventeenth century was that the earth was the centre of the universe. Even in Hume's time, the sun was considered to be the centre. Now, we know better!*

- Modern science has moved beyond Newtonian mechanics towards a world of probabilities. There is growing evidence for randomness in nature.
- Many things were thought of as impossible, such as men in space, or the ability to talk to someone on the other side of the world. These things are now thought of as commonplace.

Hume argued that accounts of miraculous events should be dismissed because the witnesses lack credibility. The Roman Catholic Church maintains a hit squad of doctors and scientists who are called in to verify claims. Hume's argument is based on the idea that intellectuals have too much to lose by making such a claim.

> *For example:*
> *Some of the most eminent scientists in the world are members of this team. The Roman Catholic Church has too much to lose from claims of miraculous events, and yet there have been 68 attested claims, supported by the Church (Vardy, The Puzzle of God, p.207). However, Anthony Flew points out that the power of such testimony may be difficult to dispute, but it does not necessarily mean that the miracle is attributable to God – the power of the human mind is still only partially understood.*

Hume's claim that religions base their credibility on miracles is not true. Apart from the miracles of Jesus (which appear to have been performed out of compassion, rather than to make any claims of authority), none of the mainstream religious movements actually make such a claim.

Hume made no mention of how a person should respond to miracles where they themselves experienced them. Experience of a miracle would count as evidence to the person.

Maurice Wiles

Wiles argues that God's action in the world would not be confined to particular instances.

> **Rather, 'the idea of divine action should be in relation to the world as a whole'.**

- There is therefore no single act of God applicable to an instance, but a constant act of God applying to the world as a whole.

Wiles considers a God that interferes in the laws of nature to be arbitrary – if God does intervene, why is there suffering in the world? Why does God not intervene where children are suffering?

Why doesn't God perform a miracle?

Natural and revealed theology

According to Aquinas (1225–1274):
- **Natural theology** is the field of theology that deals with those truths about God that can be determined by unaided human reasoning.
- **Revealed theology** deals with truths that cannot be known without some sort of disclosure experience, usually attributed to God.

Aquinas believed that the two forms were complementary: only when the former is augmented by the latter does humanity access the knowledge of God that leads to salvation.

> Aquinas has been very influential on Roman Catholic theology throughout the last seven centuries – many of his views have become accepted as a part of the Catholic faith.

The Roman Catholic Church derives its **propositional** view of faith from Aquinas's view of revelation.

Revelation discloses something which is still unknown for man from the world: the inner reality of God and his personal and free relationship to spiritual creatures.

Karl Rahner

Revelation is the 'divine broadcast', the means by which God informs mankind of the truths needed for salvation.

Revelation comes through different media:

The Old (and New) Testament prophets: Elijah, Ezekiel, John the Baptist

Jesus Christ, who through the Incarnation is the ultimate revelation of God

The Bible, which was 'inspired by the Holy Spirit, has God as its author' (First Vatican Council, 1870)

This view is that the Biblical authors were little more than secretaries, transcribing the Word of God.

John Hick gives the following illustration:
It was held that although the human mind, by right reasoning, can attain the truth that God exists, it cannot arrive in the same way at the further truth that He is Three Persons in One – thus the doctrine of the Trinity was considered to be an item of Revealed Theology, to be accepted by faith.

Much of the history of post-Reformation theology has been a battle between the proponents of natural theology, and the theologians who have believed that the Bible is the supreme source of knowledge of God.

Protestant theology

In response to the Scholastic tradition (or 'Thomist' tradition – Roman Catholic theology is based heavily on the philosophy of Thomas Aquinas), the Reformation theologians looked for an alternative to the propositional view of faith.

> The Protestant view could be characterised as a **non-propositional** view of faith. This emphasises the personal nature of God.
>
> > **Heilsgeschichte** ('history of salvation')
> > A German theological movement which emphasises the progression of revelations culminating in the revelation of God in Jesus Christ.

Protestant Christians consider the Bible as the means of this revelation.

> **Niebuhr** (1892–1971) described revelation as 'that special occasion which provides us with an image by means of which all the occasions of personal and common life become intelligible'.

> **Thomas Halyburton** (1674–1712)
> *Natural Religion Insufficient, and Revealed Necessary to Man's Happiness in His Present State* (1714)
> - Revelation augments the truths that can be accessed by reason.
> - Understanding certain truths is beyond the scope of the human mind alone.

Biblical writings
Books from the Old Testament were first committed to paper during the time of the Babylonian Exile (in the fifth century BCE) – there was some concern that the Jewish religion might be 'diluted' while away from the Temple in Jerusalem.
- The New Testament was finalised in around AD130. The complete 'canon' of the New Testament is first referred to in AD367.

> Some books were included in the canon of the Bible because of claims of authority (authorship by a respected prophetical figure, for example); others, because they made some sort of sense of the faith of the believing community.

> The idea that the scriptures were **inspired** came from the idea that each person was 'inflated' by the breath of God at birth – this breath was then surrendered at death.

> Some heroic figures (such as the prophets) were thought to have received a greater burst of the breath of God at birth – this gave them strength to accomplish their divine mission.

> The authors of the books of the Bible were believed to be 'inspired' to complete their tasks.

Authority and inspiration

Internal authority

This is the authority that derives from scholarship, moral or spiritual example, or experience.
- The great and the good who serve on ethical committees are examples of people who hold internal authority.
- People who hold authority through their status within a community can be said to have internal authority only if their status derives from their personal experience or example.

As the Enlightenment and subsequent philosophical movements eroded the authority of religious experience, **reason** came to be the prime authority.

External authority

This is the authority that is attached to a person or office.
- The Church came to hold such an authority, as the representative of God, or as the 'Bride of Christ'.

As the Church developed as an institution, arguments began to threaten the apparent position of authority of the Church. A system of councils was developed.
- A council was considered **ecumenical** when it included representatives of the Church from all over the Christian world. Otherwise, it was not considered authoritative.

Appeals could be made to respected historical figures in an effort to maintain the authority of an argument. Figures associated with the Church came to hold an authority in themselves as priests or bishops.

During various controversies in the early Church, the councils that prevailed, established what came to be held as the **Catholic faith** (catholic – κατ´ολου, of the whole).

The Holy Spirit

The Holy Spirit as *spiritus creator*	The Holy Spirit as *spiritus recreator*	The Holy Spirit as *spiritus transcreator*
The Spirit is the outreaching power of God which affects people from within.	The Spirit sustains and maintains those who receive it.	The Spirit is the power by which people can access the Kingdom of God at the end of time.

Christian theology has come to hold that the Holy Spirit is the power of God at work in the world. This Spirit was at work in the authors of the books of the Bible. There are two general approaches to the Inspiration of the Bible:

Fundamentalism

The belief that the Bible is word-for-word the Word of God. Fundamentalists apply the laws and principles of the Bible as rigorously as they can, and believe that the Holy Spirit has preserved the Bible from any error. In effect, the writers received a message which they transcribed faithfully. (For example, the Creation stories in Genesis, in which God creates the world in six days, is held to be absolutely true.)

Liberalism

The belief that the writers of the Bible were guided as they wrote their books. The Bible contains an accurate account of principles and ideas, but is not generally historically accurate. The writers were preserved from error in the theological truths that they wrote of, but need not have been kept from historical error. This accounts for the various inaccuracies. (For example, in the description of the Temple, there is reference to a large circular bowl used for burning incense. It is said to be 3 cubits round, and 1 cubit across – a mathematical impossibility.)

Definitions in religious language

Analogy	A figure of speech involving a comparison; a simile, a metaphor. *Logic:* resemblance of relations or attributes forming a ground of reasoning; the process of reasoning from parallel cases.
Metaphor	A figure of speech in which a name or descriptive word or phrase is transferred to an object or action different from, but analogous to, that to which it is literally applicable; an instance of this, a metaphorical expression. A thing considered as representative of some other (usually abstract) thing; a symbol.

Background

Realist
A philosopher who believes that a statement is true or false if it corresponds to something in reality.

Non-realist
Someone who believes that their language reflects truth insofar as it fits in (coheres) with other statements that are held to be true. The truth in a non-realist's statement would be held to be relative to the context in which it was made (for instance, the community or the age).

Analogy
Language used to inspire a sense of the meaning intended, rather than being used with a literal intention.

Analytic statement
A statement that explains its meaning within itself; e.g. the statement
'2 + 2 = 4' contains everything that you need to test its truth claims.

Synthetic statement
A statement that needs an external reference to test its meaning. A synthetic statement would need evidence to check its truth or otherwise.

Equivocal language
Words that can have completely different meanings, depending upon use and context, e.g. a bat can be a cricket bat or a flying rodent. Equivocal language about God becomes awkward because a word used can leave someone confused about its meaning. This difficulty led some philosophers to propose a **via negativa**, a negative way – see Rudolph Otto (in the section on **Religious experience**).

Univocal language
Language whose meaning is not clouded by alternative definitions. Words used about God mean the same as when they are applied in other contexts.

This emphasises what God is *not*. It concentrates on God's **unknowability**.

If language is equivocal, it becomes 'evocative and functional, rather than cognitive and descriptive'.
Despite this, believers want to make positive statements about their belief, rather than talk about what God is not!

Cognitive language
Language based on fact. Facts are known to be true or false through cognitive knowledge.

Non-cognitive language
Language that cannot be proved to be true or false through knowledge. This would include ethical, moral or emotive language.

Analogy

Thomas Aquinas (1225–1274)

Aquinas argued that we can never speak about God without using everyday language, because that is all that we have.

- We are imperfect beings using imperfect language to describe a perfect God.
- Some religious writers therefore argued for a **via negativa**. The via negativa describes God in terms of 'what God is not' (!).

> Aquinas argued that God is pure **actuality** and that humans (and the rest of Creation) are **potentiality**. God is outside time and space, and is purely simple. Since God is simple, immutable, unchangeable and so on, God is beyond human experience.

Mystics such as **Pseudo-Dionysius** argued that human language was hopelessly inadequate in trying to describe the ineffable God. Human language is not equipped to discuss the encounter between humans and God. This is the via negativa.

- Aquinas rejected using the via negativa alone because he believed that there are positive things that can be said about God – he followed Aristotle in making use of three forms of language:

Univocal	Equivocal	Analogical
Words mean the same in different situations.	The meaning of a word depends upon its context.	The meaning of a word in one context is pointed to by its meaning in another.
Green grass Green hat	Fruit bat Cricket bat	Emily is good God is good
This use of language is finite, and as such limits its subject.	*This use of language makes no connection between contexts.*	*The use of the language in one context is understood – it points on to the meaning in the other context.*

Aquinas argued that univocal language was not applied to God, since it limits its subject, and God cannot be limited.

He also argued that equivocal language was equally inapplicable – it would communicate nothing about God because there is no connection between the language uses.

Aquinas therefore argued that religious language should be **analogical**. He distinguished between two types of analogical language:

Attribution
We ascribe a quality to one thing because it is caused by another.

> *Human wisdom is a reflection of divine wisdom.*

Proportion
We ascribe a quality to one thing because it points towards another thing which has that quality.

> *Human love points beyond itself to divine love.*

Some argued that the via negativa had problems:
- It denied the positive aspects of human existence.
- W. R. Inge argued that the via negativa could lead to a denial of the importance of the self.

Symbolic language

Sign
A sign simply communicates a message by pointing beyond itself.

A person who wants to attract someone else's attention might wave a cloth.

Symbol
A symbol communicates something far more powerful.

Waving a cloth becomes more significant when it happens to be a national flag.

Often, symbolic language becomes more than if it is read literally. Because the language participates in the thing that it represents, it becomes a powerful means of communication.

Paul Tillich (1886–1965)

Religious language communicates through symbol. It is poetic and evocative.

It is religious because it demonstrates a person's **ultimate concern**. It points towards God, **being itself**.

Symbolic language serves to 'open up' new levels of reality. The language used is understandable to humans, but it points beyond itself to an ultimate reality.

- Tillich argued that a religious experience was an experience of something beyond the physical phenomena that were observed by a person.
- The experience is more than the phenomena that could be captured in a photograph. The 'religious' element of the experience is also subjective, in that someone else might observe the same phenomenon and interpret it as a perfectly normal event.

For something to be religious, it must be an experience of '**being itself**', or ultimate reality. It is an experience of **ultimate concern** and significance.

Religious language is language that points beyond the mere words towards this ultimate 'being itself'.

Ian Ramsey *Religious Language* (1957)

- Ramsey argued that religious language is symbolic and analogical.
- He referred to **models** and **qualifiers**.

A model assists us to understand the thing that it represents.

e.g. 'God is good' contains the model 'good'. We understand the human concept of goodness, and we apply it as a model to understand the nature of God.

However, we need to modify the model, because God is not good in the way that a human might be. We need to use a **qualifier**. We say that God is **infinitely good**.

Exam Advice 5: Time management

- Clearly this depends upon the exam that you are sitting! Most of the AS/A2 papers appear to take around 1½ hours, and involve answering two essay questions.
- A small proportion of the 1½ hours will be spent reading the questions on the paper, and deciding on which questions to answer.
- You therefore must keep a close eye on the amount of time actually available for your essay.
- It isn't essential to spend the entire time writing. You are being examined on your skills as a philosopher, not on your ability to use up large amounts of exam board answer booklets.
- Allow for some time at the end of the question for editing and checking.

The verification principle

David Hume (1711–1776)

> If we take in our hand any volume; of divinity or school metaphysics, for instance, let us ask, *Does it contain any abstract reasoning containing quantity or number?* No. *Does it contain any experimental reasoning, concerning matter of fact or existence?* No. Commit it to the flames: for it can contain nothing but sophistry and illusion.
>
> Hume, D. *An Enquiry Concerning Human Understanding,*1748

Unless a statement is analytical (its internal logic provides it with meaning) or synthetic (empirical evidence counts to show its truth), it is meaningless.

A. J. Ayer (1910–1989)

Ayer belonged to the **Logical Positivist** movement. The Logical Positivists believed that empirical evidence must be used to make a statement meaningful.

- A scientist's statement would be meaningful where it is based on evidence gathered through experimentation. Therefore religious statements cannot be meaningful – they cannot be verified.

A statement is meaningful if it can be assessed either by an appeal (directly or indirectly) to either:

1. the meaning of the words and the grammatical structures that constitute them, or
2. some form of sense experience.

> *'The criteria which we use to test the genuineness of apparent statements of fact is the criteria of verifiability. We say that a sentence is factually significant to any given person, if, and only if, he knows how to verify the proposition which it purports to express – that is, of he knows what observations would lead him, under certain conditions, to accept the proposition as being true, or reject it as being false.'*
>
> Ayer, A.J. *Language, Truth and Logic*

The meaning of the words

Statements that can be verified using internal logic and grammar are **analytic.**

All bachelors are unmarried.

The definition of a bachelor is an unmarried man. Everything needed to verify the statement is included in the statement.

Sense experience

Statements that can be verified using external sense data are said to be **synthetic.**

Eric is a bachelor.

We would need to find Eric and ask him about his marital status – this would provide the external sense data.

In both cases, we have everything that we need to prove whether the statement is true or false.
Remember that verification is not about the truth or otherwise of a statement – it is about its provability.

Since it would appear that religious language is not analytic and not synthetic, it would appear to be meaningless.	⇨ ⇨	It is not internally logical nor can there be external sense experience.

Problems with the verification principle

The verification principle appears to make historical statements meaningless, since they are neither analytic nor synthetic.

Statements about the Battle of Trafalgar cannot be verified through direct sense experience, nor do they contain internal logic. For example:

> 'Admiral Nelson defeated the French Fleet at Trafalgar.'

Does it contain any abstract reasoning containing quantity or number?

*The statement contains no **internal logic** which could be used to verify it.*

Does it contain any experimental reasoning, concerning matter of fact or existence?

*There is no external **direct sense experience** that can be used to verify the statement.*

Is the statement meaningless?

Following various criticisms of the verification principle, **Ayer** was forced to make some adjustments to his ideas:

Strong verification
There is no doubt as to the truth of a statement; experimentation and reason show it to be so.

Weak verification
Observation **at the time** counts to make the statement verifiable. Because Nelson was present at the Battle of Trafalgar, he would have been able to verify statements made about the event.

The weak form of the verification principle renders any statement meaningful so long as experience can render it possible.

Statements about **Jesus, Mohammed** (P.B.U.H.) and **the Buddha** can be verified because there would be sense experience to render the statements meaningful.
Statements about God as Creator may be regarded as meaningful if evidence for design in the creation of the world can be observed.

Some theologians and philosophers pointed out that often although a statement cannot be verified at the present time, it can be ultimately. Statements about life after death appear to fail under the verification principle, but if there is an afterlife, they can be verified later. This **eschatological verification** can make the statement meaningful because it can be verified **in the future**.

*Two people are journeying along a road. One believes he is travelling towards a Celestial City. The other believes the road leads nowhere. There is no way to prove the statements made about the Celestial City, and such statements are not analytic. It could therefore be argued that the statements are meaningless. However, the travellers' statements **are** meaningful because they can be verified* **'retrospectively'**
Hick, J. *Philosophy of Religion*, p.91

The verification principle simply questions a statement's meaningfulness. It does not make any claim about its actual truth. *I have blue hair* is meaningful, even if it is untrue, because it can be verified.

> Neither the verification nor the falsification principle can be verified or falsified.
> **Statements about the verification principle cannot be verified!**

The falsification principle

Antony Flew *In New Essays in Philosophical Theology* (1955)
Flew argued that religious people tend to refuse the possibility that their statements can be falsified, and so they render their statements meaningless.
- They will not allow any evidence to count against their beliefs.
For this reason, Flew argued that religious language is **meaningless.**

Flew was influenced by **Sir Karl Popper**, a philosopher of science. Popper argued that the scientific method was based not on verification but on **falsification**. A scientist proposes a hypothesis, which he then sets out to test. If the scientist knows how to show that his hypothesis might be false (i.e. what evidence he would need to count against it), then his statement is synthetic, and therefore meaningful.

He illustrated this idea using **John Wisdom's** parable of the gardener.
Flew argued that when confronted with something that is awkward regarding the existence of God, the religious person replies that God is mysterious.
- A statement can only be regarded as meaningful if something can be cited that will falsify the statement should it actually occur.
This does not mean that the statement is **factually incorrect** – a statement is regarded as meaningful if the mechanism exists to show that it is factually incorrect. Flew argues that religious language lacks this mechanism. It is not possible to falsify religious language in the same way as it is with other language.

Two people are exploring a jungle. They find a clearing that appears to have been cultivated. One believes that there is a gardener responsible for the clearing, the other disagrees.

- They test the believer's hypothesis.
- Every test fails to turn up any evidence to support the believer's claims.
Despite the lack of evidence, the believer persists, adjusting his hypothesis to suit the new lack of evidence. Each modification adds a 'qualification' to the original hypothesis, and the believer is able to persist in his claim.

It is raining outside.

To treat the statement as meaningful, we need to know what observation to make to falsify it.

We simply need to look out of the window in order to see whether the statement is factually correct. Because this 'falsifying mechanism' exists, the statement is meaningful (in fact, at the time of writing, it is a beautiful sunny day).

God is Love.

What can be done to falsify this statement?

When the atheist points out the evidence that suggests that the statement is not true, the religious person 'qualifies' the statement with further modifications. Flew called this **'death of a thousand qualifications'**.

Problems with the falsification principle

Richard Swinburne in *The Coherence of Theism* (1977)

- Religious statements are not **cognitive**, and so should not be treated as being falsifiable.

Statements can often be meaningful without there being the means to falsify them.

> *For example:*
> *The statement that a cupboard is full of toys that come to life when everyone is asleep and no-one is looking is meaningful, because we understand what it means to suggest that toys can move, even though we can never gather the evidence required to falsify the statement.*

R. B. Braithwaite

- Religious language is **non-cognitive**. The **verification principle** and Flew treat religious language as being cognitive.

A religious claim is essentially a moral statement, expressed in the terms of symbolic language.

There is no need for the religious person to believe that the story is true – they would simply need to adopt a particular behaviour pattern.

Basil Mitchell

In an essay in *The Philosophy of Religion*, Mitchell gave the story of the Resistance leader (opposite) to illustrate that, often, a person will accept a statement as meaningful simply on trust.

Although the evidence might count against their beliefs, they continue to trust in God because the evidence is not sufficient to prove them false.

Rather than religious believers refusing to allow anything to count against their belief, Mitchell was arguing that the believer's prior faith maintains their trust in God even when the evidence appears to undermine that trust.

> During a war, a Resistance fighter meets a stranger who tells him that he is the leader of the Resistance. The fighter is convinced, and trusts him completely. Sometimes the stranger can be observed working on his side, but sometimes he is seen in an enemy uniform arresting their friends. Despite the apparent evidence, the fighter remains convinced that the stranger was telling the truth.

R. M. Hare

Also writing in *The Philosophy of Religion*, in an essay called 'Theology and Falsification', Hare offered another story.

- Hare agreed that religious statements are non-cognitive.
- Religious language cannot make factual claims – but it can still influence the way that people view the world. Hare called this way of looking at the world a '**blik**'.

Religious beliefs are bliks – they affect the way people look at the world.

> Hare used the example of a student convinced that his teachers were trying to kill him. Nothing that they did to try to reassure him would shake his conviction that they were after him. The belief remained meaningful, even in the face of evidence to the contrary.

Exam Advice 6: Keywords in questions

What does the question actually want you to do?

- Analyse the question. What does the examiner want you to do with the topic?
- Make careful note of key words in the question.
- Find the words in the question that refer to the ideas that you will be referring to, and the words that tell you what you need to do with those ideas (e.g. describe, explain, evaluate, . . . ?).

Wittgenstein and language games

Ludwig Wittgenstein (1889–1951)

In *Tractatus*, Wittgenstein proposed a model of language which was based on the idea that meaning in language is based on the objects that words refer to.
Language is primarily a tool used to picture the world. Each word is like a picture.

> *The World is everything that is the case*
> *Tractatus*, 1921

Wittgenstein came to reject his early views on language. He recognised the limitations of a literal approach to language use. He came to realise that the **Logical Positivists'** view of language was too limiting.

He began to consider the way that language is defined by the functions that it performs.

He also recognised the problems that religious language faced (in terms of meaningfulness and so on).

Rather than asking questions about the meaningfulness of language, he looked at the way that language is used, and at the functions of language.
Wittgenstein proposed the concept of **language games**. Different uses of language have different rules – learning to use the language is similar to learning the rules to a different game. Games have nothing in common except for their purpose (entertainment) and their having rules. One might involve gambling and playing cards, the other a ball and a great deal of running.

> Learning a language includes learning its **grammar**, or rules of use. Consider a Norfolk school student learning German: they must build a **working** knowledge of cases, vocabulary and tenses in order to understand the language in use.

Every form of language is a self-contained 'game' with its own rules, customs and uses.

- Language cannot exist in isolation – it is a community activity, with rules of engagement, conventions of use particular to each sphere of activity.

- Religious language is a language game, and its rules apply within its system, but may be unintelligible to outsiders.

However, there is common ground between different games (e.g. religion and football) – a non believer may be able to understand some, most or even all of the rules.
The language game reflects the fact that language is a human activity. To assess the meaning of language, you must look at the activity that it refers to. The meaning is derived from the game's 'grammar', and inappropriate language breaks the rules of the language game – it could be argued that using the pronoun 'He' of God is breaking the rules of the religious language game, since ascribing gender to the concept of God is not acceptable.

Being aware of a religion's 'language game' will help in understanding the faith statements of that religion.

Some philosophers have argued that language games can become 'exclusive clubs', whereas language is a community property – it cannot be used as a secret code by one group.
- Religions also make claims of universal application of their language – belief in God is not subject to community context!

Descriptive ethics

- As its title suggests, this simply seeks to describe people's behaviour.
- It may be seen more as a branch of sociology or anthropology – it examines the choices that people make, and the values that are held by communities and societies.
- It might appear that descriptive ethics is therefore merely the preliminary stage of a serious ethical investigation.
- However, any ethical debate must start with a statement of what is happening, and of the justifications offered for that. Descriptive ethics provides this starting point.

For example:
A study of the moral values held in the USA may note that President George W. Bush is a 'born-again' Christian. That study might consider various aspects of Mr Bush's policies regarding social affairs, and it might make mention of his record as Governor of Texas. In particular, it might note his support for the death penalty. The 'descriptive ethics' approach would consider the way that Mr Bush behaves, and it might consider his stated reasons. However, the descriptive ethics approach would go no further – it would not question those reasons, nor would it make any judgements about what is right and wrong.
Descriptive ethics simply states that something is the case.

However, it should be noted that many people make everyday ethical decisions from a descriptive ethical starting point:

A motorist is pulled over by the police for speeding. As he discusses the matter, he complains that there are many other cars on the same stretch of road also speeding. He claims this as a defence for his conduct.

A teenager observes that his friends and contemporaries are choosing to smoke. He bases his decision to take up smoking on that observation.

In both these cases, the moral judgement is based on other people's behaviour. In another context, David Hume argued that you cannot derive an **ought** from an **is**. A moral decision cannot simply be based on other people's behaviour.

Descriptive ethics offers no solutions to the dilemmas of everyday life – in fact it highlights the difficulties of those dilemmas by showing the range of human responses. It can only provide the starting point for further ethical debate.

Normative ethics

This examines the norms by which people make moral decisions.

It assumes that there is a set of these norms informing the decisions people make, and it seeks to explore those norms and their applications in moral situations.

It asks questions about the 'rights' and 'wrongs' of a decision. In this way, it moves beyond the simple observations of descriptive ethics into an examination of the motives and justifications of behaviour.

For example:

Descriptive ethics would consider the fact that 500 abortions are carried out each day in the UK. It would break down these figures into various statistics, but it would draw no ethical conclusions from these figures.

Normative ethics would go on to ask whether it is right to have an abortion, and would consider the various reasons and justifications that are offered in the argument. An obvious question for normative ethics would be 'when does life begin?'

Normative ethics will consider the validity of the presuppositions behind the moral decisions, and will draw conclusions about those presuppositions.

Deontological questions
These deal with the way that a person **ought** to behave.

Axiological questions
These deal with the **values** that lie behind people's choices.

But clear distinctions must be drawn between the conclusions of the two – you cannot use a descriptive ethics statement to challenge a normative ethics statement (see the reference to Hume in the last section). You cannot derive an **ought** from an **is**.

For example:
During social unrest on an estate on Tyneside, young people excused their 'TWOCing' (Taking WithOut Consent, or stealing cars) by arguing 'everyone else is doing it'.

Stealing is wrong. No matter how many people are stealing, it remains wrong.

Normative
Should there be
*a law about
speeding?*

Deontological
What are the
*motorist's obligations
to others?*

Axiological
What values does
the motorist hold?

Descriptive
*How many motorists
actually obey the
law?*

A motorist is observed driving at 43 mph in a 30mph zone. A police officer stops her – her 'defence' is that 'no-one drives at 30 on this road'. Is this a valid ethical response?

Meta-ethics and the wider debate

Descriptive ethics deals with the way that things are.	Normative ethics deals with the reasoning behind the decisions

- It is possible to take the debate away from practical concerns, such as what people are doing, or whether they can claim to be right.
- There are presuppositions underpinning ethical debate, and these must also be discussed.
- Rather than discussing whether something is right or wrong, the debate centres on the meaning of the statements being used. In effect, the debate is about the rules of ethical debate.

For example:
> What does it mean to say that something is right or wrong?
> What do the words that are used in the debate actually mean?

- When the Logical Positivists questioned the meaningfulness of ethical language, ethicists began to examine their use of language in the face of this challenge.
- Ethical language, like religious language, does not refer to direct sense experience.

Meta-ethics looks at the basis on which ethical theories are derived. It also provides an opportunity for philosophers to agree the terms by which an ethical debate is going to proceed. This is called **prolegomena** (Greek for 'first words'), and it helps to prevent contributions to a debate working at cross-purposes.

In the late nineteenth century the Vienna Circle began to question the meaningfulness of statements being made in philosophy. The **Logical Positivists** maintained that language was not meaningful without **direct sense experience** to support statements. In particular, **A. J. Ayer** argued that religious statements were impossible to verify, and as such were meaningless.

But   **ethics is about 'real life' – the debates are about life or death issues, and about the way that people make decisions as they live their lives.**
There is a danger that meta-ethics can become 'bogged down' in the theory, and fail to provide the practical guidance that is needed to enable people to make informed ethical decisions.

Ethical debate usually provides a theory by which decisions can be made. Underpinning these are three basic approaches to ethical decisions.

Non-cognitive
Moral language is not dealing with the objective. Rather, it is a way of expressing advice for a particular situation. (For example, see R. F. Braithwaite, who claimed that religious language was a way of expressing a desired way of behaving in symbolic language.)
If moral language is non-cognitive, then it is dealing in **opinions** and **preferences**. There is no objective moral standard by which actions can be judged. As such, it is **subjective**.

Relativist
When moral language is seen as relativist, it is subject to cultural and sociological influences. Statements that are relativist depend upon **individual circumstances**. The choices made cannot be analysed and rules cannot be derived from the situation, because the circumstances are unique.

Absolutist
An absolutist ethical statement looks to an **objective** authority for its justification. This is not to say that there is a fixed moral code that exists independently of outside influence. Rather, it refers to some objective principle or idea that can be applied universally.

Where ethical decisions are made with the conviction that there is an absolute principle that can be applied in each situation, a moral code can be derived and considered. These principles, and their application, lead to a variety of attitudes towards ethical choices.

Aristotle's ethical language

Absolute and Relative

Absolute	Relative
An absolutist definition of 'good' would be something as good in itself.	A relativist definition of 'good' would be something as good in a particular context.

Good can also be defined in terms of either **outcome** (teleological, or goal-defined), or **motive** (where the reasons for the action define its being good or otherwise).

Aristotle (384–322BCE)

- Something is 'good' if it fulfills its purpose. The most obvious example if this would be a knife – a good knife is one which is sharp and which cuts well.
- This is based on Aristotle's ideas of **cause and purpose**:
  Because everything has a **Final Cause**, it is possible to discern what is 'good' by looking at the apparent purpose that a thing is to be put to.
- This is the basis for Roman Catholic morality, and the key ethical theory of **Natural Law**.
- Aristotle also spoke of the '**Greatest Good**': eudaemonia, or spiritual satisfaction. This satisfaction comes about through the fulfillment of human potential, or self-realisation.
- The eudaemonia is achieved through exercising the virtues (see the section on **Virtue ethics**), which would not simply be the pursuit of pleasure, but would include knowledge and spiritual satisfaction.
- Aristotle used the term '**good-in-itself**', meaning something that is intrinsically good.

In *Nicomachean Ethics,* he distinguished between things that are pursued for their consequences (such as money) and things that are pursued for their own sake (such as health). Aristotle's list of things that are 'good-in-themselves' includes health, sight and intelligence.

Form and matter

Reality consists of several things that make up Form and matter. The matter is what a thing is made of, and the Form is the thing's specific characteristics. A chicken is made up of a variety of materials – its matter – which come together to make a chicken. That it clucks, lays eggs, and flies, make it a chicken. When it dies, it maintains the matter, but it no longer continues in its current Form – it is now a dead chicken. Matter contains the potential to become a specific Form. All change in nature is the progression from the potential to the actual.

Causality

Aristotle used the example of rain:
1. *Material Cause – the clouds*
2. *Efficient Cause – the process by which the rain is made*
3. *Formal Cause – the Form, or nature, of the rain is to fall*
4. *Final Cause – the rain provides water for plants and animals to grow*

The Final Cause is a thing's purpose in life.

Exam Advice 7: More on planning an essay

- Remember that the plan is not going to be marked – don't spend ages crafting the plan, and neglect the essay itself.
- Jot down the points that spring to mind.
- Create a spidergram or a brain storm for an at-a-glance guide to content.
- From that, draw up a set of sub-headings to provide you with a structure for your essay.
- You don't have to stick to the plan.
- You might find it useful to define the terms that you are going to use in your essay – the examiner already knows what you mean, but it will help you clarify your thinking.

Example: 'Miracles by definition cannot happen'
Introduction
Hume's definition.
Discussion
Newton's mechanics, Quantum theory.
Wiles, Ramsey and others
Conclusion
Answer the question!!!

Moore's ethical language

G. E. Moore (1873–1958) in *Principia Ethica* (1903)
- The term 'good' is simply a non-natural, indefinable quality which is known through **intuition**.
- Moore suggested that any attempts to define the word were doomed – you can no more define 'good' than you can define 'yellow'. This was because any definition of 'good' would necessarily limit the concept, and make it applicable in only a few situations.

> The **naturalistic fallacy**
> Moore believed that the attempt to identify an ethical concept with a natural one was a fallacy: 'good' cannot be defined in terms of an invariable, specific content.

- Moore's view of ethics has become known as **intuitionism**. You may know what good is, but you cannot define it. God can only be known through intuition.

While we can point to a series of things which we hold to be 'good', we cannot define the term. 'Good' in these terms is similar to 'beautiful'.

The summum bonum

This means 'the Greatest Good'
(compare this with Aristotle's idea of eudaemonia).

The **Stoics** taught that moral virtue is the only good. All that matters is our attempt to do what's right.

The term was also used by **Utilitarians** to refer to the collective good for all.

William Ross
The Right and the Good (1930)
- Ross began from Moore's proposal that equating good with a natural property commits the naturalistic fallacy.
- He criticised Moore for committing a similar fallacy by equating the rightness of an action with its maximisation of good. He pointed out that there can be moral conflicts, making definitions of good valid only when they do not conflict with some other idea of good. As with intuitionism, what is good is self-evident.

Evil
- For some, evil is simply the opposite of good. Others see the term as synonymous with suffering.
- **Natural evil** is suffering brought about through natural processes. For example, the suffering that was a direct result of the Gujarat Earthquake was natural.
- **Moral evil** is suffering brought about through human agency. Suffering because of looting, selfishness or lack of resources would be moral evil.

The sections dealing with the theodicies are relevant to this section of the specifications. However, answers will not require detailed knowledge of the theodicies, but rather their application in the various ethical issues associated with evil.

Exam Advice 8: Writing an essay
- Your essay will be assessed on its clarity of expression.
- This means that the examiner will be looking at the way you present and explain the arguments needed to answer the question.
- Every time you make a point, it should contribute something to your overall argument. It should follow on from the previous point, and move your argument on.
- Before you introduce a new point, have you dealt with the previous part of your essay properly?
- You could think of each paragraph as being like a mini-essay. It should explain its point clearly, and draw out any ideas raised by the point. It should end with an intermediate conclusion.
- Your final conclusion should be like a summary of each paragraph's intermediate conclusion. **Make sure it answers the question!!!**

Motives for actions and outcomes

Joseph Butler (1692-1752)
- People do not normally **choose** to do evil.
- Rather, they pursue their own interests, or a cause that they identify with – evil is a by-product of this.

However, this appears to have been proved wrong by the events of recent history, in which people quite clearly appear to have chosen evil over good.

The 'right'
- Doing what is right is not the same thing as doing what is good.
- A basic preoccupation of ethics is to try to relate the right to the good.
- At a basic level, there is a **right** way to do something – the right way to cut a tenon joint, for example.

This use of the word 'right' is distinct from the idea of 'human rights'.

Right and wrong
- An act is morally obligatory (i.e. you **ought** to do it) if it would not be wrong to perform it.
- A theory of right and wrong must examine what **ought** to be done.
- It would then follow that an attempt to define **right** might depend upon the attitude of the philosopher to whether 'ought' depends upon outcome or motive.

Teleological
A thing is thought of as good or right because of its outcome (telos = goal).

- For a **teleological** approach to 'right', the word would be defined as being the most effective course of action.

An example of the teleological approach:
Ending the life of a terminally ill patient is the right thing to do because its outcome will be to stop any suffering and allow the patient to die in dignity.

Deontological
A thing is thought of as good or right because of its being right or good in itself. It may be that there are rules concerning behaviour that the act conforms to.

- For a **deontological** approach to 'right', the word would be defined as being the best action in itself. It would be right because it was a virtuous act.

An example of the deontological approach:
Ending the life of a terminally ill patient is the right thing to do because it is a compassionate action, and compassion is innately good. It is your *duty* to behave compassionately.

This distinction between outcome and motive is important throughout ethics.

Value judgements

There are three basic philosophical concerns to do with value:

On what property or characteristic do we base a thing's value?	Is value objective or subjective? Is value simply a matter of how we feel about something, or does value repose in the object itself?

What things are valuable or have value?

Clearly there can be no **empirical** evidence on which value can be based (except on a purely financial basis). The object could have value because of the way that it meets human needs, whether material, emotional or otherwise. Therefore the properties or characteristics of a thing of value are more **metaphysical**.

- Things appear to be valued differently in different contexts and cultures.

Plato's Athens valued different characteristics in a person than did his contemporaries in Sparta.	The USA holds different beliefs concerning the sanctity of life in differing contexts – the unborn child would appear more 'valuable' than the convict on Death Row.

It is alleged that manufacturers often appear to 'name their price' according to what they can get away with, rather than to the financial value of the goods they sell. Some societies have even compiled lists of 'valuable things'! People can attach value to things according to their utility, or their aesthetic appeal.

Axiological ethics

Axiological ethics focuses on what is worthy of pursuit or promoting, and what is not.
- Much current study of axiomatic ethics centres on how we can know what is of value (i.e. the epistomology of values).

Some issues

- J. S. Mill said that desire plays the same role in what we value as the senses do in our knowledge of the world. He argued that everyone desires pleasure – this leads to his contribution to the idea of utilitarianism. Judgements about value are based on emotion, and those judgements are as valid as the emotions that they are based on.

Aesthetic value

- Many things have 'value' because of a perceived quality which people admire in the object.
- In the visual arts (e.g. painting) there are huge numbers of different ways of regarding an image – some people value some styles, and not others. Styles come in and go out of fashion. The same applies to music and other arts.
- However subjective these judgements are, there may be objective grounds for valuing particular objects.
- Some have argued that beauty is an objective quality that is independent of opinion or trend. There are qualities that may be objective – qualities of nobility, honesty and so on, regarding the spirit in which the object was produced.

There has been some study of the relationship between values and identity – consideration of what is valued in society today has been within the context of modern consumerism.

Plato

Plato conceived the Forms as being arranged hierarchically; the supreme Form is the Form of the Good, which, like the sun in the myth of the cave, illuminates all the other ideas. The best parts of this mixture are beauty, symmetry, and truth, which are all closer to knowledge than pleasure.
- The Good is perfect and desired by all who know it. In the *Philebus* he wonders 'Is it pleasure or knowledge?'
- He shows that pleasure cannot be the Good; pleasures are often accompanied by false opinions, and great pleasures and pains occur in bad states of body or soul.
- Knowledge is not perfect either, because some arts are more exact than others. The Good can be neither knowledge nor pleasure alone, but a mixture of the best parts of both, which includes the sciences and those pleasures that are pure and necessary.

He finally gives the order of value as measure, beauty, mind, science, and pure pleasure.

Subjectivism, objectivism, and relativism

Subjectivism and objectivism in ethics

1. Subjectivism

Moral judgements are 'feeling-responses' to individual situations.

- This means that moral judgements are made on an individual basis, and are 'subject' to cultural and other influences. These judgements are no more than assertions of opinion regarding the moral character of a particular action, whether it is actual or hypothetical.

> **N.B.**
> There is also a debate in philosophy about subjectivism and objectivism. Although there are obvious similarities between the philosophical and the ethical treatments of the issue, there are important differences.

But such a view negates ethical debate, since everything becomes a 'matter of opinion'. In its 'hard' form, it denies the validity of ethical arguments and theories.

2. Objectivism

Moral judgements are independent of the feelings and contexts in which the actions to which they apply are being carried out.

- Moral judgements can be 'tested' using valid philosophical methods. They are rationally defendable. Objective morality often makes reference to 'duty' and to sets of rules. There is an external authority that guarantees moral judgements. This authority serves to exert a moral pressure on the individual.

But objective moral judgements are often criticised as being illusory. Empiricists argue that there *is* no objective authority – there is nothing that can be tested or experimented on.

Relative and absolute values

Relativism is the view that moral judgements are dependent on the standards and social conditions that exist when the moral judgements are being made.

Judgements depend upon:

- social norms
- acceptable practices
- religious beliefs
- levels of technology, particularly medical

> **Aristotle** and **Plato** both wrote about the ideal society. Their ideas of justice were to protect the vulnerable – yet women and slaves were lower even than the vulnerable that they thought needed protection.

Moral relativism suggests that there are no criteria by which moral judgements can be criticised, because there are no 'absolute' criteria that can apply.

> There is a good deal of anthropological and other evidence to support the moral relativists' views.
> - It should be noted that this evidence has only been brought together recently – moral absolutists such as **Kant** would have been unaware of the evidence and of its implications.
> - Recent philosophical developments have also supported the relativists' views.

Exam Advice 9: Editing an essay

- Your essay is your chance to dazzle the examiner, so you want to make it good.
- Run through a checklist to make certain you've covered all the points:
  a) Start from the Conclusion. Can you track your argument back through the discussion to the introduction?
  b) Are there any 'leaps of logic'? Look for unsupported claims or points that you have made that don't link in to the main thrust of your essay.
  c) If there are any problems, add what you need. Examiners are well used to finding 'extras' at the end of essays!

This might seem like a lot to remember in an exam. Practise it as you tackle specimen questions and past papers, and you will be able to do it automatically!

Language games

Wittgenstein rejected the idea that language was simply a range of labels to be applied to objects. He began to look at the actual use of language. He noted the various ways of using language, and he called these various systems **language games**. He argued that all language is a part of an activity, and the various language games make up our 'Form of Life'.

A word has meaning from its usage. Language is appropriate when words are used correctly: '**Meaning is use**'. Wittgenstein rejected the practice of trying to provide precise definitions of words. He felt that the various uses of a single word formed a 'family resemblance'.

At its extreme, moral relativism involves a complete lack of commonly-held values and perspectives. It becomes a kind of moral individualism.

Criticisms
- Anthropologists *have* detected commonly-held values across societies.
- The maxim 'you shall not kill' appears common to most (if not all) societies in one form or another.
- Most societies have condemned the tyrant who (ab)uses power to extend his own position at the expense of his subjects.
- Most societies recognise the need for objective jduegement in criminal cases, such as a judge and/or jury to consider disputes.

John Finnis

There are 'basic forms of good', including knowledge, life and sociability.

These principles underpin the workings of society, in which people are able to live and work. They enable dialogue between people in which there is a common understanding about the position of individuals within society as a whole.

There is a fundamental paradox in relativism – the statement 'everything is relative' is itself an **absolute** statement. If moral relativism is accepted as a universal situation, it contradicts itself!

Absolutism
The view that there are certain kinds of actions that are *always* wrong, or are *always* obligatory. This does not depend upon the context in which the action is carried out.

For example, it might be said that 'you shall not kill' is a moral absolute. Telling the truth is always right, and lying always wrong.

Note that this view is contrasted with that of **consequentialism**, where something is considered right or wrong depending upon its outcome.

Absolutism

---

1. A popular Religious Studies GCSE textbook includes this story:

As Pioneers travelled across the American West, a wagon train was attacked by Indians. A small group of settlers became detached from the train, and hid in a small wood. A woman suffocated her baby when it began to cry in order to prevent the cries giving the party away, leading to certain death at the hands of the Indians.

Jenkins, J. *Personal and Social Issues*

---

2. *Pacifism is the rejection of all violence, no matter what the provocation. Dietrich Bonhoffer was a convinced pacifist. However, he participated in the plot to assassinate Hitler, thinking that the death of one man would save the deaths of countless millions more soldiers and civilians as the Second World War dragged on.*

What is right and what is wrong in these situations?

Consequentialism is a form of relativism in that right and wrong is defined by the consequence of an action, rather than by reference to some external authority.

Deontological

The view that there are certain acts that **ought** to be carried out, and some that **ought not**. This gives rise to rules, codes and laws.

Moral absolutism is often identified as a **deontological** approach.

- **N.B.** While deontological ethics are absolutist, there are other ethical systems that are also absolutist.
- The deontological view is that certain things are **right in themselves**. They are **intrinsically** right or wrong. There is no reference to the consequence of an action.
- Some deontologists hold that while it may be wrong to kill, there may be circumstances where killing may be justifiable (though no less wrong!). An **absolutist** would not be able to make such a compromise.
- Common perceptions of absolutism correspond with traditional religious morality.
- Religious ethics are 'guaranteed' by the divine – God says that something is right or wrong, and so it is. Traditional religious ethics have been codified through systems similar to the Jewish **Torah** (Law) and the **Decalogue** (Ten Commandments). These systems derive their authority from God, and are not questioned for that reason.

Can the electric chair ever be justified as a punishment for murderers?

The **Euthyphro** dilemma:
1. Is a thing right because the gods command it?
or
2. Do the gods command it because it is good?

If God's laws are absolute (as in 1) why doesn't He command things that are cruel?
Socrates argued that God commands us to do good because it *is* good. This assumes that good is *independent* of God, and that God is not the source of standards of morality.

Theists would argue that goodness is something intrinsic to God – he *is* 'loving-kindness'. Therefore there is no conflict – God *is* good.

This assumes that God issues commands.

Absolutism (continued)

It also assumes that we can easily **interpret the commands** that are contained within the 'Word of God' (i.e. The Scriptures).	It sets God up in a **benign tyranny** – is God a good dictator? Do we have moral responsibility under such a system?

Criticisms of an absolutist view

- On a purely practical level, there may be circumstances in which a moral absolute would appear compromised.

- Moral absolutism appears to ignore the practical conditions 'on the ground'. It may be that a supposed moral absolute is observed with no regard to the 'bigger picture' in which even greater evils may be perpetrated.

- In the face of modern criticisms of moral absolutism, it has been argued that a more flexible approach to morality is needed, without compromising the absolute values being proposed.

Such a flexible approach would look at the difference between **act** and **omission**.

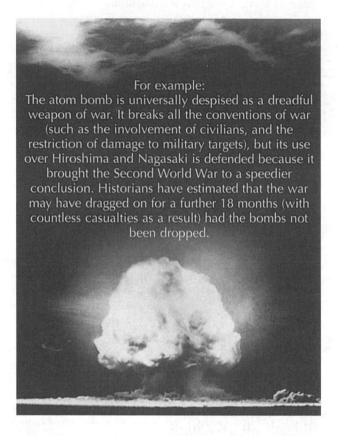

For example:
The atom bomb is universally despised as a dreadful weapon of war. It breaks all the conventions of war (such as the involvement of civilians, and the restriction of damage to military targets), but its use over Hiroshima and Nagasaki is defended because it brought the Second World War to a speedier conclusion. Historians have estimated that the war may have dragged on for a further 18 months (with countless casualties as a result) had the bombs not been dropped.

The doctrine of double effect

This states that it may be permissible to perform a good act with the knowledge that bad consequences will come about as a result. However, it is *always* wrong to perform a *bad* act in order to bring about *good* effects. The act is judged by its **intention**, rather than its **result**.

This is best illustrated with the discussion around euthanasia. A doctor deliberately administering an overdose to end the suffering of a patient has committed a 'bad act', even though his actions have brought about something good. This is not permissible. A doctor who administers palliative care, and inadvertently hastens death, has committed a good act with bad consequences.

Additional Advice 1: Using the exam board's own materials

- You can download practice questions and mark schemes from your exam boards' websites. These are intended for teachers as they prepare their classes for exams, and you may already have seen some of the questions.
- Use the titles to write practice essays. Keep to the time limits, and practice managing your time. Use the suggestions in this book to help you, or develop your own strategies.
- Be careful how you use the mark schemes. These are prepared for examiners to help them to mark essays. Remember the following points:
  a) Examiners use a system of 'positive award' – they credit what you get right, but simply ignore mistakes.
  b) The mark schemes provide a *guide* to the marking. Examiners are told to credit any reasonable interpretation of the question as long as it is in line with the specifications. Don't use them as 'model answers'!

Plato and Aristotle on virtue ethics

arete (virtue, excellence)
The quality that makes something a good example of its kind, e.g. the sharpness of a knife. For humans, arete represents the excellences that are needed for a human being to be a good human being.

eudaemonia (well-being)
The state of being content, or satisfied. This satisfaction comes about through the fulfilment of human potential, or self-realisation. Modern concepts would include material well-being (prosperity or possessions). Ancient Greek ideas were more spiritual, though bodily needs played a part.

Plato (428–347 BCE)

Plato believed that virtue was an inner state rising from a harmony of health, beauty and strength of character.

Actions are good where they enhance this inner state. Three characteristics have to be in harmony:

Wisdom
Good judgement, based on the use of reason

Courage
Taking risks calculated to be for the benefit of the self and others

Self-control
Will power, the ability to resist temptation

When these aspects of the personality are in balance, actions are just and good. Plato assumed that a person would only act badly (or unjustly) through ignorance – no-one would willingly behave badly.

Aristotle (384–322 BCE)

Plato's student divided virtues into two groups:

Moral virtues
These are characteristics of behaviour and attitude that contribute to appropriate behaviour.

For example:
courage, patience, friendliness, truthfulness, a sense of justice

Intellectual virtues
These are characteristics of thought and reason that contribute to the state of mind that leads to appropriate behaviour.

For example:
practical wisdom (balancing self-interest with that of others), technical skills, scientific skills, intelligence

These virtues combine to allow a person to live a happy and satisfying life. Some virtues are developed through habit (such as courage and temperance), others through learning and experience (such as wisdom and judgement). These virtues combine to enable the person to contribute to society.

Eudaimonia

The virtues contribute to this, the final goal of all human activity, experienced in three ways (according to Aristotle).

Pleasure
A spiritual sense of well-being

Honour
Living and working for others

Reflection
The pursuit of knowledge

Responses to virtue ethics

What do people think of Aristotle's virtue ethics?

Virtue ethics seeks the happiness of the individual – the benefits for society appear to be incidental. *I work for the benefit of society. I do this simply so that I am less likely to have my car stolen by some delinquent!*

There appears to be no room for selfless activity (altruism). Any 'selfless' act appears to be ultimately down to self-interest. *Even the apparently selfless act of making a donation to charity is accompanied by that self-righteous glow of satisfaction.*

Many people believe that Aristotle was a racist, sexist bigot. They believe that his belief that only men could access the virtues discredits the whole theory. *Aristotle's views on women, slaves and foreigners can be understood in the context of the times in which he lived. His ideas on virtue ethics, when seen in this light, can still stand.*

Modern versions of virtue ethics

Alasdair MacIntyre

MacIntyre argued for practical ethics, rooted in the 'real world'. He claimed that human communities should be at the centre of ethical life. Society's ideas of appropriate behaviour allow 'good' to be realised. Personal virtuous behaviour within society's structures allows everyone to benefit – the community is the context for this moral life.

But

- Can a virtuous person behave badly?
- Can virtuous intentions lead to vicious behaviour?
- Are the virtues culturally-defined (i.e. subjective) or are they universal (i.e. absolute)?

Phillipa Foot

Foot uses the concept of value – a wise person places appropriate value in certain goals.
Some goals are 'good in themselves', while others are 'good for the sake of something else'. A friendship based on the premise 'what's in this for me?' will be shallow, while a friendship based on trust, loyalty and companionship will be fruitful.

Foot also notes that people can 'learn' virtuous behaviour through experience.

She distinguishes between 'degrees of virtuousness' – is a person resisting terrible temptation being more virtuous than a person who is never tempted, and who never considers doing anything wrong?

Elizabeth Anscombe

Anscombe notes the way that actions have become important in judging a person's moral character. This leads to a preoccupation with rules, and attempts to read the future to work out possible consequences.

Classical Greek theories of Natural Law

Aristotle (384–322BCE)

Causality
Aristotle used the example of rain:
1. Material Cause – the clouds
2. Efficient Cause – the process by which the rain is made
3. Formal Cause – the Form, or nature, of the rain is to fall
4. Final Cause – the rain provides water for plants and animals to grow

- The Final Cause is an object's goal or aim – its purpose in life.
- Every object and action has a Final Cause, an aim or purpose.
- From this Final Cause, it is possible to establish an object or action's good.
- Once we know what an object's Final Cause is, we know what we must do to achieve this – it is this which defines our actions as good or otherwise.
- There is therefore a Final Cause to every action and object. Activity that brings about this Final Cause is **good** and activity that prevents the Final Cause is **bad**.

For example:
A knife's Final Cause is to cut. Its Efficient Cause is the cutting action, its Formal Cause the sharp edge, and its Material Cause the steel. A knife is good in so far as it can cut well, and actions using the knife are good in so far as they involve the knife cutting something.

The Stoics

- The Stoic school was founded by **Zeno of Citium** (334–262BCE). The best-known Stoic was the Roman Emperor Marcus Aurelius. The school took its name from a painted porch where the Stoics met.
- The Stoic universe was a divinely ordered one. Of paramount importance in this world view was the role of **reason**.
- Stoics believed that happiness should not be affected by events.

A wise man would naturally try to save his son from drowning, but if he failed he would not be unhappy. Rather he would see the event as part of a larger, unintelligible (to him) event, and that it was 'for the best'. The event was determined by a morally good agent, so there would be little reason to complain. This approach gives us the term **stoical** to refer to someone who takes what comes without complaint.

- The natural way to respond to this divinely ordered universe is to act through reason rather than emotion. Acts that are within the divine purpose are good. Anyone who wants to do what is good should try to see what will fit with the natural order of things.
- The Stoics believed that this natural order defined things as good regardless of their consequences. A thing is good simply because it conforms to the natural order.
- Morality was therefore seen as an expression of the individual within the universal natural law.

Thus what is good is that which conforms to the natural order of things. It is good because it conforms to that order, rather than because of any considerations of motive or consequence.

Classical Greek philosophy was lost during the break-up of the Roman Empire. Muslim scholars preserved the works of the great Greek philosophers, and these writings were gradually reintroduced during the medieval period. **Some Christians saw the 'new' philosophy as a threat, and resisted it. Others thought that Christianity and Classical philosophy complemented each other. By the end of the Reformation (the sixteenth century), there were two basic camps:**

Martin Luther and the **Reformists** insisted that human reason played no part in seeing right and wrong. God's revelation (in the Bible) was sufficient, and the Bible acts as the source of all Christian morality.

In contrast, the **Scholastics** (such as **Aquinas**) argued that God-given reason was the tool by which distinctions between right and wrong could be seen.

Aquinas on Natural Law

Thomas Aquinas (1225–1274)
- Working from a monastic Christian background, Aquinas tried to reconcile traditional Biblical Christianity with the 'new' Aristotelianism.
- Aquinas argued that God created the world with a purpose in mind. Everything, therefore, has a Final Cause (as Aristotle had said), with God's ultimate purpose as that Final Cause.
- Aquinas believed that God's purpose could be seen through the application of reason. This reason is God's gift to humanity, and it is the means by which human beings can see their Final Cause, and then choose either to follow their final good, or not to!
- This is what he called the **Natural Law**. It forms the basis of Roman Catholic moral teaching.

Sexual intercourse is the most obvious application of the Natural Law principle. This has been the principle on which the Roman Catholic teaching concerning contraception, abortion and so on has been based.
1. Sexual intercourse is the way that human beings reproduce – it brings about the fertilisation of an ovum and leads to pregnancy and ultimately to childbirth.
2. The various machinations whereby sexual intercourse 'gets going' (physical attraction, anatomy, etc.) are all part of the 'design', and therefore part of the purpose.
3. Thus sexual intercourse can be broken down as follows:
   a) Its Material Cause is the two individuals involved.
   b) Its Efficient Cause is the 'method'.
   c) Its Formal Cause is the process, from attraction to the *post-coital* cigarette.
   d) The Final Cause is the fertilisation of a new human being.

Since Natural Law would look to the Final Cause for the factors that determine whether an action is right or wrong, anything that brings about pregnancy is good, and any sexual activity that either cannot bring about a pregnancy or deliberately is prevented from doing so is wrong. This would include anal or oral intercourse, masturbation or artificial contraception.

- In this way, it appears possible to arrive at a 'good' without having to rely on unpredictable consequences, or on motive, which is subject to the whim of human nature.
- Natural Law provides a framework in which a 'universal good' can be defined, since no external reference is necessary.
- Since an act is not deemed good or bad because of its effects, a person can only be held accountable for the immediate consequences of an action. Subsequent consequences are beyond the control of the agent, who cannot be held responsible. This is sometimes called the law of **double effect**.

For example:
A Roman Catholic doctor can prescribe contraceptive pills to a woman to regulate her menstrual cycle, so preventing painful and irregular periods. Since the contraceptive effect of the pills is a secondary effect – the primary being the reason for the prescription – there is no transgression of the Natural Law principle. The doctor's prescription has the desired effect, and the woman need not become celibate. She is not taking the pills in order to prevent pregnancy (and they are not 100% reliable anyway), and so she would not be guilty of trying to frustrate the final cause of her sexual activity, namely conception.

Thompson, *Teach Yourself Ethics*, p.58

So, the Natural Law principle is used to arrive at a conclusion regarding the morality of a particular activity.
- Cynical individuals may see the example above as a 'they would say that, wouldn't they' situation. However, since the analysis of the original act (the prescribing of contraceptive pills) was that it is not sinful – the prescription was to treat a medical condition in a valid way – there is no wrong-doing.
- Any attempt to analyse an issue in the hope of establishing the right and wrong of a situation requires the issue to be broken into individual acts, and assesses the absolute morality of each individual case.

But there is a fatal flaw in the argument – it lays a great deal of weight on a very big if:
If there is a God and **if** there is a divine purpose to everything,
then we can decide what is right and wrong.
But there may not be a God, and there may not be a Final Cause. If this is the case, there is no way to establish the appropriateness of an action in terms of its Final Cause.

Some scientists, who see a naturally developing design in the universe, argue for a non-divine purpose in creation – Natural Law would therefore stand, even without a God to 'endorse' it.

Casuistry and responses to Natural Law theory

Casuistry – Natural Law in action?

Casuistry is the process by which general principles of Natural Law are applied to specific cases.

- The term has come to represent the extremes that can occur when a general law is applied to every instance. The term is used by some authors almost as an insult, applied to overly legalistic commentaries on a particular ethical situation.

In the context of the Roman Catholic Church, where Natural Law is the basis of morality, the term is often used (often by non-Roman Catholics) to attack the system.

In one famous example, a 'league table' of sexual sins was defined – rape was rated as being less serious than masturbation, because rape had the possibility of pregnancy. Masturbation was completely against the Natural Law principle that sexual activity should lead to pregnancy and childbirth.

There are various approaches to casuistry:

Probabilism	Equi-probabilism
Where there is doubt as to the morality of a situation, the best course of action would be to follow the opinion that a particular act is 'probably' lawful, even though the weight of opinion would say otherwise	Following intense criticism of probabilism, especially that it encouraged the abandonment of the Natural Law at the slightest doubt, probabilism was reformulated with certain safeguards

a) Probable opinion must be 'solidly' probable.

b) Probabilism does not apply where there is an interest that is vital either to the agent or to somebody else.

This is the system that is used in moral theology in the Roman Catholic Church.

In any event, the extremes of the Penitential Books should not affect attitudes towards the principles of casuistry, which are widely accepted in the Roman Catholic Church.

Responses to the Natural Law theory

- **David Hume** argued that '*is*' cannot lead to '*ought*'. While it is true that sexual activity usually leads to pregnancy, this cannot mean that sex is *only* for the procreation of the species. '*What is the case*' and '*what ought to be the case*' are two logically different concepts.
- Natural Law is therefore based on a false premise.
- Science has tried to explain the world in purely physical terms. There is no reference to things being the way they *ought* to be (i.e. the way they were intended be – this begs the question, 'Who is doing the intending?'), merely to the way things actually are.
- The natural order is not due to some divine intelligence – it is simply the way things are. Some scientists argue that the universe could only be the way that it is – the laws of physics and mathematics dictate the way things are. Any order or apparent purpose is due to the evolutionary process.

A response to the implications of the Natural Law theory for sexual behaviour

- The Natural Law theory argues that any sexual behaviour that is not intended to bring about pregnancy is wrong. Implicit in this idea is the suggestion that the *only* purpose for sexual intercourse is procreative.

> This highlights one difficulty with the Natural Law theory – while it may provide an objective moral good, it can be difficult to decide what a thing's final purpose is.

- However, the Church of England Marriage Service states three purposes for marriage – one of which is '**that they** [the couple] **may know each other in love**'. Sexual intercourse is here presented as a means by which a married couple can strengthen their relationship.
- In this way, sexual intercourse need not be condemned where it is not intended to bring about children.

Kant's philosophy

Deontological ethics
A deontological theory of ethics is based on the idea that an act's claim to being right or wrong is independent of the consequences of that action.

Teleological ethics
A teleological theory of ethics bases its judgements on the outcomes of actions.

Kant's philosophy

Kant took both rationalism and empiricism and looked at the good points of each. He thought that the rationalists claimed too much for reason, and that the empiricists emphasised sense experience too much. He thought that all our knowledge of the world comes from sensation, but our reason determines *how* we perceive the world around us. We all wear the spectacles of reason, affecting the way that we perceive the world.

Kant thought that we perceive the world initially as **time** and **space**. These two 'forms of intuition' precede any experience that we might have. He felt that time and space were attributes of perception, not attributes of the physical world.

Kant distinguished between **das Ding-an-sich**, things in themselves (as they really are), and things as they appear to us. We cannot know how things really are, but we can know that the things that we experience will be perceived in time and space.

Kant argued that ethical statements are **a priori synthetic**.

N.B. Utilitarians believe that ethical knowledge comes from the consequence of an action. It must therefore be **a posteriori** – after experience.

A priori — Knowledge that comes before sense experience.

Synthetic — Knowledge that requires external verification, and may be true or false.

A priori synthetic means that a statement is knowable before sense experience, but requires sense experience for verification.
A moral statement is a priori synthetic because ethical knowledge comes from pure reason (rather than sense experience) but may also be either right or wrong.

- Kant noted that people are aware of a moral law at work within them. He did not regard this consciousness as a vague feeling of something being right or wrong (compare this with the emotivist theory, where ethics appears to be simply a matter of personal preference). Rather, this consciousness was a direct experience of something powerful.
We know we have freedom because we experience moral choice (not the other way round!).

*Two things fill the mind with ever new and increasing admiration and awe the oftener and more steadily we reflect on them: the starry heavens above me **and the moral law within me**.*
Kant, I. *Critique of Practical Reason*

Kant's philosophy (continued)

Kant began with the fact that he felt a moral obligation to act in a certain way, and tried to find some sort of explanation for it.

However, Kant was aware of the 'is/ought' problem (see the sections on **Naturalism** and **Intuitionism**, and on the naturalistic fallacy). This is the difference between something being a matter of fact, and something that is regarded as an obligation (an 'ought').

Kant therefore concluded that his explorations of what is good and what is bad should begin with a **good will**. This starting point is based on Kant's observation that the attributes of the mind that are considered desirable can be subverted into something bad.

These desirable mental attributes (intelligence, wit and so on) and the desires of most people for fame and fortune are held in check by the good will. This good will is an essential part of happiness.

In this way, Kant rooted the moral choice in the will of the agent. The theories that had previously been proposed placed the choice in some external situation, whether the divinely-ordained purpose for things or the consequences of an action.

The exercise of a person's free will in an action becomes the criterion on which that action is judged.

This idea was influenced by Kant's belief that evidence alone was insufficient grounds on which to draw a conclusion – the conclusion is drawn **in the mind**. Hume's 'is/ought' distinction led Kant to conclude that empirical evidence cannot be used to define a moral good.

- Because of this, Kant believed that the senses could not be the source of moral choice.

He considered the reasons a person might have for carrying out an act, and investigated the ways in which that person's reason should be utilised.

In using their reason, the individual would have excluded three other reasons for acting – benefit, curiosity and obedience to someone in authority. Each of these three is based on something external.

Kant argued that we follow a moral command because we feel that it is our **duty**.

The three postulates of practical reason

1. Freedom	**2. God**	**3. Immortality**
To be truly free (as we believe that we are), we have to be able to carry out all of the choices available to us. If one of the apparent choices were impossible, there would be a limited choice, or even none at all.	If I feel a sense of duty, it must be because the world is designed in such a way that it matters that I act in one way rather than another. There must be some guarantee behind this sense of duty – a reward. Kant believed that this reward is happiness.	The reward does not appear accessible in this world, yet it must exist (see point 2). Kant concluded that we must look beyond this life.

These postulates are derived from Kant's theories about the use of reason (see section on **Kant's philosophy**, above).

Kant believed that the experience of the moral law leads to our awareness of freedom. This sense of freedom comes when we make moral choices.

These moral choices are independent of any thought of consequence. Acting morally is an end in itself.

A **hypothetical imperative** tells us to act in a certain way because it will tend to produce a certain result. The need for the action is conditional on our wanting the proposed result.

e.g. To get to the post office, you could go this way, or you could go that way. Either way, you'd get there.

A **categorical imperative** is a command without conditions.

e.g. You must not tell lies.

Being moral is a matter of the categorical imperative. There is nothing moral about carrying out an action simply because of the intended outcome.

The three principles of the categorical imperative

The universal law

'Act only according to that maxim (principle or rule) by which you can at the same time will that it should become a universal law'

Kant, I. *Critique of Practical Reason*
http://www.bright.net/~jclarke/kant/

This is similar to the **golden rule**, in which Jesus says **'Do to others as you would have them do to you'** (Luke 6:27-31).

However, Kant intends that a person's actions would become a law applicable to everyone.

Kant believed that acting to achieve a desired result is not a moral course of action. The *consequence* of an action cannot therefore be used in a judgement of its morality.

For example:
A man is desperately poor, and debt collectors and bailiffs threaten him. The man considers borrowing money from his friend. He knows that he cannot hope to repay his friend, but he also knows that the debt collectors will leave him alone if he can settle up with them.

If he were to borrow from his friend, the maxim he would be applying would be:
If you need money, lie about your financial circumstances in order to borrow it.
Should this become a universal maxim?

Kant said no – no-one would trust anyone, and no-one would be prepared to loan money. This would be a self-defeating maxim. Kant argued that lying is always wrong. There is no way that lying could stand up to the universal maxim test.

Humans as ends not merely as means

Act that you treat humanity, both in your own person and in the person of every other human being, never merely as a means, but always at the same time as an end.

Kant, I. *Metaphysics of Morals*
http://www.swan.ac.uk/poli/texts/kant/kantb.htm

This means that a human being is the most important factor in any moral equation. A human being can never be allowed to be the means by which a goal or purpose is achieved.

The value of a human comes from their being a rational, reasonable being. The suffering of an individual person could never be justified because a greater number of people benefit.

A kingdom of ends

Act as if you were through your maxim a law-making member of a kingdom of ends
Kant, I. *Metaphysics of Morals*
http://www.swan.ac.uk/poli/texts/kant/kantb.htm

Finally, Kant argued that to preserve the moral integrity of each individual, every individual should behave as though every other individual was an 'end'. Human beings are self-aware and have the power of reason. They are capable of autonomous moral choice-making, and should not therefore become the pawn in someone else's moral decision.

The three principles of the categorical imperative (continued)

Kant argued that each person has an intrinsic value, a value beyond price. This is because we are rational beings. We can make decisions, based on our ability to reason.

Therefore we have a duty to treat other people with respect. We should try, as far as we can, to '**further the ends of others'**.

Consider the man who is faced with the debt collectors. Suppose he needs the money to pay for medical care for his sick child. If he were to borrow money from his friend, he would be using him as a **means to an end**. This would be wrong. If he were to tell his friend the truth, and allow his friend to decide whether to loan the money, he would be showing him due respect. The friend could make the decision properly, using his reason. In this way, he would be an end as well as a means to an end.

The implications of this principle are wide-ranging. Any activity that denies the individual dignity of a human being in order to achieve its end is wrong.

The categorical imperative in action

Assuming that an embryo is a human being (this is a debatable point!), embryo research would be wrong. Scientists argue that carrying out research is for the good of humanity, but since Kant argues that a human being (in this case, the embryo) is of value in itself, the embryo becomes a means to an end.

The dropping of the atom bomb on Hiroshima is defended on strictly utilitarian grounds – the Americans argued that the war could grind on for up to two more years, with the loss of more than a million lives. The atom bomb killed a few hundred thousand, but brought the war to a speedy conclusion. However, the citizens of Hiroshima were used as a means to that end.

A person who commits a crime is punished. This is particularly problematic: if the aim of imprisonment is to protect society from a dangerous person, that person is being treated as a means to an end, namely the benefit of society. If imprisonment is to reform the prisoner, and rehabilitate him, then this is a violation of the person's intrinsic value as a human being, and an attempt to prevent the person from using their reason as they see fit. Society appears to be trying to mould the person's character – it is denying a person's right to self-determination.

However, Kant had no problem with the idea of imprisoning a person in order to punish them. If the guilty are not being punished, then **justice** is not being done.

Kant's judgement of an act is made on the basis of an individual's sense of integrity. As long as a person can justify their actions rationally, and can universalise the maxim that can be derived from an act, Kant judges the act to be right.

- The problem with this is that people are different, and their judgements appear subjective.

- No two people will have the same sense of 'good will' – their experiences of moral demands will be different.

- Most people would see the consideration of the outcome of an action as being an important part of any moral deliberation.
- If the outcome of an action turns out to be harmful to someone else, most people would feel guilty.
- The view that a person should stick to their principles 'no matter what' would appear inflexible. For example, should a person stick to the maxim 'you should not die' when being interrogated by the Gestapo about the whereabouts of their Jewish neighbours?

Therefore, a moral system that takes no account of the consequences of an act, and which remains inflexible in the face of whatever situation comes along, simply appears unrealistic and divorced from reality.

W. D. Ross (1877–1971)
Ross defined certain duties as being *prima facie* (i.e. at first appearance). He argued that we follow a particular duty unless a conflicting duty appears to make a greater claim.

Bentham and utilitarianism

Jeremy Bentham (1748–1832)
- Bentham wanted to find a way of defining right and wrong without a need for a transcendent authority.
- He was concerned about social reform – the conditions in which people lived and worked were appalling.
- In *Introduction to the Principles of Morals and Legislation* (1789) he tried to establish a way of arguing for something to be good and bad according to its benefit for the majority of the people.
- He called this the **principle of utility**.

This idea was first developed by **David Hume**. In his essay 'Why Utility Pleases' (Part 5, Book 3 of the *Treatise on Human Nature*), Hume tried to account for the fact that we tend to approve of those qualities and actions that are useful to society; that is, those that promote social utility. However, Hume's theory of ethics could not be described as **utilitarianism** in the way that the term is understood today.

By utility is meant that property in any object, whereby it tends to produce benefit, advantage, pleasure, good, or happiness, (all this in the present case comes to the same thing) or (what comes again to the same thing) to prevent the happening of mischief, pain, evil, or unhappiness to the party whose interest is considered: if that party be the community in general, then the happiness of the community: if a particular individual, then the happiness of that individual.

http://www.la.utexas.edu/labyrinth/ipml/ipml.c01.html

He established a **hedonic** or **utility calculus** by which happiness could be measured.

Duration
How long does the sensation last?

Intensity
How intense is it?

Remoteness
How near is it? How certain is it? How soon will it come?

Purity
How free from pain is it?

Richness
Will it lead to further pleasure?

Extent
How wide are its effects?

- Using this calculus, Bentham believed it was possible to measure the amount of pleasure or pain that an action will bring about. This became known as **act utilitarianism**.

The prime consideration when carrying out an action is the amount of happiness or pleasure that will ensue from the action. Laws or rules are of secondary importance.

There are problems with this theory:
- Can pleasure be quantified?
- Is pleasure the same for everyone?
- Can we make an accurate prediction of the pleasure brought about by an action?

Many people make a utilitarian judgement when they are confronted by some moral dilemma. For example, 'to speed or not to speed?': the judgement is made on the basis of pleasure (the speed itself, getting there quicker) and the risk of prosecution!

This is similar to the medical practice of 'triage' – the sorting of and allocation of treatment to patients and especially battle and disaster victims according to a system of priorities designed to maximize the number of survivors; broadly: the assigning of priority order to projects on the basis of where funds and resources can be best used or are most needed.
Webster's Dictionary (on-line)

Mill and utilitarianism

John Stuart Mill (1806–1873)

Mill felt that different forms of pleasure are of different value.
- He also recognised the frailty of human nature – a person might not strive for the highest happiness in favour of a closer, less intense pleasure.

In response to criticisms of Bentham's ideas, particularly about the value of self-sacrifice, Mill argued that sacrifice was not a good in itself, but rather only a good when it contributes to the greater good.

Mill wanted to reformulate the utilitarian theory to reflect the fact that pleasures are not all of equal value. He also wanted to take human nature into account.

Mill was the son of James Mill (1773–1836), a Scottish philosopher who worked for many years for **Jeremy Bentham**. James Mill developed utilitarianism, and wrote a pamphlet called ***On Government***. He argued for government by majority because everyone would act in their own interests, so only the greatest number could be relied upon to protect the greatest happiness of the greatest number. Mill (snr) subjected Mill (jnr) to a rigorous and intellectual education – it is claimed that John was reading Greek at the age of three!

It may be objected, that many who are capable of the higher pleasures, occasionally, under the influence of temptation, postpone them to the lower. But this is quite compatible with a full appreciation of the intrinsic superiority of the higher. Men often, from infirmity of character, make their election for the nearer good, though they know it to be the less valuable; and this no less when the choice is between two bodily pleasures, than when it is between bodily and mental. They pursue sensual indulgences to the injury of health, though perfectly aware that health is the greater good.

http://www.utilitarianism.com/mill2.htm

Mill therefore distinguished between:

Higher pleasures	Lower pleasures
Pleasures associated with the mind – intellectual pursuits, mental discipline, cultural activities, spiritual reflection, etc.	Pleasures associated with the body – satisfying the bodily need for food, water, sleep, etc.

The higher pleasures are more desirable than the lower ones. This led to Mill's famous quotation . . .
It is better to be a human being dissatisfied than a pig satisfied; better to be Socrates dissatisfied than a fool satisfied.

http://www.utilitarianism.com/mill2.htm

Where Bentham thought that laws were secondary, Mill argued that there was a more positive role for them.
- There are principles that work as a general means for securing the greater good.
- A popular example is that of lying. While there might be good reasons for lying in specific circumstances, as an overall principle, lying cannot be supported because it cannot support the greatest good for the greatest number.

'It is wrong to lie.'
Mill noted that there is some benefit to this maxim – without it people would find it hard to trust each other. He therefore proposed a rule that contributes to the greater happiness. Breaking the rule might contribute to an individual's short-term happiness, but is detrimental to long-term happiness for all concerned.

Mill argued for a system that included the individual's conscience, instead of the 'harsh, mechanistic' approach of Bentham's act utilitarianism.

Mill's revision of utilitarianism allows for the formulation of rules based on utilitarian principles. These rules promote the happiness of the greatest number, and can be used in making ethical decisions. It is therefore called **rule utilitarianism**.

Act utilitarianism	Rule utilitarianism
Each action should be judged on its ability to bring about the greatest happiness for the greatest number.	Rules should be formulated first, based on utilitarianist principles. The individual can then judge whether specific acts are acceptable.

Strong and weak rule utilitarianism
- The strong form of the theory maintains that rules established through the application of utilitarian principles should *never* be broken.
- The weak version tries to allow for the possibility that those same utilitarian principles can take precedence in a particular situation over a general rule. However, the rule would still form part of the decision-making process.

Weak rule utilitarianism accepts the need to be flexible over the implementation of a rule of utility. The rule would still need to be taken into account.

In response to Mill's version of utilitarianism, some modern thinkers have suggested that there should be a change in emphasis, so that an act can be considered good if it can be shown to produce 'enough' happiness.

Singer, Hare, and Sidgwick

Peter Singer

(in *Practical Ethics*) suggests that pleasure should not be the principal consideration in a utilitarian ethical decision.

- He proposes a utilitarian system with '**the best interests**' of the individuals concerned at the heart of ethical decision-making.
- His utilitarianist approach is to weigh up the interests of all those affected by an individual's decision.

Singer's formulation of utilitarianism replaces 'pleasure' with 'best interests'. He argues that utilitarianism stands as an ethical system unless some non-utilitarian moral rules are proposed that come with good reasons for rejecting a purely utilitarian approach.

My interests cannot, simply because they are my interests, count more than the interests of anyone else.
Singer, P. *Practical Ethics* (1993) p.12

R. M. Hare (1919–present)

In *The Language of Morals* (1973), Hare argues for **preference utilitarianism**.

The utilitarian evaluation of an action would include the preferences of the person, unless these preferences conflicted with those of others.

The 'right thing' to do is to maximise the satisfaction of the preferences of each individual involved.

This attempts to get around the problem that happiness is subjective. Under Bentham's and Mill's utilitarianism it was presupposed that there was one single idea of happiness.

Henry Sidgwick (1838–1900)

Sidgwick's main work (*the Methods of Ethics*, 1874) was not a new version of utilitarianism, but rather an attempt to see how we could arrive at a rational basis for taking certain actions.

The consequence in terms of happiness of an action need not be the motive for the action.
- Sidgwick considered it possible to look at the motives for an action in terms of utility.

An action could be considered good if its motive was to bring about the maximum good for the maximum number, regardless of the actual outcome.

This approach can be called **motive utilitarianism**.

Additional Advice 2: The A2 synoptic paper

When you finish your A2 Course, you will be tested on your knowledge and understanding of Philosophy of Religion, and of Religious Ethics. You will also be tested on your understanding of the connections between the two units.

The different boards have different approaches to the synoptic unit. You should check with your tutors to make sure you understand the unit you are studying.

Criticisms of utilitarianism

Henry Sidgwick (1838–1900) asked how we are to distinguish between two higher pleasures. How do listening to Bach and watching Shakespeare compare? Where does sporting endeavour fit in – higher or lower?

W. D. Ross (1877–1971) considered the utilitarian principle too simplistic – life's dilemmas are too complicated to rely on a single equation (i.e. the hedonic calculus). Ross considered the role of **duty** to be of some importance – what should a person do if keeping a promise acts against the utilitarian principle?

The most fundamental challenge to utilitarianism's argument comes from its claim that the only factor to be considered in deciding on the right or wrong in an action is the principle of the greatest good for the greatest number.

Justice

Justice requires that people be treated fairly. Each should be treated according to their needs.

Consider Dostoyevsky's challenge to the **free will defence** (see section on **The problem of evil**).

Imagine that you are creating a fabric of human destiny with the object of making men happy in the end, giving them peace and rest at last, but that it was essential and inevitable to torture to death only one tiny creature – that baby beating its breast with its fist, for instance – and to found that edifice on its unavenged tears, would you consent to be the architect on those conditions? Tell me, and tell the truth.

Dostoyevsky, F. *The Brothers Karamazov*, Ch.4
http://www.kosiek.com/dostoevsky/library/karamazov.txt

D. D. Raphael argues that this would satisfy the principle of utility, but most people would feel that it was terribly wrong. It is basically unfair.

Rights

The principle of fundamental and inalienable human rights appears to conflict with the idea of utility.

The idea of utility can be seen to provide grounds to deny rights such as freedom of speech, right of assembly and even of life itself.

Consider the argument proposed by Margaret Thatcher in defence of General Pinochet when he was placed under house arrest pending trial for crimes against humanity. She argued that his alleged actions (such as the torture of journalists and the disappearances of dissidents) were to secure the stability of Chile – the atrocities served a greater good.

Most people would find this indefensible.

Some would argue that this is what Mill would support in his analysis of the effect of the 'lying' argument on utilitarianism.

For most people, 'Human Rights' means the rights enshrined in the United Nations Declaration. These establish the innate value of every individual Human Being.

Criticisms of utilitarianism (continued)

Duty

Utilitarianism is also criticised because it appears to ignore the importance of duty (see sections on **The categorical imperative** and **The moral argument** for the existence of God).

For example:
A person may make a commitment to another – for example, the person may promise to do something for the other. When the time comes to carry out this action, the person finds that they would rather stay at home. They assess the utility of staying at home against the utility of meeting their commitment to the other person. The person concludes that there would be greater utility in staying at home – this outweighs the importance of their keeping their promises.

The utility of an action, measured in its anticipated consequence and benefit, is the most important factor – other considerations are over-ruled.
- Utilitarianism is based on predicted effects in the future – there is no attempt to take into account the past. In this way, past promises and obligations are over-ruled by the anticipated future benefits.

G. E. Moore (1873–1958)

Moore tried to argue against the idea that 'ought' can lead to 'is'.
He called this the **naturalistic fallacy**.
- He argued against utilitarianism – he claimed that
Mill based his idea of good on the idea of something being
desirable. He claimed that Mill defines desirable as 'what it is good to desire'.

David Hume also raised this point in his Treatise on Human Nature.

Moore argued that desires could be bad as well as good.
He also said that Mill produces an 'ought' (something we should do) from a statement of fact (namely, what is desired).

Bernard Williams (1929–present)

Personal identity consists of a person's moral commitments and values.

A person's identity is therefore to be found in what the person stands for. In a moral dilemma, a person's decision would be based on these commitments.

Utilitarianism, however, disregards personal commitments, and looks instead to an objective assessment of the consequences of an action.

Williams argues therefore that utilitarianism renders personal integrity useless in the moral decision-making process. However, in fact, people have more regard for their personal values in the moral decision-making process. Williams argues for a more 'agent-centred' approach.

John Rawls (1921–present)

Rawls argues that utilitarianism is too impersonal. In its pursuit of the 'greater good', utilitarianism disregards the rights of individuals.

Utilitarianism could therefore be used to promote a dictatorship, in which personal decisions were made to over-ride the interests of the individual in favour of the greater good of society.

Utilitarianism is therefore flawed because it ignores the rights and interests of individuals in its attempt to address the 'greater good'.

Determinism

The problem with free will and determinism is two-fold.

Are human actions causally determined or free?	What are the implications of determinism for responsibility and moral behaviour?

Determinism

This is the view that all events are completely determined by other events. The world of science is a determinist world, in that events are caused by past events.

Observable events are subject to the laws of nature	Scientific knowledge is based on the premise that events can be predicted by past events.

This principle governs everything from the smallest particle to the largest stellar body

Mel Thompson uses the illustration of a weather forecast:

'It's going to rain.'

This statement is based on meteorological analysis based on a knowledge of atmospheric conditions and the behaviour of water vapour.
Thompson, M. *Teach Yourself Ethics*, p.20

Meteorology is based on the observation of cause and effect, and involves the making of predictions based on these observations.

In this analysis, there is no such thing as an accident. Any event is caused by a series of causes that coincide to create the conditions for that event to come about.
- Most events are brought about by a chain of previous events that contribute to the situation.
- The police devote considerable resources to 'accident investigation' trying to discover the cause(s) of incidents.

On 28 February 2001 a man drove his Land Rover off the M62 motorway near Selby. The car was hit by an express train which then derailed into the path of an oncoming goods train. Ten people died in the crash.
Was this an 'accident'?

Gary Hart was found guilty of causing death by dangerous driving – he had spent the previous night talking to a girlfriend on the phone. He fell asleep at the wheel.

The world is seen as a great machine, with every event predictable. Some scientists believe that if we could know everything, then we would be able to make accurate predictions of what is to come.
- Darwin's theory of evolution is a mechanistic process – the conditions of nature affect the development of life. Know enough about the conditions, and you can predict how life will develop.
- Psychology and sociology also suggest a determinist world – to understand a person's behaviour, look at past events.

However, recent developments in quantum science suggest that the world is less predictable and more random.

Determinism (continued)

Many people have questioned whether a person's behaviour is due to:
- **Nature** – are they just 'born that way'?

or
- **Nurture** – is their behaviour affected by their upbringing?

Some characteristics are determined by our parents:
- Our physical appearance is determined by our genes, inherited from our parents.
- Some conditions, such as cystic fibrosis, are inherited.

Other characteristics may be affected by the environment in which we live:
- Children living close to major roads develop asthma.
- Research has still not yet shown that violence on television has a deep and lasting effect on children – however, a quick look in any playground may convince!

The Bell case

In 1968 Mary Bell (aged 11) was convicted of the murder of two toddlers. She spent 12 years in secure units, before being released as a 23-year-old. Throughout her imprisonment she was a difficult inmate – she was often violent, and at times self-harmed.

Her mother was a prostitute who specialised in sado-masochism. Mary would be forced to listen to her mother 'entertain' clients from behind a curtain.

Was Mary's sociopathic behaviour pre-determined by her upbringing?

While individual factors may not amount to the future being determined, a strong case can be made that we are deeply influenced by our backgrounds.

Hard determinism

This is the view that all our actions are completely governed by previous events.
- All actions stand at the end of a complex network of prior events.
- This network includes sociological, psychological, religious, political and cultural influences.
- One of these influences would not be enough to determine all future actions – the sum total of these influences would.
- The world runs to strictly applicable natural laws.

The implication of this would be that a person cannot be held morally responsible for their actions.

Soft determinism

This view holds that there is an element of determinism in human actions, but we should take moral responsibility for our actions.
- Some of our actions are conditioned by genetics and environment.
- However, to argue that all actions are determined would be to argue a form of **reductionism**.
- Within the complex web of environmental, social and genetic prior events, there is a limited amount of choice for human beings.

A 'soft determinist' would still have to define what is determined and what is open to choice.

A person who believes that determinism removes the possibility of free moral choice-making is called an incompatibilist. Where that person believes that determinism is true, they are a 'hard determinist'. Where they believe that determinism is false, they are 'libertarian'. 'Soft determinists' are sometimes called **compatibilists**, because they believe that free will and determinism are in some way compatible.

The Loeb case

In 1924, two teenagers (Nathan Leopold and Richard Loeb) were tried for the murder of a 14-year-old in Chicago. They were defended by the famous lawyer *Clarence Darrow*, who argued against the boys being given the death penalty. The boys had been brought up in privileged circumstances, and the crime was rooted in their feelings of superiority over the rest of society. Darrow argued that they were so much a product of their upbringing that they could not be held responsible for their actions and that they should be locked up to protect society, but not executed as responsible for their crimes:

'Is Dickey Loeb to blame because out of the infinite forces that conspired to form him, the infinite forces that were at work producing him ages before he was born, that because out of these infinite combinations he was born without it? If he is, then there should be a new definition for justice. Is he to blame for what he did not have and never had? Is he to blame that his machine is imperfect? Who is to blame? I do not know. I have never in my life been interested so much in fixing blame as I have in relieving people from blame. I am not wise enough to fix it. I know that somewhere in the past that entered into him something missed. It may be defective nerves. It may be a defective heart or liver. It may be defective endocrine glands. I know it is something. I know that nothing happens in this world without a cause.'

The consequences of determinism

If everything is pre-determined, there is no moral responsibility. Humans are incapable of rational decision-making if their decisions are entirely predictable based on genes, environment and society.

A person being tried for a crime can claim 'diminished responsibility' if they acted under duress. For example:
- A woman killing her husband after years of abuse.
- A drug addict stealing to 'feed their habit'.
- A father suffocating his daughter after years of mental illness.

The perception of the freedom to choose is simply an illusion. Moral responsibility is just as illusory.

Some philosophers have argued that a determinist view confuses two different types of truth.

Necessary and contingent statements

Some things are **necessarily** true – the truth of a statement is contained in its logical construction.

A necessary statement *must* be true. The statement contains a logical necessity.
e.g. All widows are women.

Some things are **contingently** true – the statement may be true or it may be false. Its truth depends upon the circumstances that it describes.

A contingent statement *need not* be true.
e.g. All women are widows

Some events are inevitable – they are pre-determined. It may be that a person's background and upbringing can be held responsible for their behaviour, but this is always the case. The person's upbringing **may not** cause them to behave in a particular way.

Determinists treat the factors that influence a person's behaviour as necessary truths.

Statements regarding the influence a person's background has over their behaviour are contingent truths.

Hard determinism relies on the world being completely predictable.
But the universe is not as mechanistic as some scientists believe.
- Recent developments in quantum physics have begun to consider the possibility of randomness in the universe – at best we can only speak of the probability of an event.

Chaos theory

This theory proposes that there is apparently random behaviour within a determinist system. This is not due to a lack of laws, but to minute and unmeasurable variations in the initial conditions affecting the outcome of an event.

The popular illustration of this is the flap of a butterfly's wing causing a hurricane on the other side of the world.

Libertarianism

By liberty, then, we can only mean a power of acting or not acting, according to the determinations of the will; that is, if we choose to remain at rest, we may; if we choose to move, we also may.

Hume, D. *An Enquiry Concerning Human Understanding*
http://www.infidels.org/library/historical/david_hume/human_understanding.html

Libertarianism is the term given to the belief that we can choose to act **despite** past events, cultural and environmental conditioning and biological influence. People who reject the concept of determinism, because it denies the possibility of moral responsibility, believe that humans have self-determination and free will.

- We are free to act, and as such we have moral responsibility for our actions.

- Our actions have moral significance – they are affected by our character, the values that we hold, and our beliefs.

Compatibilists and incompatibilists
1. **Compatibilists** believe that freedom to make moral choices is compatible with determinism – also known as **soft determinism.** Some compatibilists go further, and argue that determinism has no effect on moral decision-making.
2. **Incompatibilists** believe that determinism denies the possibility of moral responsibility. Where they believe that determinism is true, they are known as **hard determinists.** Where they believe that determinism is false, they are **libertarianists.**

Libertarianism distinguishes between types of action, and between types of cause. Humans experience freedom in ethical decision-making, even if they are physically constrained.

I can choose the direction that I travel in – I am completely free in that respect. However, I cannot break the laws of physics when I begin my journey – I cannot flap my arms to fly there.

While individual humans might come from a background that predisposes them to a life of crime, they still experience the freedom to choose. It may be that their conscience tells them that an action is wrong, or even simply that they are aware that society 'disapproves'. They can still choose.

The individual is not coerced or forced to act in a particular way. Our actions are **voluntary**.

G. E. Moore:
'I am free in performing an action if I could have done otherwise if I had chosen to do so.'

Ted Honderich argues that the compatibilist/non-compatibilist debate is based on a failure to define the term 'freedom' properly.
Determinism does not negate freedom completely – certain kinds of feelings and personal attitudes can remain. However, certain attitudes and responses based on origination will be impossible to maintain if determinism is true.

Origination is the term used to refer to the creation by free human choice of new chains of cause and effect.

Libertarianism has been accused of failing to provide an adequate explanation for the actions that humans take. It argues that humans can make moral decisions that are independent of previous 'chains of cause and effect', yet it does not take into account the importance of precedence and past experience. Our actions must be caused by something.

Predestination

John Calvin (1509–1564)

Calvin taught that God is all-powerful and all-knowing. A logical extension of this belief is that God already knows which humans will be welcomed into heaven, and which will go to hell. Clearly, if it is already decided (or predestined) who will go to heaven, then humans have no moral choice. This idea is known as **predestination**, and is supported by several writers, including St Paul:

John Calvin is most closely associated with **Calvinism**, the Protestant theological movement that emphasises:
- the sovereignty of God
- the goodness of Creation
- the authority of Scripture
- the sinfulness of humanity.

St Paul

We know that all things work together for good for those who love God, who are called according to his purpose. For those whom he foreknew he also predestined to be conformed to the image of his Son, in order that he might be the firstborn within a large family. And those whom he predestined he also called; and those whom he called he also justified; and those whom he justified he also glorified.
Romans 8:28–30

St Augustine

Will any man presume to say that God did not foreknow those to whom he would grant belief? . . . This is the predestination of saints; namely, the foreknowledge and planning of God's kindnesses, by which they are most surely delivered.
De dono perseverantiæ (428), 35

The belief has strong support from several Christian groups, and remains as one of the 39 Articles of Faith of the Church of England:

Predestination to Life is the everlasting purpose of God, whereby (before the foundations of the world were laid) he hath constantly decreed by his counsel secret to us, to deliver from curse and damnation those whom he hath chosen in Christ out of mankind, and to bring them by Christ to everlasting salvation, as vessels made to honour.

Article 17, Articles of Religion, *Book of Common Prayer*

Calvinism appeared to support the idea that salvation is from God alone, to contradict the belief that human beings can achieve salvation through their own actions (known as **Pelagianism**). A debate raged in Christianity for centuries over the role of Grace and God's agency in salvation. However, predestination as a concept clearly conflicts with the concept of free will, and also suggests that a person need take no responsibility for their actions. It would seem contrary to most concepts of justice for people to be punished if they are not responsible for their actions.

If a person is predestined to go to hell, and is not morally responsible, on what grounds are they being punished?

Pelagius taught that free will was the highest human attribute. His views were condemned by the Church in 416 and 418.

'The Last Judgement', a 12th century ikon from St Catherine's Monastery, Sinai

Other individual views on free will and determinism

Immanuel Kant (1724–1804)

In his *Critique of Pure Reason* (1781), Kant argued that there is a difference between things as we experience them, and things as they really are.

Phenomena

Things as we experience them. Everything in the world of the phenomena is determined, as our minds try to find reasons for everything. In order to make sense of the world, we impose an order, or causality, on things that we experience.

Noumena

Things as they are in reality. When we experience them, our minds impose order on the events that we perceive.

If we perceive someone acting morally, we impose an order on the events that we perceive. Through this imposing of order and causality, we can explain the actions in terms of conditioning. Kant believed that we are phenomenally conditioned (i.e. outside observers can see the cause of our actions) and noumenally free.

Kant believed that experience of the moral law leads to an awareness of moral freedom.

J. S. Mill (1806–1873)

Libertarians argue that determinism must be false, because we experience freedom of choice. When we are confronted by a moral dilemma, we are aware of different alternatives as well as of past experience. Since we are aware that we can choose to act whatever our past experiences were, determinism must be false.

*J. S. Mill argued that we only experience a **memory** of past events. In some of those events we chose one route, and in some we chose another. In every case, we followed our strongest motive – and we will do so in the present case.*

Augustine of Hippo (354–430)

In *De libero arbitrio*, Augustine argued that God's foreknowledge does not deprive us of freedom. God foreknows what each human will freely choose.

However, Augustine appeared to contradict his own view when he argued that the only way to salvation is through Grace alone.

Boethius (480–525/6)

God's foreknowledge is outside of time. Human knowledge is rooted in causality. God's knowledge is from beyond time, and is not based on the same causality. God's omniscience is beyond the confines of this linear knowledge.

In this way there can be both freedom and divine providence.

Self-consciousness and free will

With the emergence of self-consciousness, the person moves beyond the animal and purely instinctive. This heightened existence requires a new language to describe it – this includes the notion of free will. Self-consciousness includes the capacity to love, to be creative, and to make moral choices.

This view sees the determinist view as being purely mechanistic – human existence, with its capacity for self-awareness, love and creativity, is incompatible with a determinist model.

Naturalism

Naturalistic ethics involves the attempt to arrive at a moral system based on observations of human life. There are three versions:

1 Ethical terms are definable in non-ethical, natural terms

The ethical behaviour displayed by human beings should be described in natural terms, rather than by using 'technical' ethical language. This is similar to **descriptivism**. Events and actions are described in terms of the behaviour displayed. There is no attempt to derive a right or wrong from the observed behaviour.

> **Descriptive ethics** simply describes the ethical behaviour of a group of people. **It simply states what is the case.**

> **G. E. Moore** criticised this approach in *Principia Ethica* (1903). Ethics is all about what is good. It is not possible to derive what is good from what is pleasurable. Moore wanted to argue over whether 'pleasure' was 'good'. He called this the **naturalistic fallacy**.

2 Ethical conclusions are derivable from non-ethical premises

It is possible to decide on what is right and wrong from observable behaviour, rather than from ethical debate and consideration. There is no objective right and wrong – these terms are defined in terms of what is acceptable behaviour in a particular society or community. In effect, **ought** is being derived from **is**.

> **David Hume** argued that a statement that forms a conclusion as to what 'ought' to be *must* be based on a premise that includes an 'ought'.

3 Ethical properties are natural properties

This means that a natural property can be referred to in scientific situations. The ethical property is a part of the behavioural or biological make-up of an individual – there is nothing metaphysical about ethics.

David Wiggins (an Oxford philosopher) has objected that this form of naturalistic ethics is **scientism**. This term refers to the tendency to see the world in purely scientific terms.

Intuitionism

In *Principia Ethica*, G.E Moore (see last section) argued against naturalistic ethics, and for 'intuitionism'. He felt that most ethical theories had fallen into the trap identified by Hume, that of **ought/is**. He concluded that goodness is not the same as other natural properties. You may be able to say, 'a thing is good if . . .', but you will always be limiting the definition of good. Moore therefore felt that to say that something was good was similar to referring to the colour of the thing.

The example Moore used was the idea of yellow. We cannot define yellow, but we can point to things that are yellow in order to illustrate our point. It is the same with the idea of good. You cannot easily define the word, but you can point to things that are thought of as good.

This idea of yellow is based on a person's intuition. It is the same with good – we know instinctively if something is good. A thing is right if it leads to something that is good.

Everyone does in fact understand the question 'is this good?' When he thinks of it, his state of mind is different from what it would be, were he asked, 'Is this pleasant, or desired, or approved?' It has a distinct meaning for him, even though he may not recognise in what respect it is distinct. Whenever he thinks of 'intrinsic value' or 'intrinsic worth', or says that a thing 'ought to exist', he has before his mind the unique object – the unique property of things – which I mean by 'good'.

Moore, G. E. *Principia Ethica*, 1903

The idea is that what is good is known instinctively. Our obligations to other people are self-evident.

H. A. Pritchard took the idea further, by arguing that moral obligation (duty) was just as irreducible – you could not reduce moral obligation to anything else. **W. D. Ross** agreed that you cannot derive an ought from an is, but he proposed that a duty was self-evident only where it did not conflict with another self-evident duty. He said this because a person could experience a conflict of duties. This gives rise to an 'ethical dilemma', a conflict in self-evident duties. A choice must be made. These obligations are intuitive. Intuition determines the correct course of action once we have assessed the facts of the case.

Thompson (in *Teach Yourself Ethics*) gives the following example:
Children have to be taught how to behave. Consider the development and adjustment of the behaviour of a child from screaming infant to well-adjusted adult(!). The adult appears to have an innate sense of right and wrong. Is this **nature** *or* **nurture***?*
Compare this to cases of child murderers – did they have an innate sense of right and wrong which was buried in a desperate childhood, or were they simply not taught the difference between right and wrong?

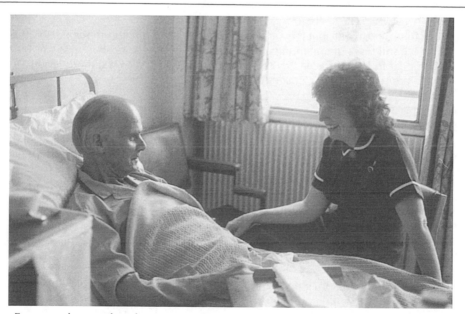

Everyone knows that the nurse is doing good.

Emotivism

The emotivist believes that:
- We make moral judgements on the basis of feelings
- Feelings lead to actions
- When we pass moral judgements, we are:
  expressing our emotions on a subject
  and
  trying to encourage others to feel the same way

> **For example, the statement, *'Abortion is wrong'* should read *'I do not like abortion'*.**
> *[When someone says] this is good, he means that he desires it. Whatsoever is the object of any man's Appetite or desire; that is it which he for his part calleth Good: and the object of his hate and Aversion, Evil . . . For these words of Good, Evil . . . are ever used with relation to the person that useth them: There being nothing simply and absolutely so; not any common Rule of Good and Evil to be taken from the nature of the objects themselves.*
>
> Hobbes, *Leviathan*, p.24
>
> **Hobbes' theory poses a problem – a conflict between duty and desire.**

> In most cases the truth about a proposition is independent of the proposer:
> *'William Shakespeare is dead.'*

> Sometimes, the truth depends on the speaker:
> *'I am allergic to cats.'*

> To include an element of moral judgement introduces the proposer's opinion of the issue:
> *'Robert Maxwell was a bad man.'*

> **A. J. Ayer:**
> 'Moral judgements are not propositions at all – they are not true or false. They do not describe anything, not even the feelings of the speaker. They are more like *exclamations*.'

Moral propositions are still propositions, but they are only true or false in relation to the person speaking. However, exclamations are still ways of communicating feelings. They can be used to mislead. Therefore, the emotive theory would appear to be proposing that moral judgements lie between pure descriptions and pure exclamations. They have some of the characteristics of both.

> **C. L. Stevenson** (1908–1979)
> *There are conflicts of belief and conflicts of attitude. If one doctor says 'operate!' and another says 'drug therapy', they are in moral agreement – there is no dispute over trying to cure the patient. They differ in their belief about how to go about curing the patient. Therefore the vast majority of disagreements about what is right is in fact disagreement about belief, and not moral disagreements at all.*
>
> *Ethics and Language*, 1945

'If we give up our nuclear weapons, other countries will follow our example.' This is a factual statement, which can be supported by evidence, and we can *verify* the statement. 'I'd rather die or live under a Communist dictatorship rather than support the use of such weapons.' This is a moral preference. There is no way of verifying it.

A moral judgement has a double function. It describes the attitude of the speaker, and it seeks to persuade the listener to that attitude. Even where a moral statement is made to no-one at all, it still has this persuasive quality – Stevenson calls it 'self-persuasion'.

Fletcher's situation ethics

Joseph Fletcher (1905–1991)
Situation Ethics (1966)
Fletcher was an American theologian. He was suspicious of fixed rules. He thought that it was unwise to follow the rules of **casuistry**.

The Roman Catholic Church has maintained a system based on Aquinas and the Natural Law. Rules about right and wrong are deduced from the perceived divine purpose for individual acts and objects.

ʾαγαπη
agape
– the New
Testament word
for *Compassion*

- Fletcher felt that the individual should be of paramount concern. Each ethical situation should be judged in its own context.
- He also wanted to preserve the Christian principle of love.
- He therefore proposed an **agapeistic calculus.**
- The basic principle that underlies this system is the 'duty' to do whatever is the most loving thing. **'Love your neighbour as yourself.'**
- This is not proposed as a rule or law. The calculus does not say *what* a person should do in any given situation. Rather, it provides a framework in which the person can decide how best to behave. The calculus *'informs'* that situation.

A person following situation ethics would take each situation as it came. They would come to a judgement as to the best way to respond by assessing the most compassionate option.

- Fletcher rejected any sense of a moral absolute. He agreed with the criticisms of **casuistry** – that each situation is different, with different circumstances. Any attempt to apply a general rule to a specific situation could overrule the interests of the people involved. Often the most compassionate, human approach would be to lay aside the rule and proceed with the interests of the individual at heart.

In Fletcher's system, this Christian compassion is to be exercised in the context of a **personal** God. Since the Christian God is a personal God, morality should be person-centred. **Conscience** is seen in this context as the term for the process by which a decision is worked through in each situation.

Fletcher's theory involves the following principles:

- Only one thing is intrinsically good – love itself. The criteria by which actions can be judged rest solely on this principle. Actions are good where they help human beings, and bad if they do not.
- Justice is simply love in action. It is love at work in the community.

This principle of love in action is universal. Love wills the good of the neighbour regardless of who they are. The end justifies the means. Since love is the end in all cases, any action carried out in the name of love can be judged to be good. Love is always the end, and never a means to another end. Love does not lay down principles that should be followed in all circumstances. The decisions are made **situationally**.

Situation ethics has often been (crudely) summarised in the words of the Beatles song 'All you Need is Love'. But what exactly *is* love?

'The meaning of love'

The Greeks have four words for love:

1. ψιλος **philos** friendship	2. στοργη **storge** family love	3. ερος **eros** erotic love	4. ʾαγαπη **agape** compassion
The bond between colleagues, friends, etc.	The love between parent and child	Lust!	Selfless love. There is a famous passage in the First Letter to the Corinthians that summarises the Christian attitude to agape:

If I speak in the tongues of mortals and of angels, but do not have love, I am a noisy gong or a clanging cymbal. And if I have prophetic powers, and understand all mysteries and all knowledge, and if I have all faith, so as to remove mountains, but do not have love, I am nothing. If I give away all my possessions, and if I hand over my body so that I may boast, but do not have love, I gain nothing. Love is patient; love is kind; love is not envious or boastful or arrogant or rude. It does not insist on its own way, it is not irritable or resentful; it does not rejoice in wrongdoing, but rejoices in the truth. It bears all things, believes all things, hopes all things, endures all things. Love never ends. But as for prophecies, they will come to an end; as for tongues, they will cease; as for knowledge, it will come to an end. For we know only in part, and we prophesy only in part; but when the complete comes, the partial will come to an end. When I was a child, I spoke like a child, I thought like a child, I reasoned like a child; when I became an adult, I put an end to childish ways. For now we see in a mirror, dimly, but then we will see face to face. Now I know only in part; then I will know fully, even as I have been fully known. And now faith, hope and love abide, these three; and the greatest of these is love.

1 Corinthians 13

- The word **love** has been affected by popular usage. When people talk of being **'in love'** they usually refer to some sort of emotion or feeling associated with attraction to another human being.
- It could also refer to the biological attraction associated with the identification of an appropriate mate and the continuation of the genetic code.

Fletcher's situation ethics (continued)

Other theories
Fletcher rejected two of the main approaches to ethical decision-making:

> Fletcher criticised this system as being a recipe for moral anarchy. Without an external point of reference, anyone can claim moral authority for their actions, and differing opinions will come into moral conflict.

1. **Antinomianism** – This approach is completely situationist. There are no rules, laws or principles. The situation itself will provide the solution – we can find this solution through intuition.
2. **Legalism** – This system provides rules by which people can make their moral decisions. Often there are scholars who make it their business to interpret and apply the rules to new situations previously unknown to the law. Eventually a system of commentaries on the law develops, enabling each new generation to apply the law to their own unique situation. The moral system operated by the **Pharisees** in first-century Palestine appears legalistic.

> Fletcher saw this system as being the opposite extreme. The law cannot cope with new technological advances – how could the Bible possibly address the problems raised by gene therapy and stem cell research?

- Fletcher argued that neither extreme can work. The only viable system of ethics must be based on love.
- Each situation must be assessed in terms of the most loving response.
- In some ways the theory would appear to be similar to that of **utilitarianism**, in that the act is judged by its results. Fletcher wrote that the 'good' (the pleasure principle) for Bentham and Mill is replaced by the principle of agape.

Criticisms of situation ethics
- A person who operates a situational moral system will not be able to maintain a coherent approach to moral decision-making. Each decision is made within the context of its situation – no consideration is taken of previous experience. Many critics claim that the theory fragments complex moral issues into a series of situations. There is a danger, it is claimed, of missing the 'big picture'. The immediate situation could involve a particular act, but the wider situation could contradict this judgement.
- Situation ethics appears to put the emphasis on the individual – there is no collective ethical framework.
- The absolute principle 'act situationally – act with the greatest love' is a law. Rather than replace law with a principle that can be applied situationally, Fletcher has provided a single law that is as easily broken as any other.
- The notion of a 'situation' is often not as clear-cut as the theory requires. The act that is being considered can involve more people than simply those involved in the immediate situation.
- Situation ethics is a relativistic theory – a person's interpretation of 'love' may vary according to their outlook.
- Where there are conflicting interpretations of the requirement of love, two people may find that they disagree as to the most loving response to a situation. In such a situation, there is nothing to support one intuitive loving response against another. This would promote moral vagueness, where it would be difficult to be specific about the correct approach to an ambiguous situation.
- Often, the most loving response would appear to be a clear-cut decision. However, the consequences of a chosen action might prove to be disastrous.
- A chosen act does not necessarily have to be a good act simply because it appears to be the most loving act. It could be that the act flies in the face of popularly-held ethical opinion.
- The theory does not take into account human nature. Human beings can often only act out of self-interest. By the same token, a person's judgement often can be affected by their emotions – this can also cloud their ability to respond in the most loving way.

Because people are 'only' human, it may be realistic only to expect a person to respond in the **most loving way they can**.

Proportionalism

Paul Tillich (in *Morality and Beyond*, 1963) argued for a position somewhere between the purely situationist position and the legalist approach. He noted that a lack of outright rules would cause everyone to be forced to re-evaluate their moral framework in the face of each situation. This would be an impossible to maintain.

Thus, moral laws derived from **Natural Law** provide firm moral guidance that would, under normal circumstances, not be over-ruled. If a sufficiently proportional reason should occur, it would be arguable that the moral law should be ignored.

> Proportionalism holds that there are certain moral rules that can never be broken unless there is a sufficiently proportional reason for doing so. This reason is situationally based – it must be sufficiently serious to merit the overturning of a normally definitive rule.

Proportionalists make a distinction between acts that are **right** and acts that are **good**. It is possible for a person to have a good intention but only be able to carry out this intention by performing an act that would appear wrong. The wrong act is performed in the context of the situation – the intention, and the intended outcome, are good. Taken out of context, the action would be seen as wrong. Seen in the context of the situation, the action may be morally right.

> **Bernard Hoose**, a supporter of the idea of proportionalism, argues that account must be taken of the consequences of an action, though he does not suggest a framework for this. In many cases, intuition would be used to judge the action (unlike utilitarianism, where the action is judged right or wrong through the use of the **hedonistic calculus** through which the effects of an action can be assessed by their contribution to the greater good.

Proportionalists argue that a person will know that a reason for ignoring a moral law has cropped up. We can see that there are few reasons to justify lying, cheating, stealing or murder. However, there *may* be reasons to ignore the rules – the individual will assess the situation, and judge the act's intrinsic good (or bad) against the consequences.

Additional Advice 3: Making connections in the synoptic paper

> For most of the people reading these notes, A Level Religious Studies will have involved papers on Philosophy of Religion and Religious Ethics. Some people may have been entered for either Philosophy or Ethics and some other paper (New Testament, or Buddhism perhaps).

> The synoptic paper requires you to examine the connections between your two A Level subjects. These notes concentrate on the approach to questions on Philosophy and Ethics.

> The exam boards have specific content to study for the synoptic exam, and you should be absolutely clear on what is likely to be asked of you. You should also make full use of the specimen and past papers for the synoptic papers.

> Because the various boards have a range of content topics in the synoptic papers, you will not find notes on specific topics here. Instead, there are suggestions to help you approach the synoptic unit.

> If you have a sound grasp of the different elements of the Philosophy and Ethics courses, you should find the connections between them reasonably straightforward!

Synderesis and Aquinas

Synderesis

In the New Testament of the Bible, the Greek word used for conscience is 'syneidesis'. The term 'synderesis' was first used by **Aristotle**, and became well-known when **St Jerome** referred to the 'gleam of conscience'.

> **Synderesis** – the ability of the mind to understand the first principles of moral reasoning.

St Paul referred to conscience as bearing witness to the requirements of the law. These uses refer to the conscience as the means by which a person knows that they have done wrong.

St Bonaventure (1217–1274)

Bonaventure thought that synderesis was the drive that directed a human being towards the good. It governs behaviour and provides rules for a good life.

> Bonaventure was a Franciscan theologian, who was less influenced by **Aristotle** than by his contemporary, Aquinas.

As such, Bonaventure's view of conscience is a **voluntarist** view.

Thomas Aquinas (1224–1274)

Aquinas believed that synderesis is the means of distinguishing between right and wrong. It is a natural part of mental activity – it provides an individual with moral guidance.

> Synderesis takes the basic principles of behaviour and applies them, through the conscience, to individual situations.

> **Synderesis is never mistaken.** An individual only does wrong when the conscience makes mistakes when it applies synderesis to a situation.

Aquinas believed that the conscience was binding, but that it could be mistaken – the error was to be treated in one of two ways:

> **1.** A **factual mistake**, where the individual did not know that a general rule applied to a particular situation.
> *The individual is not responsible for the wrongdoing.*

> **2.** A mistake that is due to **ignorance of a rule** that the individual should have known.
> *The individual is responsible for the wrongdoing.*

Conscience is the activity that takes place when reason is making right decisions. It is the process of weighing up good and bad.

> **Synderesis** is right reason, the awareness of being able to do good and prevent evil.

> **Conscientia** distinguishes between right and wrong, and makes moral decisions.

Butler on conscience

Joseph Butler (1692–1752)
Butler argued that the conscience is the means by which an individual makes a moral decision. Every human being has the ability to reflect on moral issues, and they also have an awareness of two basic and possibly conflicting principles, **self-love** and **love of others.** Conscience directs us towards concentrating on the interests of others and away from love of the self.

Joseph Butler was Bishop of Durham from 1750, and a supporter of 'natural theology and ethics'. This is a system of theology based on reason alone, without the support of revelation.

Self-love
This is a desire for happiness for the self. It is not a passion or emotional response, nor is it merely instinctive. It is 'who can reflect upon themselves and their own interest or happiness, so as to have that interest an object to their minds'.

Benevolence
This is a desire for the happiness of others.

Conscience 'adjudicates' between these two interests. It behaves as a guide, a gift from God to show the way towards the 'good'. Because it is from God it should be obeyed without question. It has universal authority in all moral judgements.

Intuition The mind is able to perceive abstract concepts or truths normally thought to be beyond empirical experience.

- Where Aquinas argued that conscience is the voice of reason, Butler argued that conscience comes from intuition.
- Butler believed that individuals make moral decisions without any thought to the sanctions of an external law. 'Man is a Law to Himself.'
- The obligation to obey the law is, through its source in human nature, put there by God. The demands of the conscience are compelling without any recourse to an external authority. The conscience is self-authenticating.

N.B. Butler gave conscience absolute authority – he required that the conscience be followed without question.
- The conscience may be misled, or misinterpreted.
- Intuition is impossible to cross-reference – given 'absolute authority', it could lead a person to behave in a way that does not provide for the happiness of others.

Additional Advice 4: Planning for the synoptic paper

It would be worthwhile to begin your planning for the synoptic paper from the start of your revision course.
- Your synoptic paper is an important part of the course. It is worth 20% of the final A2 assessment, so don't neglect it!
- When you work on each part of either the Philosophy or the Ethics papers, keep separate notes to make clear the possible links between topics.

Freud's ideas of the ego and the superego

Sigmund Freud (1856–1939) is best known for his analysis of the human psyche. He believed that the key to human behaviour was in people's instincts and desires.

See also section on **The challenge to religious belief from psychology**.

- Behaving instinctively is often contrary to the interests of the community. Because of this, people frown upon certain types of behaviour. Instinctive desires are suppressed from an early age, and Individuals develop an **ego** with which to interact with society. Society's disapproval of 'inappropriate' behaviour is internalised by the **super-ego.**

This internalisation deals with the ego's suppressed anger and bewilderment at the requirements of society. However, in doing so, it leads to the development of a 'guilty conscience'.

- Freud also suggested that a child identifies closely with its parent. Its super-ego becomes an 'inner parent', rewarding the good behaviour and punishing the bad.

For example:
- *A young child explores its genitalia in the bath.*
- *Its mother says 'Don't do that – it's dirty.'*
- *The child feels bad – something it enjoyed has caused its mother to be angry.*
- *This feeling is suppressed, and the super-ego turns it into a 'guilty conscience'.*

The super-ego divides into the conscience and the ego-ideal

Ego-ideal	**Conscience**
This represents the rewarding parent – it gives rise to feelings of pride and satisfaction.	This represents the punishing parent – it causes feelings of guilt and discomfort for immoral acts.

Freud's analysis of human behaviour is often seen to be discredited by his florid account of the effects of sexuality on the psychological development of human beings.

However, others have developed Freud's ideas. They have argued that the conscience develops through past experience:

Children learn their moral behaviour from their parents, carers and teachers.

Parents encourage good behaviour and admonish bad. ⇨ The way they do this affects the moral development of the child.

The admonishments can be displays of anger, disappointment or even controlled violence (i.e. a smack). ⇨ The child becomes anxious as it tries to avoid the displeasure of the adult. Eventually this anxiety is felt when the child simply considers an immoral act. This is the conscience.

Newman and Piaget on conscience

John Henry Newman (1801–1890): Conscience as God-given

The Roman Catholic Church accepted Thomas Aquinas's account of the conscience as the voice of reason. Newman came from an Anglican background, though he became a Roman Catholic Cardinal.

> Aquinas had argued that following the conscience could never lead to immorality so long as the conscience was properly informed. Ignorance was no excuse, and an individual acting immorally out of ignorance was responsible for their actions.

- He adopted a more intuitionist view of the conscience. He believed that the conscience was the voice of God, informing the individual's moral decision-making.
- Since the conscience is the voice of God, following the promptings of the conscience is following the laws of God.

> *If, as is the case, we feel responsibility, are ashamed, are frightened, at transgressing the voice of conscience, this implies that there is One to whom we are responsible, before whom we are ashamed, whose claims upon us we fear.*
>
> http://www.newmanreader.org/works/grammar/chapter5-1.html

Jean Piaget (1896–1980): Conscience as cognitive development

Piaget was a Swiss psychologist who became influential in the field of child development.

A child's moral development occurs in stages through time, and moral reasoning is dependent on the stage of underlying cognitive development.

Piaget argued that children go though four **stages of cognitive development**:
- Sensorimotor (0–2 yrs)
- Pre-operational (2–7 yrs)
- Concrete operational (7–12 yrs)
- Formal operational (12 + yrs)

During this last stage children develop logical thought.

Piaget suggested two **stages of moral development:**

1. **Heteronomous morality** is the type of moral awareness demonstrated by children aged 5–10. Children demonstrating this level of moral development look beyond themselves for moral guidance. They tend to see rules as inflexible, and expect immediate punishment when they break a rule. An act is seen as immoral through its observable consequence.

   hetero – other
   nomous – law

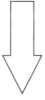

2. **Autonomous morality** is the type of moral awareness demonstrated by children aged 10 + . Children demonstrating this level of moral development develop their own set of rules. They begin to understand the nature of rule-making as a social construction for the benefit of all.

   auto – self
   nomous – law

Adults can operate with a mixture of the two stages – the move towards the second stage is usually observed when the child is less dependent on others for moral authority.

The basic facts of abortion

Abortion	*The act of giving premature birth with loss of the fœtus, especially in the period before a live birth is possible; (the procuring of) induced termination of pregnancy to destroy a fœtus.*

- In the UK 'social' abortion is legal up to the 24th week of pregnancy. Beyond that, a termination can be carried out throughout the later stages of pregnancy if there is a serious threat to the life and health of the mother, or if the baby is very seriously disabled.
- This law dates from 1991. It revised a previous law passed in 1967. Prior to 1967 the deliberate termination of a pregnancy was illegal (this law was first passed in 1803). The social changes that took place in the 1960s, and the increasing liberalisation of sexual ethics throughout that decade, led to a change in the expectations both of women and of society.
- Under current legislation, a woman seeking to have a pregnancy terminated must be referred to a clinic or hospital by their GP and by another doctor.

'Pro-choice'
This group argues that a woman is perfectly capable of making the decision to terminate an early pregnancy. There is no need to seek the permission of two doctors (a process which many women find traumatic and demeaning).

'Pro-life'
This group argues that the life of the fœtus is of paramount concern, outweighing the rights of the mother. Some would agree that a termination would be appropriate under certain extreme medical circumstances.

N.B. A doctor who cannot in conscience refer a woman to have a pregnancy terminated can 'opt out' and refuse to provide counselling about abortion and artificial contraception. They would therefore simply refer the patient to a colleague.

The 1967 Abortion Act established the limit for a termination under normal circumstances to be 28 weeks. Medical technology is now capable of treating babies born at 23 weeks, giving them a good chance of survival. This led to the 1991 Act revising the limit to 24 weeks (see section on **The current legal position**, below).

Terminating a pregnancy when fœtal abnormalities are detected.
- Where a woman is aged over 35, or there is a family history of some genetic disorder, tests can be carried out on the fœtus to determine whether it will be born healthy.
- A pregnancy can be terminated at any stage where *serious* abnormalities are detected.
- There is growing controversy over this form of 'selective' genetic screening by abortion; in particular, the Disability Movement has expressed concerns over the value of life where a disability is detected.

The current legal position in the UK

Under current legislation, the fœtus is protected from 24 weeks – prior to this time, the pregnancy can be terminated.

This 24-week period was established based on medical practice, which has established that babies born at 24 weeks are 'viable', and with intensive care can survive.

In 1967 the original Abortion Act established this 'viability' stage as being at 28 weeks. This was because medical technology had not succeeded in treating babies born before that stage.

The Human Fertilisation and Embryology Authority (HFEA) closely regulates the use of sperm and ova for research or infertility treatment. This body has laid down rules that govern the 'harvesting', use and disposal of embryos, sperm, and ova.

The regulations require that any infertility treatment must take into account the welfare of any child that might result from the treatment, but no mention is made of the possible rights of the embryo or fœtus – except to say that any disposal of material should be 'sensitive'.

When does life begin?

Despite the advances in medical technology, there is considerable debate over when life actually begins (see sections on **Augustine** and **Aquinas**, above).

Life begins at conception
See section on **The Roman Catholic view**, below. Note that the Roman Catholics do not hold a monopoly on this view!

When debates flare up about the rights of the fœtus against the rights of the mother, the *actual* life of the mother is compared with the *potential* life of the fœtus.

Life begins some time after conception
The law appears to suggest that a fœtus becomes a viable life at 24 weeks. Supporters of the argument note that there is a difference between **potential** and **actual** life. While the Roman Catholic argument, as put forward in the various Papal Encyclicals, argues that life begins at conception, in fact anything born before 24 weeks is barely viable.

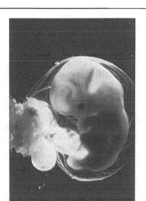

At six weeks an embryo begins to develop genitalia.

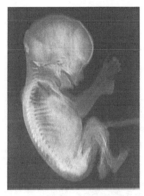

At 24 weeks a fœtus becomes a viable life independent of the mother.

Does life begin at birth?

For centuries this was the established point at which life began. Various rules were established regarding the protection of the unborn – in Exodus there are references to the punishments due to someone who kills or injures a pregnant woman. The law explains that the offence is only punishable by death if the woman herself dies. If the assault brings on a miscarriage, then only a fine is payable.

Does life begin some time before birth?

The embryo/fœtus is *not* part of the woman's body.
- Others argue that the embryo/fœtus is distinct from (if completely reliant on) the mother.
- Genetic tests have shown that the embryo is biologically distinct from its mother. Even when it is still a single cell, it has a separate biological identity. As such it is an individual. It is, to all intents and purposes, 'foreign tissue'.
- Its 'support system' – the placenta, umbilical chord and amniotic sac, are formed by the embryo, and are distinct from the mother.
- The science of 'in vitro fertilisation' (IVF – literally 'in glass fertilisation') has shown that the embryo can be fertilised and can exist briefly outside a woman's body – it is suggested (and not only in science fiction) that artificial wombs will be developed.

It is also argued that the embryo's dependence on the mother for survival is little different from the baby's dependence – both can be supported by a woman other than their own biological mother.

The embryo/fœtus is part of the woman's body.
- The embryo/fœtus is still a part of the woman's body Some believe that the unborn embryo is a part of the woman's body until such time as it can survive by itself (i.e. is viable). This would imply that the fœtus has the same rights as an organ or limb until it is viable. Therefore, any research or termination carried out on the fœtus before 24 weeks is no different from research carried out on any other human tissue. However, the HFEA states that *any* handling of such human tissue should be conducted in a spirit of sensitivity.

Fœtal research

1. Cloning
- This is the extraction of the nucleus from the cell of a human being, and inserting it into the cell of another, producing an exact replica of the original human.

Cloned tissue will be genetically identical to the original – this will be useful for organ and tissue transplantation, where there has traditionally been a risk of tissue rejection. The cloning of an entire human being is more problematic – doctors in South East Asia claim already to have completed such a procedure. Some would ask why we would need to clone a human being.

> Cloning does not mean that the planet will be over-run by Saddam Hussein clones – a complete cloned replica of Saddam would need to have identical experiences as well as an identical genetic make-up!

2. Fœtal screening
- This is the procedure that is carried out to see whether the fœtus is suffering from any abnormalities (see also the section above on **Abortion**)

Some parents have argued for the right to screen embryos for desirable (or undesirable) characteristics – one family has had treatment in Italy whereby only female embryos were implanted, since they wanted a baby girl. This is illegal in Britain.

3. Stem cell research
- This is the harvesting of the basic cells that have the potential to become any part of the human body.

Stem cell research could help with the treatment of degenerative diseases such as Parkinson's.

Religious views

The **Roman Catholic Church** argues for the sanctity of life – it has been an implacable opponent of all aspects of embryo research, IVF and abortion.

The **Protestant Churches** have taken a more liberal approach. The use of abortion as a form of birth control is opposed, but '**therapeutic abortion**' and a carefully restricted programme of research on embryos, have been tentatively accepted.

Additional Advice 5: Synoptic specification content

The various boards differ on their synoptic content, so make a list of your particular board's requirements. You may not need to learn or revise anything extra, but you should be absolutely clear on how the various parts of your Philosophy and Ethics papers connect.

Making the Connections
- In a sense, the Connections paper is asking 'so what?'.
- It looks at the implications for a particular theory, but takes those implications beyond the topic itself.

For example:
A. J. Ayer argued that religious language could not be verified. It was therefore meaningless.
- What are the implications of Ayer's proposition for ethical language?
- Is religious language, as Braithwaite suggests, simply ethical preference expressed in symbolic language?

The Roman Catholic view on abortion

Embryo – a fertilised egg up to 8 weeks of development
Fœtus – a fertilised egg beyond 8 weeks of development

Source: HFEA

The debate regarding the rights of the unborn hinges on the question: **When does life begin?**

- **St Augustine** believed that the soul was implanted into the unborn child at **46 days**. He had no evidence for this!
- **St Thomas Aquinas** believed that there was something of a gender imbalance: **90 days for girls**, and **40 days for boys**.

The debate is moved further by the Roman Catholic Church, which has taught since the sixteenth century that the soul enters the body at the point of conception. Various Biblical quotations are cited to support this:

Jeremiah 1:5

Before I formed you in the womb, I knew you.
God tells the prophet that his prophetic purpose has been decided before he was conceived.

Psalm 139:13, 15

For thou didst form my inward parts, thou didst knit me together in my Mother's womb.
My frame was not hidden from me, when I was being made in secret, intricately wrought in the depths of the earth.

Luke 1:24-38

The Angel Gabriel tells Mary that she will conceive and carry Jesus. Jesus is 'planned' before He is conceived.

Luke 1:44

For behold, when the voice of your greeting came to my ears, the babe in my womb leaped for joy.
When Mary meets with her pregnant cousin Elizabeth (who is expecting the birth of John the Baptist), the unborn child reacts to Mary's voice.

Revised Standard Version

These quotations, and others, are seen to support the idea that a child is valued by God from conception. Various Popes have added pronouncements (Encyclicals) to the body of scriptural and Church support for the 'life from conception' argument.

In particular, **Pope Pius XI** issued the Encyclical *Casti Connubi* in which he spoke of the sacredness of life, especially of the unborn. He wrote that the life of an unborn child is as sacred as that of its mother. (*Casti Connubi* was an Encyclical letter on the Importance of Christian Marriage issued in December 1930.)

- This was further reinforced by the **Second Vatican Council** which met in the early 1960s.

The Roman Catholic Catechism contains a summary of Roman Catholic doctrine. Roman Catholics are required to demonstrate their understanding of the Catechism at their Confirmation. The Catechism states:

Endowed with 'a spiritual and immortal' soul, the human person is 'the only creature on earth that God has willed for its own sake.' From his conception, he is destined for eternal beatitude.

Catechism 3:1:1:1

Pope Paul VI issued an Encyclical entitled ***Humanæ Vitæ***, which also argued for the rights of the unborn.

Ethical theory and abortion

Most forms of embryo research and abortion are acceptable to utilitarianism (though the greater good may *not* be served by eradicating genetic diseases – the consequences may be disastrous). The issue hinges on the rights of the mother and the rights of the fœtus – it may be argued that the mother has a duty of care for the unborn child until she decides whether to carry the child to term (within the 24-week boundary). The child's rights have to be considered along with the rights of the mother and of any other children that the mother may have. The rights of the child could be seen to be outweighed by its **potentiality** for life – when taken alongside the **actual** life of the woman and any other children, the unborn child's rights may be overlooked. In all cases, **situation ethics** would argue for compassion and sensitivity. 'No unwanted child should be born' (Fletcher).

Judith Jarvis Thompson (1929–   ): the right to choose

Thompson's argument begins by supposing that the fœtus is a person from the point of conception. She defines her argument from this starting point in terms of the **right to life**:

> [Imagine that] you wake up . . . and find yourself back to back in bed with an unconscious violinist. He has . . . a fatal kidney ailment . . . you have been kidnapped and the violinist's circulatory system was plugged into yours so that your kidneys can be used to extract poisons from his body as well as your own.
>
> Thompson, J. J. in Singer, P. *Applied Ethics*, 1986, p.39

The violinist requires this treatment for nine months. To unplug him would mean certain death. Does his right to life outweigh your own right to choose?

This argument looks at the right to life of the mother over and against the right to life of the fœtus.

- If the woman's life is threatened by the fœtus, then the woman's right to life could be argued to be stronger.
- In the case of the violinist, the 'life support' person is under no obligation to remain plugged into the musician.
- In the same way, the woman's rights are stronger than those of the unborn child.
- The woman's right to choose what happens to her body is of greater importance than the rights of the fœtus.

This makes the issue of abortion a matter of 'rights', and may obscure the ethical dimension of the issue.

When the debate hinges on the woman's right to choose, the ethical judgements based on that right to choose may need to take into account her choice to have sexual intercourse.
- If the woman freely chose to take part in a sexual liaison, she should be prepared to accept the consequences.
- The person linked to the violinist did not choose freely to be connected to the patient.
- There are others who may also have a right to choose – the father, the grandparents, and even the fœtus.

Peter Vardy criticises the view that the woman's right to choose is paramount. He points out the need to accept that others' rights are also important. He also argues that the logical conclusion of Thompson's argument would be that an individual has absolute rights over their body.

For example:
A person could be morally free to mutilate themselves in order to improve revenue from begging.

Much of the argument about abortion is presented in extremely emotive language. There have been notorious cases of pro-life campaigners murdering doctors at abortion clinics – there is something of a contradiction in a pro-life campaigner taking a life . . .

146

Voluntary euthanasia and the UK law

This is the term used to refer to a painless and dignified death. It is commonly held to refer to the practice of assisting a patient who is suffering from some terminal and painful disease.

΄ευ – **good**   θανατος – **death**

- The aim is to ensure that the patient is given the opportunity to take some control of their final days, and to allow them to die in as pain-free, dignified and managed a way as possible.

A popular expression would be '**mercy killing**'.

The legal position in the UK
- Suicide is *not* illegal in the UK (this was made law in the **Suicide Act** of **1961**).
- Assisting a suicide is illegal and is a criminal offence.
- Any person who carries out actions that are deliberately intended to bring about the death of another is culpable under the **Homicide Act** of **1957**. Where it can be shown that the actions were carried out for compassionate reasons, the charge can be reduced to manslaughter on the grounds of **diminished responsibility**.
- Anyone found guilty of 'aiding, abetting, counselling or procuring' the suicide of another person could be imprisoned for up to 14 years. However, in practice, where a person has assisted suicide for compassionate reasons, a suspended sentence has often been handed down.

Voluntary euthanasia
- This is the term used for euthanasia at the request of the patient concerned. The patient is able to give full, informed consent.
- Usually the patient is suffering from a terminal and debilitating disease. Death is preferable to continued, but painful, life.
- The pain being experienced can also be the pain felt by close friends and relatives who have to watch the patient die.
- Euthanasia is therefore based on **anticipated results**. The decision to seek euthanasia is based on the anticipated benefits for the patient and for the relatives.
- It is this form of euthanasia that is the popular concept held in debates and in the public perception of euthanasia.

The principle of voluntary euthanasia is usually rooted in the idea that a human being has the right to die in dignity and free from pain. Patients who seek euthanasia as a solution to their condition suffer from a wide variety of diseases, including multiple sclerosis, cancer or some other disease that leaves them lucid (i.e. capable of rational thought) but in very great physical discomfort.

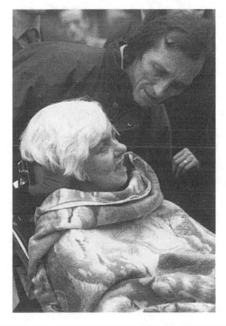

Diane Pretty (d. 11 February 2002) – a motor neurone disease sufferer who wanted to end her life with dignity.

147

Euthanasia definitions

Non-voluntary euthanasia

- When a patient is unable to request euthanasia, their relatives, friends or doctor may seek to end their life – usually because the patient is in considerable suffering, or is in **PVS** (permanent vegetative state).
- In the case of PVS there have been considerable legal and ethical difficulties. A person can be kept alive on a respirator indefinitely, despite considerable brain damage. In such cases, it may be that the patient regains consciousness (eventually – some textbooks cite cases of patients who exist in such a state for over 20 years, before reviving!), or it may be that they do not. The patient's relatives presumably consider this condition to be undignified. There is also considerable suffering on the part of the relatives, who have to maintain some kind of vigil at the bedside – their relative is to all intents and purposes dead, but they cannot begin to grieve.

In such cases, death is often defined as the cessation of certain fundamental brain functions:

Whole brain death	Upper brain death	Brain stem death
This is the definition of death based on the entire brain ceasing to function.	This is the absence of consciousness, thought and emotion – the qualities usually associated with personhood.	The brain stem is the part of the brain that controls physiological and anatomical function. Death is therefore the cessation of function in that part of the brain, the person ceases to be the person that they were.

Involuntary euthanasia

- This is the term used when someone is killed in order to prevent their further suffering, but their consent is not sought (even though they are capable of expressing their opinion).
- It may be that they *have* expressed an opinion, but it is judged to be in the patient's best interest that their life is ended in a humane way.
- The people who carry out the actions that end the patient's life have motives associated with preventing unnecessary suffering.

The difference between involuntary euthanasia and murder would appear to be a matter of motive alone!

Active euthanasia

- Something 'positive' is done to bring about the end of a person's life – *popularly referred to as a **'mercy killing'***.
- This could be the injection of a drug, or the administration of sleeping pills or a pillow.

Passive euthanasia

- Treatment is withdrawn or not administered in the first place – thereby bringing about the death of the patient. This would include turning off a life-support machine.

Suicide

In the United Kingdom, there is no law that deals directly with voluntary euthanasia. Cases where a person has helped someone to die are prosecuted either under the law dealing with murder, or under the law on suicide.

Murder
The **Homicide Act 1957** states that murder is punishable with life imprisonment. However, the court can reduce this punishment for compassionate reasons. The sentence can be reduced, or the charge reduced from murder to manslaughter through diminished responsibility.

Diminished responsibility
s.2(1): Where a person kills or is party to the killing of another, he shall not be convicted of murder if he was suffering from such abnormality of mind ... as substantially to impair his mental responsibility for his acts and omissions in doing or being party to the killing.
s.2(3): A person but for this section would be liable, whether as principal or as accessory, to be convicted of murder shall be liable instead to be convicted of manslaughter.

Suicide pacts
s.4(1): It shall be manslaughter and shall not be murder for a person acting in pursuance of a suicide pact between him and another to kill the other or to be a party to the other being killed by a third party.

This means that, while it is not a criminal offence for a person to commit suicide, it is a criminal offence either to assist in a suicide, or to provide the means for a person to commit suicide.

Moves to promote euthanasia

Dr Jack Kevorkian

Kevorkian has become famous (or infamous) as the doctor who supports euthanasia in America. He invented a machine called the **mercitron**, which provided a way for a patient to bring about his or her own death without effort – literally 'at the flick of a switch'.

His first patient ended her life after a struggle against Alzheimer's disease.

Kevorkian has provided a means for patients to bring about their own death without any intervention or assistance (save for the setting up of the machine). However, he has been prosecuted under laws in the USA for assisting suicide and for manslaughter. Kevorkian's case has raised important issues for the medical profession.

I will follow that system of regimen which, according to my ability and judgment, I consider for the benefit of my patients, and abstain from whatever is deleterious and mischievous. I will give no deadly medicine to any one if asked, nor suggest any such counsel.
Part of the Hippocratic Oath
http://classics.mit.edu/Hippocrates/
hippooath.html

- Under the Hippocratic Oath it is argued that a doctor cannot do anything to provide for anything other than the cure of a patient – still less, do anything to bring about their death.

Any action that is intended to bring about the death of a patient is in direct contravention of any moral medical code. However, it may be that the doctor can bring about the death of the patient indirectly.

The administration of morphine, a powerful painkiller, is widespread in the treatment of cancer. Excessive morphine use is lethal – a doctor can administer morphine intending to reduce the suffering of the patient, and the patient can die as a result.

- In this case, the doctor may feel that it is appropriate to administer potentially lethal doses of morphine simply to allow the patient a pain free end to their life. The intention is to prevent pain, not to kill.

Some would say that the doctor need not be held responsible – this is known as the law of **double effect**. The doctor is only responsible for the results of their own intended action. Subsequent or unforeseen results are beyond their responsibility.

Australia and Holland

- On 25th May 1995 the Northern Territory in Australia passed the **Rights of the Terminally Ill Act (ROTI)**.
- In November 2000, Holland also passed an act legalising euthanasia.
  In both cases there was considerable anxiety about protecting the rights of the vulnerable.

Living wills

Some people have drawn up quasi-legal documents in which they record their desires and wishes regarding their treatment.

Usually these are an attempt by the patient to state their wishes regarding euthanasia while still mentally sound, and before they become incapacitated.

- Instructions are issued to doctors and to relatives regarding the means by which the patient is to face their final moments.
- Some people have included in these documents wishes regarding the circumstances of their death – they have requested their relatives to be present (almost like a funeral).

Providing the living will is properly completed and witnessed, it is legally enforceable under Common Law. The person completing the will would need to demonstrate mental competence at the time the will was drawn up. They would also need to be fully aware of the implications of the will. The living will could not be used to refuse basic care (such as washing), or to prevent medical staff from offering food and drink (though it could refuse food intravenously).

Under current British Law, euthanasia is illegal. A living will cannot make provision for euthanasia.

Ethics and euthanasia

Euthanasia is usually seen as a utilitarian act – an action carried out on the basis of perceived outcomes. However, it may also be regarded as a response to suffering and terminal illness embedded in the principles of compassion – in this way it may be justified under the principles of situation ethics.

However, the action that brings about the end of a person's life would appear to be directly against the Biblical principle 'You shall not kill'. This verse is variously translated 'kill' or 'murder' – the debate hinges on this!

The practice of euthanasia radically changes the relationship between doctor and patient.

The **Roman Catholic** view was summed up by Pope John Paul II in *Evangelium Vitae*. In it, he states clearly that euthanasia is a violation of the law of God. Life is an **extraordinary gift** from God.

On a practical (and perhaps cynical) level, there are concerns about euthanasia, particularly over the possibility of unscrupulous relatives seeking the early demise of a rich aunt by arguing for mercy killing – when we say 'put her out of her misery', do we really mean 'put her out of our misery'?

Emotive arguments against euthanasia have included references to the Nazis' attempts to 'deal' with a variety of groups of people in pre-war Germany.

From society's point of view, euthanasia poses awkward questions regarding the value of individual persons – is human dignity based solely on a person's usefulness to society?

Ethical theories and euthanasia

A situationist might argue that 'rules' about the sanctity of life should not apply. The most important consideration is the suffering of the patient. **Situation ethics** argues that the 'correct' response is the most compassionate.

However, **deontological arguments**, such as the **categorical imperative**, take the position that euthanasia could never be a **universalisable** principle. Killing can never be right, and it can certainly never be made into a law applicable to everyone. Some might also argue that the patient is using themselves as a means to an end!

Additional Advice 6: Preparing for synoptic questions

As you revise, you should be looking for possible links between topics in Philosophy and Ethics.
- As you maintain a file of connections, look through your notes on a regular basis. Use specimen questions and past papers to help you to formulate sample essay titles to use for your revision.
- Use the synoptic specimen questions, and past papers, to establish the links and connections between the areas of Philosophy and Ethics that your board's specifications require.
- Use the assessment objectives from the specimen mark schemes to help you to form the links between the topics.

Introduction to environmental ethics

Environmental ethics divides into two parts – the ethics of the human relationship with animals, and issues associated with the planet.

Animal rights	**The natural environment**
Should ethical theories apply to animals as much as humans? This debate may be labelled **non-human rights**.	What responsibility do we have towards the planet we live on? This issue is often referred to as **conservation ethics**.

Recent scientific developments seem to suggest that the planet is being irretrievably affected by human activity:

- Species are becoming extinct at an alarming rate.
- Tropical rainforest is being destroyed.
- Global warming appears to be causing a disastrous rise in sea level and also causing significant changes to world climate conditions.

Clearly these are worrying developments – note that the ethical dimension of the issue is unclear.

> If we have an ethical responsibility towards *all* life-forms on the planet, then we have a responsibility to stop destroying the environment.

> Since many people regard ethics as being concerned with the limiting of suffering and the maximising of pleasure (whether directly or indirectly), the environment might not seem an ethical issue.

> If we define ethics as behaviour that affects other people, then an ethical consideration of the environment would be restricted to the way that environmental exploitation affects people.

Humanity's effect on the environment

It could be argued that all life-forms have an effect on the environment, from ants to elephants. However, in the last 3000 years humans have had a powerful effect – landscapes have been altered by human activity, and few areas of the planet have been left untouched.

- The environment becomes an ethical issue when the exploitation of the natural world affects the happiness and well-being of human beings.

A developing world country building a dam in a valley has something of an ethical dilemma.

The damming of the valley will result in the destruction of people's homes and livelihoods. It will cause the displacement of wildlife and the loss of vegetation.	However, the dam will provide jobs and develop industry. This will generate much-needed income for the government and the local region.

To build or not to build?

Was the flooding in Eastern Europe in summer 2002 the result of global warming?

Conservation ethics

This is the best-known form of environmental ethics – it is based on the idea that the environment should be protected for the benefit of humanity.

Many people are concerned about the dangers of climate change.
- They campaign to protect the environment from the projected effects of this climate change.
- This is not necessarily because of any **intrinsic** value in the environment itself. It is of **extrinsic** value in that it provides the means for the pleasure of humanity.
- Their campaign is to protect the environment for future generations.

The recent efforts by governments at Kyoto (in 1997) following the agreements reached in Rio in 1992 are based on this principle. The environment is to be protected so that humanity can continue to thrive.

This view can be traced back to Aristotle, who argued for a hierarchy of living organisms. The better the ability to reason, the higher they would be up the hierarchy.
- Aristotle's philosophy was a deep influence on Thomas Aquinas.
- Aquinas in turn was a considerable influence on the development of Christian philosophy. The Christian view can be traced back to the Bible.

In like manner we may infer that, after the birth of animals, plants exist for their sake, and that the other animals exist for the sake of man, the tame for use and food, the wild, if not all at least the greater part of them, for food, and for the provision of clothing and various instruments.

Aristotle
http://classics.mit.edu/Aristotle/politics.1.one.html

In the Creation story in Genesis, God gives the created world to Adam and Eve. Adam is given 'dominion' over the fish, the birds, and every living creature on the earth (Genesis 1:26).

This 'dominion' includes the notion of responsibility. Christian tradition speaks of humanity as 'stewards' of Creation. Christianity today argues for this stewardship approach:
That this Synod (1992), affirming its belief and trust in God the Father who made the world, believe that the dominion given to human beings over the natural order is that of stewards who have to render an account [to God].

Church of England General Synod
http://www.cofe.anglican.org/view/environ.html

Some Christian thinkers take a hard-line approach, seeing the world as a gift from God for the 'use' of humanity.

- Others (such as St Francis of Assisi) take a different view, seeing Creation as a gift from God for humanity to enjoy 'in partnership' with its fellow inhabitants.

However, Christian teaching is clear that the planet was given to humanity, and that humanity has control. Christian environmental ethics tends towards an approach that seeks to protect the environment in order to enhance and continue human enjoyment of it.

Singer's environmental ethics

Peter Singer in *Practical Ethics* (1993)

Singer takes a **preference utilitarian** stance on many ethical issues. He notes that most Christians seek to conserve nature in order to protect the lifestyles of vulnerable peoples who are affected by changes to the environment.

Singer suggests that as the unspoilt parts of the world shrink, they acquire a 'scarcity value' that argues for preservation as a bequest for future generations. *These unspoilt regions tend to be specialist ecosystems that are difficult to recreate or restore.*

- Singer argues that these areas should be referred to as 'World Heritage' sites. They have been inherited from our ancestors, and we should leave them for our children. He suggests that this would be a suitable course of action even though future generations may not appreciate the legacy.

Climatic climax vegetation

Where specialist conditions (such as at the equator) apply, specialist ecosystems develop. Tropical rainforest is a highly specialist and evolved ecosystem – clearing rainforest in order to develop farmland often fails because the climate and the soil conditions do not favour crop-growing.

Singer suggests that we should preserve these 'World Heritage' wildernesses as a legacy to future generations. He suggests that they should be able to choose between developing an appreciation of the 'built environment' and of unspoilt country. He compares such an act of conservation with the campaign to preserve Venice.

Singer's environmental ethics is basically a humanist approach. He offers an androcentric (or anthropocentric – 'man-centred') view of conservation concerns. He extends this ethic to include **sentience** as a consideration for ethical behaviour – see section on **Animal rights**.

Vardy disinguishes between two forms of human-centred environmental ethics:

'Strong' androcentric

Humans are at the centre of the universe, and that is where they should be.

'Weak' androcentric

We can only understand the universe from a human point of view.

These arguments are based on the fact that we can only understand the universe from a human point of view. We can imagine life as a dog, but we can never really know what it is to be a dog, or to experience that life.

It is possible to see the universe in terms of the interests of other life-forms. This begs the question 'how (or why) are other life-forms of value?'

One way to answer this question is to see everything on the planet as interdependent. Every creature takes a place in some sort of food-chain. Each creature, however insignificant on its own, forms part of a greater whole, and as such could be seen as valuable.

- *This is an extrinsic value – the creature is only valuable in so far as it relates to other creatures. It has no value in itself.*

Ecological pyramids

Biologists use this term to refer to the relationship between different levels in an ecosystem. They use the idea to represent the relationships between the various factors that effect life in an ecosystem.

While the ecological pyramid is a technique used in biology, it can demonstrate the eco-holist's view that all life is inter-dependent. Consider the 'Pyramid of Number' that represents the numbers of different organisms in a particular ecosystem: The animal at the top of the pyramid (e.g. a lion) relies on the next level down for its food, and each level then depends on the next. Should the environment change, and a large number of organisms in the base layer of this pyramid die, the lion's food supply would in turn be compromised.

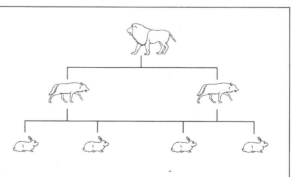

The eco-holist emphasises the fact that the lion's existence is closely linked to the existence of even the smallest organism. *For a good example of this idea, think of the song 'Circle of Life' in the Disney film 'The Lion King'.*

Deep ecology

This movement began when Aldo Leopold, an American ecologist, argued for a 'land ethic' based on a whole-earth approach to environmental ethics. The term 'deep ecology' came from an article written by **Arne Naess**, a Norwegian philosopher who had campaigned for environmental conservation in Norway in the 1970s.

Shallow ecology
Naess argued that a 'shallow' approach to ecology involved seeking to improve the environment in order to improve things for human beings – clean water, and countryside for rambling and sightseeing.

Deep ecology
In contrast, this approach values the environment for its own sake. The environment should be preserved regardless of its benefits for humanity.

By an ecosophy I mean a philosophy of ecological harmony or equilibrium. A philosophy as a kind of sofia (or) wisdom, is openly normative, it contains both norms, rules, postulates, value priority announcements and hypotheses concerning the state of affairs in our universe. Wisdom is policy wisdom, prescription, not only scientific description and prediction. The details of an ecosophy will show many variations due to significant differences concerning not only the 'facts' of pollution, resources, population, etc. but also value priorities.
Naess, A. quoted on
http://www.deep-ecology.org/drengson.html

The created order is valuable in itself, rather than for what it can do for humanity. This value is independent of any value that a person might attach to the environment.

Naess (and his collaborator, George Sessions) argued that humanity has no right to compromise the environment except to 'satisfy *vital* needs'.
• The deep ecologists also argue that these principles apply to river systems, landscapes and entire ecosystems.

But all living creatures are of equal worth because they are equally valuable – whether human or fish. What is this 'equal worth' based on?

Some deep ecologists argue this on the basis of the interdependence of living creatures and plants within ecosystems. Each creature or plant occupies a unique point in this system, and other creatures and plants rely on each other for their survival.

This is not necessarily the case.

Peter Singer argues that individual organisms cannot hold a claim of intrinsic value – no individual organism is essential for the survival of the ecosystem.

He also argues that the fact that there are interrelationships between organisms does not mean that there is equal worth. The value of an organism may simply be because it contributes to a greater whole. He suggests that deep ecology should concentrate on ecology at the species or ecosystem level.

Eco-holism

This view of ecology is based on a species-level concern for the value of organisms.
It assumes that a species or an ecosystem is valuable in its own right.
As such, an entire species, or a specific ecosystem, is of intrinsic value.

- This would lend support to the movements that seek to preserve specific environments such as the rainforests and deserts.

However, there may be a philosophical problem with ascribing value to something that does not have self-awareness. Most ethical systems are based on the principle that self-aware life has value because it has some sort of moral responsibility.

Arguments to save the rainforests can be based on:
- Their impact on the world climate system
- Their 'heritage' value to future generations
- Their value 'in themselves' as climatic climax vegetation systems

The Gaia hypothesis

James Lovelock argued for an interdependence between the living world and its non-living environment.

Gaia was the Greek Goddess of the Earth.

- Traditionally, it was believed that the inorganic conditions on earth have influenced the development of life. See sections on **The anthropic principle** and on **The teleological argument** for the existence of God.
- The Gaia hypothesis argues that there is a more **symbiotic** relationship between the inorganic (abiotic) and organic (biotic) worlds.
- Life on earth serves to stabilise the climate and other conditions on the planet surface.

The Gaia hypothesis is not unlike the thermostat that operates a domestic central heating system. The thermostat switches on the boiler when the temperature in the house drops below the set temperature. Life on earth provides a similar control feature.

For example:
Over the past 4 million years the sun has increased its luminosity. This should have overheated the planet, yet we are still here.
As the planet warmed, plankton levels were increased, removing CO_2 from the atmosphere. As the plankton died, they sank to the seabed, removing the CO_2 from the system altogether. This allowed the planet to cool (i.e. the greenhouse effect in reverse).

Perhaps life regulates the physical and chemical environment of the planet so as to maintain suitable planetary conditions for the good of life itself. If so, then the planet can be thought of as a single, integrated, living entity with self-regulating abilities.

Although Lovelock (a British scientist), and his collaborator Lynn Margulis (a microbiologist) argued for a scientific hypothesis, their idea has been 'adopted' by theologians as a further example of the teleological principle at work.

Rainforests are under threat
Does eco-holism offer an answer?

Animal rights

The traditional Christian view is that God gave humanity 'dominion' over all other living creatures (Genesis 1:26) for:

- Sport – either as racing animals or as something to chase, torment or kill
- Work – as pack animals, to draw carts and ploughs, or as a means of transport
- Entertainment – either as exhibits in zoos or for sport (see above). Some would include pets in this category!
- Experimentation – whether to improve medical care for humans, or to push back the boundaries of human knowledge
- Food – we eat animals
- Clothing – we wear animal skins as clothing
- Companionship – we keep animals as pets

In recent years there has been a reaction against the view that animals are inferior to humans, and can be used for whatever we want. As living conditions for humans have improved, the extreme cruelty that animals have been subjected to has come under increasingly close scrutiny.

| **N.B.** | *Many people have an emotive response to the question of animal rights.* |

Animals are not moral creatures.
Morality is about making ethical choices. Most animals behave instinctively, and do not make choices.
- We are therefore under no moral obligation to treat animals with respect.
- Justice is not a concept that can be applied to animals.
Animals can therefore be used for the benefit of humanity.

Animals should be worthy of the same (or similar) respect as humans.
Animals are of value in themselves – their ability to choose is of secondary concern.
- **Peter Singer** argues for equal rights for certain species – he compares the mental capabilities of a chimpanzee with that of a human with some mental incapacity.

Peter Singer argues that distinguishing between different creatures, and treating animals badly because of this assumed distinction, is **speciesist**.

- Arguments about the sanctity of life apply as much to animals as they do to humans.

- Animals' responses to basic sensations like pain are the same as human responses.

- Humans would never be treated the same way as many animals would.

Singer believes that there is no moral basis for assuming that one species is superior to another.

The debate appears to be between the rights of animals and the interests of humans. **Roger Scruton** suggests a middle way:

Humanity should not be lessened by its treatment of animals.
- It may be justifiable to research a cure to childhood cancer using animals, but any suffering should be kept to a minimum.
- Humanity is lessened by its enjoyment of the suffering of animals. Many people object to fox hunting, but not because they believe that the foxes should be left alone – they object to the way that humans *enjoy* the hunt.

Human sexuality and sexual development

It has been said that nature is basically an orgy on a massive scale.

- The entire creative process in nature is engaged in various forms of sexual activity – the drive is to produce offspring, and so continue the genetic line.

Almost every activity undertaken by a living organism is to enhance the possibility of the continuation of the species. Sexual activity (including the processes of child-rearing and training to produce the next generation) is the creative power behind life on earth.

- In humanity (although it is carefully disguised) the procreative process has been at the heart of much of human creativity.
- The instinctive urge to procreate is often suppressed because of social conventions, but remains at the heart of much of human culture.

Most human societies have constructed rules to try to control the sexual drives (mainly of men) – largely these efforts have been to try to limit the spread of sexually transmitted disease (STD), or to provide a stable environment for the rearing of the resulting children.

N.B. These controls have largely been justified by regard to the consequences of behaviour – a thing becomes right or wrong because of the desirability of the outcome.

Human sexual development

An embryo begins to develop genitalia at six weeks from conception. Hormones are released which dictate sexual development.

From an early age, the sexualisation of a child takes place. Subliminal messages establish gender expectations – despite parents' best efforts, girls still play with dolls, and boys try to smash things up. Parents establish expected behaviour standards.

In the main this is to do with public behaviour, but at a more intimate level, attitudes to sex and sexuality are being reinforced. In particular, attitudes to the naked body and to genitalia are established.

Once children become adolescents, sexuality becomes a much higher priority. The body undergoes massive changes as it matures sexually.

Once adolescence is fully underway, the child becomes much more sexually aware. In particular, issues of sexual orientation (and more probably of opportunity) become important. In some cultures, ceremonies are organised whereby the individual is 'initiated' into the adult world.

As the individual becomes a fully-fledged adult, sexual activity tends to become directed towards another individual – this may be an attempt to establish a monogamous relationship. Sometimes this is formalised as **'marriage'**.

In the animal kingdom, the process of achieving sexual maturity varies in complexity, and is linked to the need for the parent to rear the child. An elephant takes several years to achieve maturity, and a mature elephant will play a considerable part in the nurture of its young. A bluebottle, however, is sexually mature in a relatively short time, and plays no part in caring for its offspring.

The biology

Sex and relationships are therefore part of the process by which species effect the survival of their kind. The more developed the organism, the more complicated the process. Elephants, dolphins and apes take longer to mate, gestate and rear their offspring, so their relationships are more complicated.

It has been argued that there is no ethical dimension to sexuality – it is purely a matter of biology.

The introduction of effective, easily accessible and useable contraception has freed women from their fertility, and allowed for the move towards a more equally balanced society.

- Many of the reasons for sexual morality (such as STDs and unwanted pregnancies) have become controllable by means other than behavioural. Sexuality has become 'de-moralised'!

However, religion in particular has been anxious to introduce a moral dimension to sexuality.

Christian attitudes to sexuality

In Biblical societies, the role of women has provoked some controversy – women have been traditionally subservient to men.

- Women's lives have largely been at the mercy of their menstrual cycle, and in particular their fertility. In primitive societies, women stayed at the camp to look after children, while the men went off to hunt.
- Sexuality, and in particular pregnancy, placed women in a position where they were rendered powerless by their own biology.
- In Judaism, this is reinforced by the Creation story, where God creates Eve to be Adam's 'helpmeet'.

As societies developed, women were able to establish a more 'matriarchal' position, where they became the 'power behind the throne'. However, they were still subject to their fertility.

Men in power found that sexuality posed a threat to their position of control. The most powerful man would still find himself subject to sexual urges that he could not control.

- These became identified with the women who were seen as inspiring them.
- Partly in an attempt to control these sexual urges, religion promoted marriage as a suitable context for sexual activity. This fulfilled the concern that sexuality might be out of control, and also provided the biological requirements for child-rearing.

Current religious teaching combines a regard for the biology of sexuality with a consideration of its psychological dimensions. Sex is seen as having both reproductive and of psychological potential:

Reproductive potential
Sexual intercourse has obvious reproductive potential! Within the marital relationship, sex and children are seen as an essential part of the couple's life together.

Psychological potential
Sex also has the power to unite a couple in mutual love (the Church of England Marriage Service calls it 'knowing each other in love').

Obviously, sex also has a very negative potential – it can be used as an instrument of power and degradation. In certain circumstances, sex can be psychologically and biologically damaging.

Much of Christian sexual morality is bound up in the teachings of **St Paul** (the early Church's greatest missionary) and **St Augustine of Hippo** (a fourth-century North African Bishop).
Some Christian moralists have argued that sexual desires are so damaging that total abstinence is preferable.

St Paul taught that sexuality was a necessary part of the physical world, but should not be all consuming. He argued that it was necessary for a man to be married in order to direct his sexual urges in an appropriate way.

St Augustine taught that sex was once pure and innocent, but Adam and Eve corrupted the world through **the Fall**. We experience the 'fallout' of this through barely controllable sexual urges – this is the stain of **original sin** passed through sexual intercourse from generation to generation.

Augustine converted to Christianity. However, he left a 'mistress' by whom he had a son, and he had embraced Roman sexual morality with some enthusiasm. It may be that a combination of guilt for this past life, and also guilt for missing it, led Augustine to develop such a dark view of sex.

St Augustine said '*To many, total abstinence is easier than perfect moderation*'.

Celibacy
The state of living without sexual intercourse. Often part of vows made in a religious context.
- This could be from religious conviction (as in the growing movement among American teenagers to take a vow of celibacy – many carry cards stating that they will not have intercourse until they are married).
- The traditional home of the celibate has been either the priesthood or the cloister. Benedict made celibacy one of the vows taken by those Christians who joined his order. This vow is taken to devote the person's life completely to the Church and to God. Sexuality is 'put on hold' for the benefit of others.
Some people take on celibacy within marriage as the relationship deepens and moves beyond the physical.

Ethical theory and sexuality

Natural Law

The application of the Natural Law theory to the field of sexual ethics is the best-known ethical issue confronting Christianity.

The Roman Catholic Church has traditionally applied this principle in its ethical teaching.

- See the section on the **Natural Law theory** for the implications of the theory for Roman Catholic sexual behaviour.

- Any sexual activity that does not include the potential for conception is seen as 'un-natural'. The traditional view of sexual activity is therefore for the purpose of 'having children' (i.e. this is sex's 'Final Cause').
- Therefore any activity that does not carry with it the potential for conception is considered wrong – this would include masturbation and the use of artificial contraception. Activities that still carry the possibility of conception, such as rape or sexual intercourse during a woman's 'safe' period, are acceptable because they do still carry the possibility of conception.
- **Sex is therefore entirely associated with conception, pregnancy and childbirth.**
- However, there is some disagreement over the scope of the **Final Cause** of sexual intercourse. Arguments that limit the purpose of sexual intercourse to the purely biological deny the various other aspects of sexuality – within a permanent relationship (e.g. marriage) it brings the couple closer together and strengthens their relationship.

Utilitarianism

Utilitarianism sees itself as essentially practical. It does not attempt to limit sexual activity, but rather argues for 'appropriate direction'. As long as no-one is left injured, offended or psychologically damaged by a sexual encounter, there is nothing that utilitarianism can find to condemn in the activity.

Throughout the issue of sexuality, the emphasis is on potential harm. Therefore, utilitarian teaching about promiscuity and 'safe sex' has been an effort to limit potential harm.

Utilitarianism therefore argues for 'responsible behaviour', rather than condemning certain types of behaviour as being sinful, wrong or evil.

Sexual relationships as contracts

The emphasis of this approach to sexual ethics is that of the promotion of 'consensual sex'.

Sexual intercourse should be in a context of mutual and informed consent, and should not involve physical or mental force.

This would exclude any sexual activity that is conducted where one or other of the parties involved was incapable of understanding or preventing anything that was to take place.

Consensual sex cannot take place unless *both* parties are fully aware of the significance of what is to happen, and are *both* in a position to stop it from going any further.

However, this appears to be an almost legal or financial approach to sex. While it may protect people from mental or physical harm, it denies the emotional and spiritual dimension.

The **Kantian** principle that no-one should become a means to an end (see section on **The categorical imperative**) would condemn any sexual activity that was conducted in a context of coercion or manipulation.

Love

Christian teaching about love in the context of relationships and sexual ethics focuses on the interaction between the four loves.

A relationship based purely on *eros* (i.e. lust) will tend to be hedonistic (i.e. purely for pleasure). The Marriage Service emphasises the need for companionship and mutual respect, as well as the need for sexual attraction.

The Christian ethic is compassion – see the section on **Situation ethics**. A relationship which involves *agape* as well as companionship and lust will evolve beyond the physical into a relationship of selfless mutual concern and service.

Justice in Plato's Republic

Plato presented a dialogue in which he explores various theories on the nature of justice.

Thrasymachus:	**Glaucon:**
Conventional justice promotes the interests of rulers. The only reasonable basis for ethics is self-interest.	If everyone operates from self-interest, everyone will end up suffering somehow by being exploited by others. Conventions and rules protect everyone from the selfishness of everyone else.

Plato went on to suggest that society is like a human body. All the parts need to be in proper working order for the general health of the whole. Justice offers the happiest life, whereas injustice is like a sickness.

- Plato thought that for society to work to the advantage of all, it should be governed by **philosophers**(!).
- He believed that philosophers were able to make unbiased decisions, based on the needs of society as a whole. He also thought that ordinary people should obey the philosopher rulers.

> Of course, philosophers are not as altruistic as Plato would like to think. They would have their own presuppositions, values, and self-interests which would conflict with the needs of the whole of society.

Self-interest

In *Republic*, Plato presented the argument that justice is in the interest of the strongest. Laws are imposed simply because the strongest are 'in charge' – they are backed up by the authority of the status of the ruler.

Compare this with Marx's dialectical materialism.

Karl Marx believed that:
- All religious, moral and political life is rooted in economics.
- People have needs and desires (material, social, etc.), and society structures itself to meet those needs and desires.
- This has given rise to a capitalist society, where the the workers produce goods and services, and rich industrialists and landowners profit from their labours.

Plato also presented a similar argument in *Thaetetus*. He described Protagoras's views: the wind feels cool to one person, but hot to another. Values are dependent on the context in which we find them.

Protagoras
A Greek philosopher in the fifth century BCE, who argued that moral rules are not absolute rules, but are social conventions.

Plato tried to define a means by which society can exist without self-interest causing it to disintegrate.

Plato's ideal society

He defined a society in which there are three layers – these correspond with the three elements within the individual.

The ruler
This level corresponds to the reason in the individual.

Plato believed that reason should always be in control of the body.

The soldier
This level corresponds to the will in the individual.

The reason was the means by which reason controlled the baser instincts.

The worker
This level corresponds to the appetite in the individual.

The bodily appetite needs to be controlled if self-interest is to be kept in check.

A person who is unjust is governed by his appetites.
Justice is the state in which a person behaves in a way ruled by his reason. The philosopher is able to consider his appetites and govern them with his reason, whereas someone who knows only their appetites cannot be ruled by anything else.

The ideal society

Plato's ideal society is an authoritarian state. He claimed that only those who know what the 'Good' is should rule.
- He believed that a rigorous academic training would prepare rulers for their role.
- Once this training was complete, a person should know what the Good is – they would then be ready to rule.

A person with such a training, and a knowledge of the Good, would govern the state with a view to maximising the happiness of the state as a whole.

Plato believed that for society to be just, it had to be ruled by reason. Only reason gave access to the Form of the Good; therefore only reason gave access to knowledge of Good. Plato argued that philosophers should rule a state if that state is to be ruled with justice.

David Hume (1711–1776)

It is impossible to achieve justice based on what people deserve. People will never be able to agree on what each individual actually deserves.
Instead, Hume argued for a justice that protected the property of each person, even though people are unequal.
He did not argue for equality of property – he believed that to achieve this would be impractical. People are unequal in their abilities and some will simply do better than others.

Rules and laws

How are rules made?
- Some rules are created by legislators to control society (whether this control is benign or not, and whether the rule is with the consent of the people).
- Some rules come about through custom and social convention.
- Some rules are based on the consent of the people.

> For example, the American Declaration of Independence and the Constitution: new citizens of the USA must declare their allegiance to the Constitution – they give their consent to the laws being proposed. This forms a **social contract** where there is an agreement between the people and society itself, whereby the people are agreeing to abide by certain rules for the benefit of everyone.

Thomas Hobbes (1588–1679)

Hobbes lived during the English Civil War, when life was unpredictable and violent. He argued that society requires a social contract to operate. The ruler acts as protector, guaranteeing the rights of the individual within the social contract. The people agree to live under that rule, which is absolute, if the danger of social disintegration is to be avoided. The ruler has to be above the law if this rule of law is to be preserved, and people cannot 'opt out' of the system. Simply living within the bounds of the state involves agreement with its rules.

John Locke (1632–1704)

In *The Second Treatise on Civil Government,* Locke argued that people had to give up some of their individual rights to the community. However, he felt that absolute authority lay with the institutions of state, not with the ruler. Individuals have rights – freedom of speech, belief, etc. – which government has to preserve and protect.

Jean-Jacques Rousseau (1712–1778)

Rousseau proposed arguments similar to Locke. He saw the social contract as guaranteeing individual liberty. The social contract involves people and rulers working in partnership to their mutual benefit.
- He also argued that people have two primitive emotions: self-preservation and sympathy (the revulsion felt at the suffering of others).
- He felt that 'civilisation' creates inequality and resentment because it promotes ideas of personal property and consequent inequality.
- This destroys the simplicity of the 'primitive state' where people live together in a spirit of co-operation.

Thomas Paine (1737–1809)

Paine left Thetford for America, and became a guiding light behind the American Declaration of Independence. He argued that there is a social contract that guarantees individual liberty so long as no harm is done to others.

Rules and laws (continued)

John Stuart Mill (1806–1873)

In *On Liberty*, Mill noted that a social contract could force a minority to conform to the wishes of the majority. He therefore proposed that the majority could only impose its values on a minority where the minority was doing something that was harmful to the interests of the majority.

John Rawls (1921–present)

Rawls tries to establish a framework in which the notion of justice can be defined.

Rawls begins with a situation something like William Golding's story *Lord of the Flies*. Imagine some people are lost on a desert island with no hope of rescue.
- They would organise themselves in order to maximise their chances of survival.
- In part, this would be to ensure that the society that they created would last, in order to maximise the chances of survival for their successors.

In *A Theory of Justice* (1972) Rawls argues that a society establishes its definition of justice in terms of a **social contract**.

This is based on two concepts:

1. Each individual has equal rights to maximum liberty without compromising the liberty of others.

2. Inequality should be tolerated only if it benefits the least fortunate in a society.

The contract is based on a hypothetical situation where everyone in a society imagined themselves in an 'original position' of equality.

Decisions concerning the nature of the social contract would be made under this '**veil of ignorance**'.

Any decision would be made out of self-interest, but because the veil of ignorance left each individual uncertain of their position in society, self-interest would require them to legislate to protect the most vulnerable, just in case they were a member of that group.

The social contract would therefore involve, first, the preservation of personal liberty and, second, the solution of the problem of socio-economic inequalities.

These two concepts would inform the underlying political and economic structures, rather than affect individual choices.

Rawls opposes utilitarianism because he believes that the greatest good cannot be pursued without minorities experiencing injustice.

Punishment

Theories of punishment

1. Retribution

Having been found guilty, the offender deserves to receive the appropriate punishment.
- Some would argue that it would offend natural justice for a person to 'get away with it'.

For example:
The public often demands that an offender should receive a punishment – sometimes the Home Secretary adjusts a sentence to reflect better society's view of a particular offence.

2. Protection

Ethics in society is about protecting the vulnerable from the powerful (see above, Rawls).
- A person could be locked away from society to protect other people.
- They could be locked away to prevent them from committing the offence again.

For example:
Rapists and paedophiles receive lengthy sentences partly to reflect the nature of their crimes, and partly to prevent them from offending again.

3. Reformation

The offender is put though a programme that is designed to reform their character.
- On release, they should be able to take their place in society again.

For example:
Sex offenders receive prison sentences that often include attendance at a rehabilitation course. They receive psychiatric treatment for the condition that leads them to offend.

4. Deterrence

When the offender is punished, this acts as to deter other people who might consider committing the same offence.

For example:
The Romans crucified rebelling slaves along the main roads into Rome to warn anyone considering a rebellion. London Bridge was often decorated with the heads of executed prisoners mounted on spikes.

5. Vindication

The offender is punished in order to maintain respect for the law. Justice must be seen to be done.
- Other people see that the law means business, and respect for the law is maintained.

For example:
Recent debates about the relaxation of the law concerning the use and possession of cannabis have been sparked by the suggestion that the police may not arrest people found to be in possession – the law appears weak and unenforceable.

Additional Advice 7: Know what the examiner wants

The objectives used by examiners tell them to look for the ability to combine the two fields of study, using appropriate evidence and supporting the argument with appeals to the views of scholars. You should therefore treat the Synoptic Paper in the same way as you would the other papers.
- Look in the Mark Schemes that are published with Specimen Questions to see exactly what the examiner will be looking for.

Reasons for war

In international law, war is armed conflict between two or more governments or states.

Where the conflict affects large parts of the world, and involves most of the nations, it is known as a **world war**. Where the fighting is between two or more factions within political boundaries (such as a particular country) it is a **civil war**. Custom and diplomatic activity have defined a series of rules concerning the execution of war and the treatment of enemy personnel when taken prisoner. For centuries, one of these customs has been the status of non-combatants (such as civilians), though the increased mechanisation of war, and advances in the technology of weapons of mass destruction, have made civilians increasingly a part of any military campaign.

Wars can be waged for a wide variety of reasons:

In response to armed invasion	To try to gain territory from a neighbouring nation	To counter a threat to peace and stability
e.g. the Falklands War, where British armed forces regained the Falkland Islands from an Argentine force	e.g. the wars waged by the English against the French throughout most of the medieval period	e.g. Israel's war in the Lebanon

To support a less-powerful nation in its struggle against a superior military force	Because a treaty exists which obliges a nation to go to war in support of another nation
e.g. the Gulf War, where a coalition of military powers went to war against Iraq to reclaim Kuwait. It is arguable that the Gulf War was waged to protect Western access to oil.	e.g. the various treaties that were in operation in 1914, which led to most of Europe going to war.

In the case of World War II, most of these reasons applied!

Philosophical ideas about war

Philosophy has had a varied relationship with armed struggle:
- Plato's opinions of Athenian politics were formed during the disastrous Peloponnesian War.
- Augustine wrote *Civitas Dei* (The City of God) after the Visigoths sacked Rome in 410.
- Hobbes wrote *Leviathan*, in which he characterised life as being 'nasty, brutish and short' after the English Civil War.
- After the horrors of the First World War, most of the intellectual map of Europe was altered completely (compare Elgar's music pre-war, such as his *Cockaigne* overture and the *Pomp and Circumstance* marches, with the desolation of his post-war *Cello Concerto*). In some cases, philosophers were enlisted to justify militaristic and nationalistic standpoints, as the various nations struggled to redefine themselves in the aftermath of the war.

For most religious people, war is a difficult issue because it is often a very complex one. The rules of international politics and of sovereign statehood make an opinion on the justification of war rarely a straightforward opinion.

The notion of a just war
The different religions have different interpretations of the justification of war.

Islam – the jihad
Jihad is spoken of on two levels: the internal, spiritual struggle against evil, and the external struggle against the forces that represent evil. Jihad is the duty of all Muslims. There are four ways they may fulfill a jihad: by the heart, the tongue, the hand, and the sword. These refer to the inner, spiritual battle of the heart against vice, passion, and ignorance; spreading the word of Islam with one's tongue; choosing to do good and avoiding evil with one's hand; and waging war against non-Muslims with the sword.

Christianity
Various Christian philosophers have tried to identify the conditions in which it could be justified to enter into armed struggle. Unlike Islam, Christianity has never supported the notion of a **holy war**. Although the Crusades were described as such, they were never fought according to the rules that Christianity has tried to apply to war. All Christians abhor violence, and war is always seen an *unholy*. Attempts to justify war are never intended to excuse the violent actions of war, merely to try to explain the circumstances when war could be regarded as an acceptable *last resort*. In such circumstances, war would be very much the lesser of two evils.

For example:

The Archbishop of Canterbury declared his support yesterday for Nato's action in the Balkans, describing it as a fight against evil.

In his Easter sermon at Canterbury Cathedral, Dr George Carey said that the 'evil of ethnic cleansing' was leading to 'the crucifixion of Kosovo'. In his strongest statement on the crisis, he said that military action was necessary to help save the lives of innocent people. 'Military action thus far is recognition that the civilised world cannot stand idly by and accept that evil can triumph', he said.

Until yesterday Dr Carey had made no comment on Nato strikes other than to say that the use of force was a cause for 'regret'. Now he has joined Cardinal Basil Hume, the leader of the Roman Catholic Church in England and Wales, in backing Nato's action. Last week Cardinal Hume said the Alliance's 'humanitarian motives' in the Balkans were 'honourable' and intended to save lives.

The Archbishop challenged the 'voices' that claimed people no longer needed to hear the Christian message. 'We have outgrown such myths', they say. 'Humankind can take care of itself; we have the capacity, the moral strength and the ability to handle our own problems without recourse to God.' 'But reality hardly bears this out,' Dr Carey said. He called on Christians not to give in to 'darkness'. He said that 'songs should continue and candles shine', despite the fact that the world was 'still racked by bloodshed and conflict'.

The Daily Telegraph, April 1999

Philosophical ideas about war (continued)

The arguments for a just war

The 'rules' of a just war came to be divided into two theories. The theory of *jus ad bellum* dealt with what makes it right to go to war, and the theory of *jus in bello* dealt with acceptable behaviour during a war. For a war to be 'just' it would need to meet the following conditions:

Jus ad bellum	**Jus in bello**
• It must be waged by a recognised authority. • It must only be undertaken in a just cause. • It should be a last resort. • There must be a formal declaration of war. • There should be reasonable hope of success.	• The means of waging the war should be 'proportional' to its intended aim (i.e. the war should not constitute a greater evil than it is fighting to prevent). • It should not harm the innocent (i.e. the civilian population).

More recent conflicts (such as the air attacks on Baghdad, Belgrade and Kabul) have made these criteria more relevant than ever.

- The use of 'smart weapons', with laser guidance and pin-point accuracy (when they are pointed at the correct targets), make warfare an almost clinical activity.
- NATO spokespeople use the term 'collateral damage' to refer to civilian casualties during air raids.

> During the First World War, increasingly indiscriminate weapons (such as poison gas attacks, air raids and sustained sea and land artillery bombardments) began to infringe the rules concerning the non-involvement of civilians, and the proportionality of war.

Modern approaches to the idea of a just war have reduced the justification of war to two principles:

Jus ad bellum – when it is justifiable to take up arms War can only be justified as a response to aggression.	**Jus in bello – how those arms should be used** War should never involve civilians.

> The justification of armed defence in the face of unprovoked aggression creaks when that defence involves the bombing of thousands of unarmed and defenceless civilians; for example, the bombing of Dresden. However, some people have tried to argue that a nation makes its population vulnerable to such attacks when it undertakes an act of aggression – despite this, it is argued that a civilian's right to life is not compromised by his or her government's activities!

> Equally, there is a philosophical awkwardness about the idea of a war not involving the innocent, since wars tend to be caused by the activities of politicians, but fought by soldiers. How far does a soldier renounce his right to life when he joins up? Can a conscript be considered an innocent?

167

The weapons of war

The first weapons of mass destruction were the gas attacks launched by the German army from the trenches around Ypres in 1915. The gas was indiscriminate, and it operated less at the behest of the armies that used it, and more at the whim of the weather.

Since then, weapons have become increasingly violent and have killed more and more people. Today, the 'weapons of mass destruction' that keep people awake at night are:

Biological weapons
Agents that cause the spread of disease, such as anthrax.

Chemical weapons
Chemicals that are highly damaging, or fatal, such as nerve agents.

Nuclear weapons
Bombs which unleash the power of either nuclear fission or nuclear fusion. Entire cities are flattened, thousands killed, and radiation released into the environment to cause further death and injury for years to come. It has been argued that for most of the last 50 years, 'peace' has been maintained because of the huge nuclear arsenals of NATO and the then Soviet Union. MAD, or 'mutually assured destruction', has ensured that no-one has dared to press 'the button'.

It would appear that a greater threat to nuclear holocaust is posed by less-stable countries, such as India and Pakistan, developing nuclear weapons. Terrorist groups are perfectly capable of producing a small nuclear device ('small' being enough to level most of greater London!).

There have also been concerns about other less-spectacular weapons that have been used in various theatres of war.

- Anti-personnel land mines were developed to maim and disable enemy soldiers, and if used according to set rules (which include keeping some sort of record about where the things have been planted) have been used for much of this century without causing ethical problems. However, in Angola, Cambodia and Bosnia land mines have been 'sown' indiscriminately, and now cause horrific damage to civilians years after the end of the conflicts that the weapons were a part of.

Other anti-personnel devices have included:
- special lasers designed to blind enemy troops
- 'dum-dum' bullets that are designed to cause as much damage as possible without necessarily killing the victim
- the use of depleted uranium in artillery rounds as a means of penetrating tank armour, but (allegedly) causing radiation sickness in the people who were in the tanks when they were hit
- thermo-baric weapons, which cause an intense fire, sucking the air from buildings. The resulting loss of air pressure causes horrific injuries.

'Smart technology' has transformed the way in which some countries have waged war. First seen in the Gulf War, these are weapons that use computer and laser technology to target with amazing accuracy. Cruise missiles were programmed with street maps of Baghdad such that they were observed to fly past a BBC reporter's hotel and turn the corner at the end of the street. Laser-guided bombs were dropped down factory chimneys from 15 000 feet. A government building in Belgrade was utterly destroyed, without (apparently) causing much more than superficial damage (and panic) in a hospital next door.

Assuming that they are properly programmed (i.e. not with the co-ordinates for the Chinese Embassy, by mistake), are these weapons in line with the guidelines for a just war?

Although these weapons are developed and used primarily by the 'West', it is important to remember that the majority of wars are fought in the developing world. While it may be important for philosophers to work out the rules by which civilised countries can go to war, the wars being fought in Africa and elsewhere are unlikely to be fought according to any rules at all.

Business definitions

Business – a definition

> 'Business': Trade, commercial actions or engagements
>
> *(Oxford English Dictionary)*

Businesses can involve individuals or groups of individuals. Groups usually organise themselves and establish themselves as 'companies' under laws governing the behaviour of such groups.

- Sometimes, the 'market' perceives a value in the business concerned, and interested groups can purchase 'shares' in the business. For an injection of cash into the business, shareholders can expect to share in the success (or failure) of the business. These shareholders can come to wield considerable power!

A business can be anything from an individual working from home (such as a computer engineer or a childminder) to a multi-national (such as Shell or Microsoft).

Businesses can be involved in one of three areas of industry:

Primary
Industries engaged in the extraction or production of raw materials.

Secondary
Industries engaged in manufacturing or processing, to produce an end product.

Tertiary
Service industries, such as leisure, retail and support services.

Businesses can operate either in a free market or in conditions designed to favour one group of businesses over another.

The free market
Most businesses, whether local or global, operate in a **free market**. This means that usually the cheapest bid gets the trade, and bids are based on what the client is prepared to pay. Where groups in competition with each other produce services or products, 'healthy competition' drives down the prices as the groups vie with each other for the client's custom.

An alternative would be the system operated by some governments, where tariffs and taxes are charged on imports in order to protect home industries from competition from overseas.

Business and politics
Mainstream British politics has largely divided into two approaches to social welfare, with different emphases on economics and business.

The left
Socialism, following Marx, holds that economic activity should be for the benefit of society as a whole. Industries should be owned and run by the state, to support a welfare state system whereby the poor and disadvantaged are supported by the economic activity of the rest of society.

The right
Capitalism, favoured by more right-wing political systems, supports a complicated system of free-market economic activity. Individuals are encouraged to take part in economic activity and to strive to improve their personal lot in life.

What does business have to do with ethics?

At a basic level, ethics deals with the relationships between individuals and groups of individuals. Business introduces a commercial dimension to these relationships, *ergo* ethics is concerned with business.

The activities of **small businesses**, such as builders and plumbers, can be of ethical concern.

For example, 'cowboy' builders have been accused of carrying out unnecessary work, of raising invoices for work that hasn't been carried out, and of taking an unreasonable length of time to complete work.

The activities of **large companies** also cause some concern.

For example, the four main supermarket chains have recently been investigated by the UK government for unfair trading. They have been accused of using their market strength to drive down prices paid to the producers, while charging unnecessarily high prices to the consumer.

Developing world
• Countries which are developing an industrial base.

Developed world
• Countries with a well-developed industrial base.

Multi-national companies often have interests on every continent on earth, and their activities can range from 'high-tech' computer-based industry to traditional heavy industry. Their profits can be larger than many countries in the **developing world**. Often their business interests can conflict with the personal and social interests of the populations of developing countries, and their activities can be seen as exploitative and even corrupt.

For example, the activities of certain multi-national sportswear manufacturers have been a cause for concern for many years. It is alleged that workers in factories in the developing world are paid minimal wages, and work in dangerous conditions, to produce famous brand sporting goods.

Ethicists have begun to look at the way that commercial interests conflict with the personal and social interests of people involved in the business, and also the consumers. In particular, the growth of **bio-industry** and the attempted patenting of parts of the human genome, and the sale of human tissue (anything from kidneys to eggs), have caused considerable concern.

Money

Originally, humans secured things that they wanted either by swapping (bartering), by stealing, or simply by getting them (by hunting, growing, scavenging or whatever means presented themselves).
- When people began to specialise and provide services that other people wanted, a system began to evolve that enabled goods to be exchanged for other goods or services.

Originally, the barter system would be simple – food for a repaired wheel, for example. When people began to value precious metals, these became an important part of the barter system. A small quantity of gold is easier to carry than a cartwheel, and so money began to develop.

An 'exchange rate', where the value of a quantity of (say) gold was established, defining its worth against certain goods and services, also developed. This was based on the amount of gold a customer was prepared to hand over for goods or services (or *vice versa*).

Religious teachings on money

Buddhism

The Buddha considered that everything in the material world is condemned to a life of suffering. A person seeking happiness is doomed unless they can shake free from the trappings of materialism. He called the process the **Four Noble Truths**.

1 All life is suffering.
2 Suffering is caused by wanting things
3 To stop the suffering, stop wanting things
4 This can be achieved by living a life of reasonable austerity, concentrating only on what the body needs.

Christianity

Jesus's teaching on money was similar to that of the Buddha. He warned against undue attachment to money, saying:
For it is easier for a camel to go through the eye of a needle than for a rich man to enter the kingdom of God.

Luke 18:25

Most commentators accept that this is a reference to a gate in the City Walls in Jerusalem. The gate was too narrow for a camel to pass through without removing its pannier baskets. The interpretation of this is that anyone who is attached to their money will be unable to access the Kingdom of Heaven.

- Both teachers argued that greed and avarice lead to sinful behavour, and cause individuals to behave in an unethical way.
- Since religions claim to place individuals at the heart of both the decision and the result of an action, the use of money becomes an important issue in ethical decision-making.
- Today, the Churches act in many ways as the conscience of the nation, warning about (for example):
  - banks closing rural branches (at the expense of rural customers) in order to ensure profits for shareholders.
  - the commercial activities of bio-industrial organisations, especially over cloning and infertility treatments.

The ethical theory of business

Micro-ethics
- Micro-ethics deals with the transactions that take place at a one-to-one level. This involves an examination of the nature of business carried out between individuals and in individual situations.

It can also involve the way that individuals are treated by employers and by businesses. In a wider context, it deals with relationships between businesses. Key to this is the idea of justice.

Macro-ethics
- Macro-ethics deals with the 'wider picture' of the rules by which business is conducted.

It also involves the economic theories that underpin business activity, and the terms that are used in these discussions.

Molar-ethics
- Molar-ethics deals with the power balance in business, and the responsibilities of the 'bosses' (who are a small minority) and the businesses that they run.

There is a long tradition in religion and philosophy dealing with the ethics of commercial activity.

Aristotle made a distinction between the day-to-day operations of a household, and the purely commercial activity that was purely for profit. He felt that the latter was immoral, especially when the rates of profit were excessive.

Jesus is recorded as having forced money-lenders and market traders out of the Temple precincts. The money-lenders changed Roman coinage into Temple currency (the Roman coins carried an image of Cæsar – forbidden by Jewish law), usually at an unfavourable rate of exchange. The market traders sold animals for sacrifice – the animals had to be pure and free from blemish, but it is doubtful that the traders were careful to prevent unsuitable animals from being sold.

Charging interest on loans was banned by Papal Decree in the Middle Ages. It did not take a genius to see that a Papal Decree only applied to Christians, and non-Christians, especially Jews, took advantage of this to set up banks. Jewish financiers bankrolled much of the Crusades. The success of these businessmen became a source of resentment for Christians, and led to racial tension, and even riots, lynch mobs and murder. A classic expression of this racist attitude is found in the character Shylock in Shakespeare's *The Merchant of Venice*).

As societies began to urbanise, finance and commerce became increasingly important. Protestant Christians took little notice of the Pope, and **Adam Smith** (a Scottish economist) developed an economic system that relied on free trade and enterprise.
Milton Friedman (an American economist) argued that 'the social responsibility of business is to increase its profits'. A business's *only* responsibility was to its shareholders. This is a hard-line capitalist view, which held sway during the 1980s, but is now being replaced by a softer attitude.

Current issues in business

Business is being encouraged to take a more 'responsible' attitude to society. A 'middle way' between pure capitalism and socialism is proposed – this is the **stakeholder economy**, in which the wider influences of business define its responsibilities. These include consumers, investors and employees, as well as suppliers, retailers, and even the people who live near to factories, shops and other installations. Today, business ethics has begun to address many of the difficulties associated with the growth of the free trade system, and its effects on the lives of people around the world.

UK supermarkets
- In the UK there are four major supermarket chains, which together control the vast majority of the retail grocery trade.
- Farmers have expressed concern that the supermarkets appear to have artificially depressed the prices paid to the agriculture industry for food products, yet the prices on the shelves continue to rise.
- The supermarkets are accused of profiteering – of forcing down the prices they pay, while failing to pass these savings on to the consumer. Instead, the shareholders benefit.
- Their activities appear to have closed down the traditional British high street. The numbers of independent grocers, butchers and so on have halved in ten years.
- The supermarkets appear to be able to dictate public tastes. They can create demand through advertising and loss-leader offers.

Genetically modified (GM) food
- Biological concerns aside, the genetic modification of food raises business concerns. GM plants and foods have generally been created, and are being promoted, by multi-nationals such as Monsanto. These multi-nationals usually also fund the research that universities are carrying out into GM foods.
- Some of the seeds being promoted as drought- and disease-resistant, and therefore ideal for sale to the developing world, have been developed so that the plants are sterile. This means that farmers cannot use the seeds from these plants to grow next year's crops – they have to buy new seed each year.

Trials of GM food have led to protests in the UK.

Fair trade
- The terms of trade with Africa have attracted the attention of ethicists.
- In the early 1970s, Western banks loaned money to developing world countries to facilitate the development of infrastructure.
- The developing countries would grow cash crops to sell to the West for 'hard currency' which would enable them to pay back the loans.
- In the free market, the crops have not been able to attract sufficiently high prices to repay the loans. Further, smaller independent farmers are disadvantaged by the activities of larger multinational-owned farms. The Banana Wars between the USA and the EU are an example of this.

Index

Page numbers in **bold** refer to significant sections devoted to a single philosopher.

36584